SHORTLIST

New York
2013

WHAT'S NEW | WHAT'S ON | WHAT'S BEST

timeout.com/newyork

Time Out
New York

Contents

Don't Miss: 2013

Itineraries

New York by Area

Essentials

Published by Time Out Guides Ltd
Universal House
251 Tottenham Court Road
London W1T 7AB
Tel: + 44 (0)20 7813 3000
Fax: + 44 (0)20 7813 6001
Email: guides@timeout.com
www.timeout.com

Editorial Director Sarah Guy
Management Accountants Clare Turner, Margaret Wright

Time Out Guides is a wholly owned subsidiary of Time Out Group Ltd.

© **Time Out Group Ltd**
Chairman & Founder Tony Elliott
Chief Executive Officer David King
Chief Operating Officer Aksel Van der Wal
Editor in Chief Tim Arthur
Group Financial Director Paul Rakkar
UK Chief Commercial Officer David Pepper
Time Out International Ltd MD Cathy Runciman

Time Out and the Time Out logo are trademarks of Time Out Group Ltd.

This edition first published in Great Britain in 2012 by Ebury Publishing
A Random House Group Company
Company information can be found on www.randomhouse.co.uk
Random House UK Limited Reg. No. 954009
10 9 8 7 6 5 4 3 2 1

Distributed in the US and Latin America by Publishers Group West (1-510-809-3700)
Distributed in Canada by Publishers Group Canada (1-800-747-8147)

For further distribution details, see www.timeout.com

ISBN: 978-1-84670-290-7

A CIP catalogue record for this book is available from the British Library.

Printed and bound in Germany by Appl.

The Random House Group Limited supports The Forest Stewardship Council (FSC®), the
leading international forest certification organisation. Our books carrying the FSC label are
printed on FSC® certified paper. FSC is the only forest certification scheme endorsed by the
leading environmental organisations, including Greenpeace. Our paper procurement policy
can be found at www.randomhouse.co.uk/environment .

Time Out carbon-offsets all its flights with Trees for Cities (www.treesforcities.org).

New York Shortlist

The **Time Out New York Shortlist 2013** is one of a series of annual guides that draws on Time Out's background as a magazine publisher to keep you current with everything that's going on in town. As well as 2013's key sights and the best of its eating, drinking and leisure options, it picks out the most exciting venues to have opened in the last year and gives a full calendar of annual events from September 2012 to August 2013. It also includes features on the important news, trends and openings, all compiled by locally based editors and writers. Whether you're visiting for the first time in your life or the first time this year, you'll find the *Time Out New York Shortlist* contains all you need to know, in a portable and easy-to-use format.

The guide divides central New York into four areas, each containing listings for Sights & Museums, Eating & Drinking, Shopping, Nightlife and Arts & Leisure, and maps pinpointing their locations. At the front of the book are chapters rounding up these scenes city-wide, and giving a shortlist of our overall picks. We also include itineraries for days out, plus essentials such as transport information and hotels.

Our listings give phone numbers as dialled within the US. Within New York you need to use the initial 1 and the three-digit area code even if you're calling from within that area code. From abroad, use your country's exit code followed by the number (the initial 1 is the US's country code).

We have noted price categories by using one to four $ signs ($-$$$$), representing budget, moderate, expensive and luxury. Major credit cards are accepted unless otherwise stated. We also indicate when a venue is **NEW**, and give Event highlights.

All our listings are double-checked, but places do sometimes close or change their hours or prices, so it's a good idea to call a venue before visiting. While every effort has been made to ensure accuracy, the publishers cannot accept responsibility for any errors that this guide may contain.

Venues are marked on the maps using symbols numbered according to their order within the chapter and colour-coded as follows:

❶ Sights & Museums
❶ Eating & Drinking
❶ Shopping
❶ Nightlife
❶ Arts & Leisure

Map Key	
Major sight or landmark	
Hospital or college	
Railway station	
Park	
River	
Freeway	478
Main road	
Main road tunnel	
Pedestrian road	
Airport	✈
Church	✚
Subway station	Ⓜ
Area name	SOHO

Time Out **New York** Shortlist 2013

EDITORIAL
Editor Lisa Ritchie
Copy Editor Ros Sales

DESIGN
Senior Designer Kei Ishimaru
Guides Commercial Senior Designer
Jason Tansley
Picture Editor Jael Marschner
Picture Researcher Ben Rowe

ADVERTISING
Sales Director St John Betteridge
Advertising Sales (New York)
Mellisa Keller, Dan Kenefick

MARKETING
Senior Publishing Brand Manager
Luthfa Begum
Group Commercial Art Director
Anthony Huggins
Circulation & Distribution Manager
Dan Collins

PRODUCTION
Group Production Manager
Brendan McKeown
Production Controller
Katie Mulhern-Bhudia

CONTRIBUTORS
This guide was researched and written by Joshua M Bernstein, Sarah Bruning, Adam
Feldman, Howard Halle, Sophie Harris, Richard Koss, Gia Kourlas, Ethan LaCroix, Marley
Lynch, Amanda MacBlane, Amy Plitt, Anne P Quigley, Lisa Ritchie, Jonathan Shannon,
Chris Schonberger, Bruce Tantum, Allison Williams, Carl Williott and the writers of *Time
Out New York*. The editor would like to thank Daryl Coke.

PHOTOGRAPHY
pages 7, 9 Ilenia Martini; 13, 15, 19, 39, 68, 89, 92, 150, 159 Time Out New York; 16
Caroline Voagen Nelson; 25, 26, 33, 49, 52, 79 (top and right), 82, 111, 128, 161
Michael Kirby; 29 Jonathan Perugia; 36 Countdown Entertainment, LLC; 37 Marc Whalen;
38 (top) gary718/Shutterstock.com; 38 (bottom) Debby Wong/Shutterstock.com; 41, 47,
79 (left), 121, 133 Ben Rosenzweig; 42 Jolie Ruben; 45 nadirco/Shutterstock.com; 46,
55, 56, 99, 164 Wendy Connett; 50 Songquan Deng; 51 vvoe/Shutterstock.com; 63 Lee
Magill; 64 Virginia Rollison; 75 Grant Asken; 102/103 Stuart Monk/Shutterstock.com;
114 Allison Michael Oren; 127 © MoMA, New York; 134, 137 Alys Tomlinson; 147 Paul
Wagtouicz; 163 Beth Levendis; 167, 175 Benoit Linero; 168 Phillip Ennis; 178 Z NYC
Hotel.

Cover photograph: Brooklyn Bridge by fotog/Getty Images

MAPS
JS Graphics (john@jsgraphics.co.uk).

About **Time Out**

Founded in 1968, Time Out has expanded from humble London beginnings into
the leading resource for those wanting to know what's happening in the world's
greatest cities. As well as our influential what's-on weeklies in London, New York and
Chicago, we publish nearly 30 other listings magazines in cities as varied as Beijing
and Mumbai. The magazines established Time Out's trademark style: sharp writing,
informed reviewing and bang up-to-date inside knowledge of every scene.
  Time Out made the natural leap into travel guides in the 1980s with the City Guide
series, which now extends to over 50 destinations around the world. Written and
researched by expert local writers and generously illustrated with original photography,
the full-size guides cover a larger area than our Shortlist guides and include many
more venue reviews, along with additional background features and a full set of maps.
  Throughout its rapid growth, the company has remained proudly independent,
still owned by Tony Elliott four decades after he started Time Out London as a single
fold-out sheet of A5 paper. This independence extends to the editorial content of all
our publications, this Shortlist included. No establishment has been featured because
it has advertised, and no payment has influenced any of our reviews. And, for our critics,
there's definitely no such thing as a free lunch: all restaurants and bars are visited
and reviewed anonymously, and Time Out always picks up the bill.
For more about the company, see www.timeout.com.

Don't Miss 2013

ANY POINT
OF VIEW™

Observation Deck at Rockefeller Center®
50th Street Between 5th and 6th Avenue
Open Daily from 8am to Midnight
212-698-2000 | topoftherocknyc.com

TOP
OF THE
ROCK®

High Line

Sights & Museums

Despite the lingering effects of the recent economic slump, several projects that seemed to be in limbo for years surged forward in 2012. The most notable of these was the redevelopment of the World Trade Center. Visitors to Ground Zero can now pay their respects at the powerful new memorial, and crane their necks to admire New York's tallest skyscraper, which is nearing completion on the site. However, the National September 11 Museum will not open in autumn 2012 as originally planned, and at time of writing a completion date had not been set (see box p63).

Another long-term project that has made further strides is the High Line (see p97), a 1.5-mile defunct elevated train track on the west side that's being converted into a stylish, slender park. Since the first stretch (from Gansevoort Street in the Meatpacking District to 20th Street in Chelsea) made its debut in 2009, it has joined the ranks of the city's most popular attractions. The second leg, continuing up to 30th Street, opened in spring 2011, and negotiations are underway to move on to the third and final section, which skirts a privately owned rail yard that's being developed into a mixed-use complex.

The elevated park-cum-promenade cuts through the city's prime gallery district, so it's fitting that the Whitney Museum of American Art (see p146), which hosts a high-profile biennial of current creative talent, is building its new base alongside it. The Renzo Piano-designed museum broke ground in 2011 and is expected to open in 2015, with 50,000 square

AMERICAN MUSEUM ᴼꜰ NATURAL

Close by.
Worlds away.

Minutes from Midtown, adventure awaits.
Come for an hour or spend the day
time-traveling through space, fossil halls,
ancient cultures, new worlds, and more.

Open daily | Central Park West at 79th Street
212.769.5100 | amnh.org

feet of indoor gallery space as well as a rooftop that will be used for exhibitions. Together with the New Museum of Contemporary Art (see p77), a striking off-kilter structure built on the Bowery five years ago, it represents a considerable culture shift downtown.

While many of the city's art venerable institutions have been in place for decades, even stately Museum Mile is evolving. Once the Museum for African Art (www.africanart.org) debuts its dramatic new building at 110th Street and Fifth Avenue, it will lengthen the strip by several blocks. The nomadic museum had hoped to move into its new digs by late 2012, but completion has been delayed by insufficient funding. Across Central Park on the Upper West Side, the city's oldest museum, the New-York Historical Society, has embraced the digital age with a high-tech revamp that brings its extraordinary trove of artefacts, art and documents to vivid life (see box p150).

Of course, a priority for first-time visitors will be to see some of the world-class collections for which the city is famous. The Metropolitan Museum of Art (see p143) is renowned for its European painting and sculpture, Islamic art, Greek and Roman collection and an ever-changing array of blockbuster travelling shows. The Museum of Modern Art (see p130) contains some of the most famous artworks of the 19th century through the present; it's also worth checking out its cutting-edge affiliate, MoMA PS1 (see p165) in Queens.

The Guggenheim (see p146), in Frank Lloyd Wright's landmark building, is another New York essential. If you want a bit of background, then the Museum of the City of New York (see p145) provides fascinating insight, while

SHORTLIST

Best new/revamped
- National September 11 Memorial (see p62)
- New-York Historical Society (see p152)

Best for local insight
- Lower East Side Tenement Museum (see p77)
- Museum of the City of New York (see p145)
- New-York Historical Society (see p152)

New York icons
- Chrysler Building (see p135)
- Empire State Building (see p129)
- Statue of Liberty (see p65)

Best free
- Brooklyn Bridge (see p162)
- Governors Island (see p57)
- National Museum of the American Indian (see p62)
- National September 11 Memorial (see p62)
- Staten Island Ferry (see p65)

Best urban oases
- Central Park (see p137)
- The Cloisters (see p158)
- High Line (see p97)
- New York Botanical Garden (see p161)

The 'big three' museums
- American Museum of Natural History (see p151)
- Metropolitan Museum of Art (see p143)
- Museum of Modern Art (see p130)

Best museum buildings
- New Museum of Contemporary Art (see p77)
- Solomon R Guggenheim Museum (see p146)

enjoy the ride™

FREQUENT DAILY DEPARTURES:
- 84 Pier 84 (West 44th Street)
- C Christopher Street
- B Battery Park
- S South Street Seaport
- D DUMBO Fulton Ferry – Pier 1

NEW YORK WATER TAXI

SAM HOLMES

HOP-ON/HOP-OFF: ALL-DAY ACCESS PASS
with free 9/11 MEMORIAL VISITOR PASS

9/11 MEMORIAL | OFFICIAL TRANSPORTATION PARTNER

BEST TOURISM TRANSPORTATION 2007-2011

The 9/11 Memorial provides reservations free of charge.

212.742.1969 | www.nywatertaxi.com

the Lower East Side Tenement Museum (see p77) brings New York's immigrant history to life.

It may have been surpassed by 1 World Trade Center in height, but the Empire State Building (see p129, is still New York's most famous skyscraper. Although there can be long lines to ascend to the observation deck, it's now open until 2am and late-night viewings are usually less crowded (and the illuminated cityscape is spectacular). Another option is the Top of the Rock observation deck, perched above Midtown's Rockefeller Center (see p131). The art deco tower gets one up on the Empire State by allowing a view of that iconic structure. On the subject of spectacular views, following a renovation that closed the interior of the Statue of Liberty (see p65), the crown is scheduled to reopen to the public in autumn 2012.

New-York Historical Society p11

Slicing up the Apple

This book is divided by neighbourhood. Downtown is the oldest part of Manhattan and also the most happening. At the tip of the island, the Financial District contains the seat of local government and the epicentre of capitalism. Elsewhere, the character of many downtown neighbourhoods is in a state of continual evolution as the forces of gentrification and fashion take hold. Over the past decade trendy bars, boutiques and galleries have been moving into the erstwhile immigrant neighbourhood of the Lower East Side. Former bohemian stomping ground Greenwich Village still resounds with cultural associations, but today is more moneyed and has the restaurants to prove it; to the west, leafy, winding streets give way to the Meatpacking District's warehouses, now colonised by designer stores, eateries and

nightspots. The once-radical East Village brims with bars and restaurants. Former art enclave Soho is now a prime shopping and dining destination, along with well-heeled neighbour Tribeca, while Little Italy is being crowded out by ever-expanding Chinatown and, to the north, boutique-riddled Nolita.

In Midtown, Chelsea contains New York's main contemporary-gallery district. Rivalled only by rapidly gentrifying Hell's Kitchen to the North, it is also one of the city's most prominent gay enclaves. Once mainly commercial, the Flatiron District has evolved into a fine-dining destination and nearby Union Square attracts foodies four days a week to New York's biggest farmers' market. Among the skyscrapers of Midtown's prime commercial stretch are some of NYC's most iconic attractions. Here, Fifth Avenue is home to some of the city's poshest retail, while Broadway is the world's most famous theatreland. Love it or loathe it, garish Times Square (see p122) is a must-gawp spectacle.

Uptown, bucolic Central Park (see p137), with its picturesque lakes, expansive lawns and famous zoo, is the green divider between the patrician Upper East Side and the less conservative but equally well-heeled Upper West Side. Between them, these wealthy locales contain the lion's share of the city's cultural institutions: most museums are on the UES – the Metropolitan Museum of Art and others on Fifth Avenue's Museum Mile, in the stately former mansions of the 20th-century elite – but the UWS has the Metropolitan Opera, the New York Philharmonic and the New York City Ballet at Lincoln Center (see p155). Further north, regenerated Harlem offers vibrant nightlife, soul food and plenty of cultural history.

Making the most of it

First, accept that you can never see it all. The typical week's visit to the city will involve some tough choices. Similarly, it's self-defeating to attempt to hit all the major collections in one visit to an institution as large as the Met or the American Museum of Natural History. So plan, pace yourself and take time to enjoy aimless wandering in picturesque areas like the West Village or Central Park.

Because the city's museums are privately funded, and receive little or no government support, admission prices can be steep. However, these usually include entry to temporary as well as the permanent collections, and many institutions offer one day or evening a week when admission fees are either waived or switched to a voluntary donation (and remember, 'suggested donation' prices are just that). Be warned that many museums are closed on Mondays – except on some holidays, such as Columbus Day and Presidents' Day.

Despite recent budget cuts, the subway (see p184) is still highly efficient and runs 24 hours a day. It is generally well populated, clean and relatively easy to navigate. It will often get you from one end of the city to another more quickly (not to mention more cheaply) than a cab. Charge up a MetroCard and you can travel seamlessly by subway and bus. Of course, you should keep your wits about you and take basic precautions, but New York these days is a pretty safe place. But the best way to get to know the city is by walking. Manhattan is a mere 13.4 miles long and 2.3 miles across at its widest point, and once you've mastered the grid, it's easy to find your way (although it gets a little trickier downtown).

Don Antonio p17

Eating & Drinking

Dining out is one of New York's truly great passions. Food is entertainment here, and the most celebrated chefs attract rock-star followings. For visitors, there's no better way of tapping into the city's zeitgeist than by venturing into its restaurants and bars.

One of the most exciting restaurants to open in recent years comes courtesy of chef Andrew Carmellini, a haute-cuisine vet who made his name cooking family-style Italian at Locanda Verde (see p70). In spring 2011, he opened the Dutch (see p69), channelling his experiences road-tripping across the States into an exuberant menu that highlights NYC institutions like the oyster bar while delivering impulsive comfort food from across the country (hot fried chicken, a cracker-domed rabbit potpie).

Culinary fusion has an obvious appeal in a city that prides itself as an ethnic melting pot. Korean-American superstar David Chang continues to draw fans to his cadre of buzzy restaurants, including Momofuku Ssäm Bar (see p87). But more recently, a new cast of gastronomic renegades have come to the fore. At Parm (see p74), fine-dining refugees Rich Torrisi and Mario Carbone remix the Italian-American tradition with polished upgrades on classics like chicken parmesan and baked clams, as well as inventive tasting menus at the adjacent Torrisi Italian Specialties. Across town, restaurateur Ed Schoenfeld and chef Joe Ng bring farm-to-table zeal to the ancient art of dim sum at RedFarm (see p98).

Nouveau scene-maker Gabriel Stulman has built a mini empire in a stretch of the West Village affectionately named Little Wisco (a nod to his home state of Wisconsin). The most recent addition to his stable, Perla (see p95), is perhaps the most ambitious, pairing bold riffs on humble Italian fare with Stulman's trademark bonhomie.

New Yorkers love Italian food, from humble pizzerias to Michelin-starred white table cloth joints. Even in a crowded market, Michael White stands above the fray. Over the past few years he's criss-crossed Gotham, erecting standard-bearing beacons of Italian cuisine: gleaming seafood temple Marea (see p132) on Central Park South; the hushed fine-dining hotel restaurant Ai Fiori in Midtown East; and seasonal pizzeria Nicoletta in the East Village. For an introduction to his exceptional handmade pastas, head to the raucous Bolognese trattoria Osteria Morini (see p70).

There was a time, around the turn of last century, when grand hotels were the place to find the best restaurants in New York. You'll find a return to form at the NoMad (see p115), an opulent throwback from chef Daniel Humm and Will Guidara of Eleven Madison Park renown. No meal is complete without the show-stopping chicken for two – amber-

hued, with foie gras, brioche and black truffle stuffing under its skin – or a classic cocktail in the elegant barroom run by mixology wiz Leo Robitschek. For a more casual (though no less decadent) repast, head to the nearby Ace Hotel, which Spotted Pig duo Ken Friedman and April Bloomfield have turned into an all-hours fooderati clubhouse. The gastropubby Breslin Bar & Dining Room (see p112) offers excellent grub from morning till night, and across the hotel lobby the equally mobbed John Dory (see p113) focuses on seafood.

The East Village has a knack for sprouting reasonably priced eateries that draw cult followings. Find superlative slow-roasted pork sandwiches at Porchetta (see p87), outrageously popular ramen at Japanese import Ippudo NY (see p86) and the city's best burritos at Cal-Mex transplant Dos Toros (see p86). Northern Spy Food Co (see p87) has become a locavore staple for its earnest (and delicious) devotion to seasonal cooking.

While gastronomes take pride in haute-cuisine temples like Per Se (see p154) and Daniel (see p148), you'll find equal devotion to more humble classics. The city's best burger is a source of constant

RedFarm p15

debate, with many critics giving their budget-patty nod to celebrated restaurateur Danny Meyers' Shake Shack chain (see p154). The Neapolitan pizza craze has shown no sign of flagging, either, though the latest trend to take hold is the montanara – a puffy, golden-crusted pie that's flash fried before hitting the oven. Find standout examples at Don Antonio by Starita (see p123).

New York's farm-to-table movement is perhaps most robust in Brooklyn, where cheaper rents and a DIY spirit have made the borough a refuge for young, risk-taking chefs. The nerve centre of the movement is Roberta's in Bushwick (261 Moore Street, at Bogart Street, 1-718 417 1118, www.robertaspizza.com), which has its own rooftop garden and plays host to the Heritage Food Network's sustainable-eats radio station. Brooklyn has also begun to establish itself as a destination for cutting-edge cooking. If you're looking to splurge, and can plan ahead, you'll find some of the city's most accomplished cooking in an upscale supermarket. Chef's Table at Brooklyn Fare (200 Schermerhorn Street, at Hoyt Street, 1-718 243 0050, www.brooklynfare.com/chefs-table) serves as a stage for a daily-changing, 15-course meal from self-taught masterchef César Ramirez. Reservations are only accepted on Mondays at 10.30am, six weeks in advance.

Elsewhere, there are cheek-by-jowl Asian restaurants in Chinatown, while Koreatown, the stretch of West 32nd Street between Fifth Avenue and Broadway, is lined with Korean barbecue joints and other eateries. Further afield, Harlem offers soul food and West African cooking, while the melting pot that is Queens counts Greek (in Astoria) and Indian and Latin American (in Jackson Heights) among its globe-spanning cuisines.

SHORTLIST

Best new
- Buvette (see p97)
- The Dutch (see p69)
- Earl's Beer and Cheese (see p148)
- The NoMad (see p115)
- RedFarm (see p98)

Best cheap eats
- Cafe Edison (see p122)
- Dos Toros (see p86)
- Parm (see p74)
- Shake Shack (see p154)

Where to blow the budget
- Brushstroke (see p69)
- Chef's Table at Brooklyn Fare (see left)
- Corton (see p69)
- Per Se (see p154)

The classics
- Bemelmans Bar (see p148)
- Grand Central Oyster Bar & Restaurant (see p136)
- Katz's Delicatessen (see p78)
- Keens Steakhouse (see p118)

Best seasonal fare
- ABC Kitchen (see p112)
- Blue Hill (see p94)
- Northern Spy Food Co (see p87)

Best for carnivores
- The Breslin Bar & Dining Room (see p112)
- The Cannibal (see p113)

Best cocktails
- PDT (see p87)
- Pegu Club (see p70)
- Bar Pleiades (see p146)

Best local brews
- 508 GastroBrewery (see p67)
- Blind Tiger Ale House (see p97)
- Jimmy's No 43 (see p86)

Some of these further-flung locales are now attracting big-name chefs. Marcus Samuelsson has heralded an uptown renaissance with Red Rooster (see p158). In 2011, Quebecois toque Hugue Dufour put Long Island City on the food map with his snout-to-tail cooking at the short-lived M Wells; look out for his much-anticipated follow-up, M Wells Dinette at MoMa PS1 (see p165), as well as a rumoured steakhouse-cum-boathouse.

Veg out

In spite of the city's obsession with locally sourced produce, new vegetarian restaurants are few and far between. While it's not strictly meat-free, Jean-Georges Vongerichten's ABC Kitchen (see p112) – a 2011 *Time Out New York* Food & Drink Award winner for Best New Restaurant – has become a bastion of Greenmarket cookery, with a mix of healthy and decadent cuisine that puts seasonal produce in the spotlight. Dirt Candy (see p85), from talented chef Amanda Cohen, serves sometimes sinful, always sophisticated meat-free eats, while Pure Food & Wine (54 Irving Place, between 17th & 18th Streets, 1-212 477 1010, www.pure foodandwine.com) draws loyal devotees for its refined raw-food ethos and innovative beverage program highlighting seasonal cocktails and biodynamic wines.

The big tipple

New York continues to be a cradle of cocktail culture. Many of the early adopters of classic cocktail revivalism were unmarked, speakeasy-style bars, usually with vintage looks to match. Although locals might be starting to tire of the game, seeking out these 'secret' boozing spots is part of the fun –

from the dark alley that leads to the Back Room (see p78) to the fake phone booth at PDT (see p87). The scene also thrives in Brooklyn, most notably in Williamsurg at spots such as Maison Premiere (298 Bedford Avenue, between Grand & South 1st Streets, 1-347 335 0446, www.maison premiere.com) – a throwback New Orleans-Style boîte specialising in absinthe-based tipples.

The craft-beer revolution that's swept the country has a firm foothold in NYC, too. Scrappy producers like Sixpoint and Barrier Brewing Co have brought attention to the local brewing scene. The most dependable spots to sample the local offerings are cultish beer bars like Jimmy's No 43 (see p86) and Blind Tiger Ale House (see p97). La Birreria crafts its own housemade cask ales on a rooftop above Mario Batali's gastromarket Eataly (see p115), while the Cannibal (see p113) specialises in esoteric beers and artisanal meats.

While wine doesn't drive the boozing scene like cocktails and beer, a new breed of vino bars is tossing out the pretence and putting an emphasis on funky, affordable lists that reflect the tastes of the owners. The poster child of this movement is Terroir (see p88), which recently opened its third location in Murray Hill after conquering the East Village and Tribeca.

Where there's smoke…

The only legal places to smoke indoors are either venues that cater largely to cigar smokers (and actually sell tobacco products) or spaces that have created areas for smokers. Try Circa Tabac (32 Watts Street, between Sixth Avenue & Thompson Street, Soho, 1-212 941 1781) or Hudson Bar & Books (636 Hudson Street, at Horatio Street, 1-212 229 2642).

In God We Trust p23

Shopping

One of the best cities in the world to drop some of your hard-earned cash, New York offers anything you could possibly want to buy, and – as long as you're prepared to shop around or hit some sample sales – at the best prices. Locals may complain about the 'mallification' of certain neighbourhoods such as Soho, but for visitors, these retail-rich areas are intoxicating consumer playgrounds. As America's fashion capital, and the site of the prestigious Fashion Institute of Technology and other high-profile art colleges, the metropolis is a magnet for creative young designers from around the country. Not only does this ensure the shops and markets are stuffed with unique finds, the Garment District is a hotbed of open-to-the-public

showroom sales (see below). While the recession hit the retail sector hard, it has been a boon for bargain-hunters, and there's also been a silver lining for some small businesses. As rents in Manhattan have become more affordable, young designers and boutique-owners from the outer boroughs have migrated to areas like the Lower East Side that were previously beyond their reach. Shopkeepers are also becoming more creative, launching pop-up shops and hedging their bets with mixed-use businesses, such as the Dressing Room (see p81), which combines a bar and boutique. Increasingly, small shops are selling a combination of goods, and the vintage trend, appealing to the environmentally aware and budget-conscious alike, is stronger than

ever. Dear: Rivington (see p80) divides its retail space between designer clothes and vintage home accessories, while Voz (see p90) sells a mix of new and vintage garb, furniture and design objects.

Retail hotspots

Although many of the city's retail-rich districts are within walking distance of each other, and you can zip quickly between others on the subway, because of the dense concentration of shops in some areas (for example, the Lower East Side or Madison Avenue), you might want to limit yourself to a couple of areas in a day out. Generally speaking, you'll find the most unusual shops downtown and in parts of Brooklyn.

Although Soho has been heavily commercialised, especially the main thoroughfares, this once edgy, arty enclave still has some idiosyncratic survivors and numerous top-notch shops – don't miss tucked-away design store Kiosk (see p71). Urban fashion abounds on Lafayette Street, while Broome Street is becoming an enclave for chic home design. To the east, Nolita has been colonised by indie designers, especially along Mott and Mulberry Streets.

Once the centre of the 'rag' trade, the Lower East Side used to be associated with bargain outlets and bagels. Now a bar- and boutique-laden patch, it's especially good for vintage, streetwear and local designers, such as Chuck Guarino's rockin' menswear line Thecast (see p83), and Victor Osborne's hip handcrafted hats (see p83). Orchard, Ludlow and Rivington Streets are hotspots. North of here, in the East Village, you'll find a highly browsable mix of vintage clothing, streetwear and records alongside stylish home and kids' goods, but shops are more scattered than on the Lower East Side.

SHORTLIST

Best new
- (3x1) (see p71)
- Fivestory (see p149)
- The Hoodie Shop (see p81)
- Obsessive Compulsive Cosmetics (see p81)

Best vintage and antiques
- Doyle & Doyle (see p80)
- Mantiques Modern (see p108)
- Voz (see p90)
- What Goes Around Comes Around (see p72)

Taste of New York
- Russ & Daughters (see p83)
- Union Square Greenmarket (see p116)
- Zabar's (see p155)

Best books and music
- Downtown Music Gallery (see p76)
- Other Music (see p90)
- Strand Book Store (see p90)

Local labels
- Alexis Bittar (see p71)
- In God We Trust (see p71)
- Erica Weiner (see p76)
- Thecast (see p83)

Best for gifts
- Bond Street Chocolate (see p88)
- Kiosk (see p71)

Best bargains
- AvaMaria (see p76)
- Bit+Piece (see p76)
- Century 21 (see p67)

Cutting-edge designs
- Opening Ceremony (see p72)
- The Future Perfect (see p90)

Best New York institutions
- Barneys New York (see p149)
- Bergdorf Goodman (see p132)

DON'T MISS: 2013

YOUR GUIDE TO ARTS, ENTERTAINMENT AND CULTURE IN THE WORLD'S MOST EXCITING PLACES

timeout.com

Over on the other side of the island, the one-time down-at-heel wholesale meat market, stretching south from 14th Street, has become a high-end consumer playground; the warehouses of the Meatpacking District are now populated by a clutch of international designers, including Diane von Furstenberg and Stella McCartney. Meanwhile, the western strip of Bleecker Street is lined with a further cache of designer boutiques.

Most of the city's department stores can be found on Fifth Avenue between 38th and 59th Streets, in the company of chain stores and designer flagships (the parade of lofty names continues east on 57th Street). The exceptions are Macy's, in Herald Square, and Bloomingdale's and Barneys, which are both on the Upper East Side. The Uptown stretch of Madison Avenue has long been synonymous with the crème de la crème of international fashion.

It's also well worth venturing across the East River. Williamsburg abounds with idiosyncratic shops and one-off buys. As well as the main drag, Bedford Avenue, North 6th and Grand Streets are good hunting grounds for vintage clothes, arty housewares and record stores. There are further treasures in Cobble Hill, Carroll Gardens and Boerum Hill, especially on Court and Smith Streets and Atlantic Avenue; the latter has mainly been known for antiques, but cool clothiers have started to move in.

Keep it local

Of course, many of the country's most popular designers are based in New York, from established names like Diane von Furstenberg and Marc Jacobs to newer contemporary stars such as Phillip Lim, Thakoon Panichgul and Marcus Wainwright and David

Neville of Rag & Bone (see p100). Made-in-NYC items – jewellery by Erica Weiner (see p76), makeup from Obsessive Compulsive Cosmetics (see p81), accessories from In God We Trust (see p71) or cards printed at Bowne & Co Stationers (see p67) – are chic souvenirs. Stores that stock local designs among their wares include Castor & Pollux (see p100), Honey in the Rough (see p81), Opening Ceremony (see p72) and the Future Perfect for interior items. There are also opportunities to buy goods direct from emerging designers at popular weekend markets such as the Brooklyn Flea (see box p42).

Famous names

Of course, many visitors to New York will simply be looking to make the most of the incredible variety of big brands on offer in the city. For young, casual and streetwear labels, head to Broadway in Soho. Fifth Avenue heaves with a mix of designer showcases and mall-level megastores. Madison Avenue is more consistently posh, with a further parade of deluxe labels.

If you prefer to do all your shopping under one roof, famous department stores Macy's (good for mid-range brands), Bloomingdale's (a mix of mid-range and designer), Barneys (cutting-edge and high-fashion) and Bergdorf Goodman (luxury goods and international designer) are all stuffed with desirable goods.

Sniffing out sales

New York is fertile bargain-hunting territory. The traditional post-season sales (which usually start just after Christmas and in early to mid June) have given way to frequent markdowns throughout the year: look for sale racks in boutiques, chain and department stores. The twice-a-year Warehouse Sale at Barneys (see p149) is an important fixture on the bargain hound's calendar. And of course, as New York is home to numerous designer studios and showrooms, there is a weekly spate of sample sales. The best are listed in the Shopping & Style section of *Time Out New York* magazine and www.timeout.com/newyork.

Racked (www.ny.racked.com), Top Button (www.topbutton.com) and Clothing Line (1-212 947 8748, www.clothingline.com), which holds sales for a variety of labels – from J Crew and Theory to Tory Burch and Rag & Bone, at its Garment District showroom (Second Floor, 261 W 36th Street, between Seventh & Eighth Avenues) – are also terrific resources.

Chief among the permanent sale stores is the famous Century 21 (see p67) – it's beloved of rummagers, but detested by those with little patience for sifting through less than fabulous merchandise for the prize finds. A second Manhattan location opened on the Upper West Side in 2011, but we recommend braving the original for breadth of stock and, sometimes, deeper discounts. Loehmann's (see p108) can also come up trumps. Nordstrom Rack, the discount arm of the department store (www.nordstrom.com), is worth checking out. Recently, however, smaller discount boutiques have opened in the city offering more personal service and less of a scrum (see box p75).

Have a rummage

Flea market browsing is a popular weekend pastime among New Yorkers. Chelsea's Annex Antiques Fair & Flea Market may be consigned to history, but the area retains the covered market Antiques Garage (see p108), although at time of writing there were rumours it might relocate; it has a sibling outdoor market in Hell's Kitchen. There are also some worthwhile antiques stores in the neighbourhood, including the wonderfully eclectic Mantiques Modern (see p108). Make the pilgrimage to one of the deservedly popular Brooklyn Fleas to browse everything from vintage jewellery and crafts to salvage and locally made foodstuffs. For fine antiques, with prices to match, head for Madison Avenue in the 1960s and 70s.

Consumer culture

Chains like Barnes & Noble (www.barnesandnoble.com) still dominate the book scene, but well-loved independents, such as the Strand Book Store (see p90), home to 18 miles of books, have been holding their own for years. Housing Works Bookstore Café (see p71) doubles as a popular Soho hangout. For art books, as well as cool souvenirs, don't forget museum shops – MoMA Design & Book Store, attached to the Museum of Modern Art (see p130) and the New Museum Store (see p77) are both terrific.

When Other Music (see p90) opened opposite Tower Records in the East Village in the mid 1990s, it boldly stood as a small pocket of resistance to corporate music. Its Goliath now shuttered, Other Music rolls on, offering a well-curated selection of indie-rock, world music and experimental sounds. Tucked away in a Chinatown basement, the Downtown Music Gallery (see p76) is an essential stop for seekers of avant-garde jazz and new classical.

Santos Party House p26

Nightlife

The discotheque may have had its origins in occupied Paris during World War II – apparently, the Nazis weren't too keen on jazz, dancing and high times, driving such pursuits underground – but it was in New York City that the modern concept of clubbing came into being. Hallowed halls such as the Loft, Studio 54, the Paradise Garage and Area are imbedded in nightlife's collective consciousness as near-mythic ideals. But in this millennium? Well, the city can no longer claim to be the world's clubbing capital; the balance of power has shifted eastward to cities like London and Berlin. Still, with this much history (not to mention eight million people ready to party), New York nightlife can never be counted out – and the scene today is as strong as it's been in years.

Recently, there's been a burst of roving shindigs, sometimes held in official venues but more often tossed in out-of-the-way warehouses and lofts. By their nature, these parties can be a bitch to find out about for those not in the loop. Some of the best, particularly if you're a fan of underground house and techno, are run by the teams at Blkmarket Membership (www.blkmarket membership.com), ReSolute (www.resolutenyc.com) and Mister Saturday Night (www. mistersaturdaynight.com); a visit to www.timeout.com/newyork should help to clue you in.

Don't rule out the clubs themselves, though, as there are still plenty of fabulous DJs playing music of all persuasions. Cielo (see p101), an intimate and beautiful Meatpacking District venue, boasts underground jocks playing over one of the city's best sound systems. On the other end of the dance-club spectrum, Pacha is the club of choice for followers of big-name superstars, with the likes of Skrillex, David Guetta and Erick Morillo regularly presiding over the dance floor. Santos Party House is another good bet, particularly when Danny Krivit takes the spot over for the soulful-house-and classics oriented 718 Sessions (www.dannykrivit.net).

Some of the city's best parties only take place occasionally or are seasonal. Warm Up, a summertime soirée held every Saturday during July and August in the courtyard at MoMA PS1 in Queens (see p165), attracts kids who like nothing better than to boogie down to some pretty twisted DJs and bands. The (usually) monthly Bunker bash, one of New York's top techno get-togethers, takes place in Williamsburg's Public Assembly (70 North 6th Street, between Kent & Wythe Avenues, 1-718 782 5188, www.beyondbooking.com/thebunker). The house-music-loving Verboten crew tosses top-shelf, one-off affairs all over the city (www.verbotennewyork.com).

And, of course, there's the Sunday-night tea dance Body & Soul (www.bodyandsoul-nyc.com), helmed by the DJ holy trinity of Danny Krivit, Joe Claussell and François K. The formerly weekly affair now only pops up a few times each year – but it's still a spectacle, with a few thousand sweaty revellers dancing their hearts out from start till finish.

For those who like a bit of bump-and-grind in their after-dark activities – and really, who doesn't? – the city's burlesque scene is as strong as it's ever been. Some of the best producers and performers – they often cross over – are Doc Wasabassco (www.wasabassco.com), Shien Lee (www.dancesofvice.com), Jen Gapay's Thirsty Girl Productions (www.thirstygirlproductions.com), Angie Pontani of the World Famous Pontani Sisters (www.angiepontani.com) and Calamity Chang, 'the Asian Sexation' (www.calamitychang.com).

Live and kicking

New York is among the greatest cities in the world to see live music.

Joe's Pub

Manhattan and Brooklyn are packed with venues, from hole-in-the-wall dives to resplendent concert halls. Plan accordingly and you can catch more than one world-class show on any given night.

For larger seated shows, try the posh theatres in midtown and further north. The palatial art deco Radio City Music Hall (see p132) gives grandeur to pop performances, while Harlem's Apollo Theater (see p160) still hosts its legendary Amateur Night competition, as well as fancy galas from the likes of the Jacksons. In addition to classical performances, Carnegie Hall (see p126) hosts jazz mavericks like Keith Jarrett and neoclassical stars like Joanna Newsom, and Jazz at Lincoln Center's Allen Room (see p156), has a million-dollar view that threatens to steal even the good shows.

Some of music's biggest acts – Jay-Z, Bruce Springsteen, Britney Spears – play at Madison Square Garden (see p120), which is currently undergoing a face-lift. Terminal 5 (610 W 56th Street, between Eleventh & Twelfth Avenues, 1-212 260 4700, www.terminal5nyc.com) is a three-floor, 3,000-capacity behemoth hosting indie superstars (Florence and the Machine) and dance-y acts (Chromeo, Girl Talk).

The rock scene's heart, however, beats downtown and in Brooklyn. The clubs dotting the East Village and Lower East Side are too many to count, but don't miss the Mercury Lounge (see p83), the no-nonsense spot that launched the career of the Strokes, among others. Joe's Pub (see p91), the classy cabaret room tucked inside the Public Theater, continues to present great acts of all genres. For medium-size acts, the Bowery Ballroom (see p83) is Manhattan's hub, while its sister venue in Brooklyn, Music Hall of

SHORTLIST

Best new/revamped
- 54 Below (see p124)
- Madison Square Garden (see p120)
- XL at The Out NYC (see p181)

Best for indie bands
- Bowery Ballroom (see p83)
- Cake Shop (see p83)
- Mercury Lounge (see p83)
- Union Pool (see p28)

Hottest dancefloors
- Cielo (see p101)
- Santos Party House (see p76)
- Sullivan Room (see p96)

Best jazz joints
- Smalls (see p101)
- Village Vanguard (see p101)

Most storied venues
- Apollo Theater (see p160)
- Carnegie Hall (see p126)
- Radio City Music Hall (see p132)

Best for rising stars
- Joe's Pub (see p91)
- Le Poisson Rouge (see p96)
- Metropolitan Room (see p116)

Best gay spots
- Fairytail Lounge (see p125)
- Henrietta Hudson (see p101)
- XL at The Out NYC (see p28)

Best for laughs
- Carolines on Broadway (see p125)
- 92YTribeca (see p72)
- Upright Citizens BrigadeTheatre (see p109)

Best dance parties
- 718 Sessions at Santos Party House (see p26)
- The Bunker (see p26)
- Warm Up (see p26)

DON'T MISS: 2013

Williamsburg (66 North 6th Street, between Kent & Wythe Avenues, 1-718 486 5400, musichallof williamsburg.com), hosts bands such as Sonic Youth, Arctic Monkeys and Antlers, often on the day after they've played Bowery Ballroom.

Williamsburg is an essential stop for indie-rock aficionados. Union Pool (484 Union Avenue, at Meeker Avenue, 1-718 609 0484, www.union-pool.com) offers up-and-coming acts, excellent DJs and a sweet photo booth. Take a ten minute stroll and you'll hit cute local spot Pete's Candy Store, offering everything from whimsical folk music to poetry and bingo (709 Lorimer Street, between Frost & Richardson Streets, 1-718 302 3770, www.petescandystore.com).

Working the room

The cabaret scene is a confluence of opposites: the heights of polish and the depths of amateurism; intense honesty and airy pretence; earnestness and camp. One thing's for sure, it's a quintessentially New York experience. Although the storied Oak Room in the Algonquin Hotel closed for good when the hotel underwent refurbishment in late 2011, classic performance spaces live on, including Café Carlyle in the plush Upper East Side hotel (35 E 76th Street, at Madison Avenue, 1-212 744 1600, www.thecarlyle.com), although cover is high and dinner is often compulsory. A worthy alternative is the Metropolitan Room (see p116), which offers top-notch shows at reasonable prices. A new cabaret venue, 54 Below (see p124), opened in summer 2012, showcasing a mix of Broadway luminaries and edgier talent.

If it's laughs you're after, the city's myriad comedy clubs serve as both platforms for big names

and launchpads for the stars of tomorrow. The looming presence of TV sketch giant *Saturday Night Live*, which has been filmed at Rockefeller Center since 1975, helps to ensure the presence of theatrical comedy; more influential in the day-to-day landscape, however, is the improv and sketch troupe Upright Citizens Brigade, which migrated from Chicago in the 1990s. Its theatre has been the most visible catalyst in New York's current alternative comedy boom, and it expanded with a second space in the East Village in 2011.

Out and about

The passage of 2011's Marriage Equality Act in New York State cemented NYC's status as the gay capital of the US (sorry, San Francisco). Today, you can walk through the current It gaybourhood, Hell's Kitchen, and see couples happily canoodling on the street. It's also the location of New York's first gay luxury hotel, the Out NYC (see p181). The property's XL Nightclub is one of the few all-gay megaclubs left in the city, but there are plenty of popular roving events courtesy of promoters including Maggie C (www.maggie cevents.com), FV Events (www. fvevents.com) and Josh Wood (www.joshwoodproductions.com).

You'll find thriving queer subcultures all over town. Bearded boys and tattooed girls mingle at laid-back mixers in the East Village, while serious music fiends often take over historic West Village venues like the Stonewall Inn (see p101) and the Monster (80 Grove Street, at Seventh Avenue South, 1-212 924 3558, www.manhattan-monster.com), offering a house-party vibe that's considerably more welcoming than the gay blowouts of yore.

Times Square p122

Arts & Leisure

Given the impressive sweep of New York's cultural life, it's easy to be overwhelmed by the number of events on offer. From enormous stadia to tiny Off Broadway stages, from revival cinemas to avant-garde dance venues, the choices are endless. With a little planning, however, you can take in that game, concert or show that will make your visit more memorable. Consult *Time Out New York* magazine or www.timeout.com/newyork for the latest listings.

Classical music & opera

A new generation of entrepreneurial groups like the International Contemporary Ensemble (ICE), Alarm Will Sound, New Amsterdam Records and numerous upstart opera companies have brought an electrifying new energy to New York's classical music and opera scene. These musicians possess a potent mix of formal training and street cred, contributing to a rejuvenation of even the most staid of New York's music institutions.

At Lincoln Center (see p155), the renovated Alice Tully Hall has inspired exciting programming, including the three-year-old White Light Festival, an exploration of music's spiritual power that takes place each autumn. The Metropolitan Opera (see p156) forges ahead under the adventurous – and occasionally controversial – guidance of general manager Peter Gelb and new principal conductor Fabio Luisi. The 2012/2013 season boasts new productions of *Rigoletto*

Broadway's
Longest-Running
Musical...EVER.
THE
PHANTOM
OF THE OPERA
Telecharge.com | 212.239.6200
MAJESTIC THEATRE, 247 West 44th Street

and *L'Elisir d'Amore* as well as three complete rounds of Robert Lepage's flashy Ring Cycle in spring 2013. At the New York Philharmonic, which plays at Lincoln Center's Avery Fisher Hall (see p156), music director Alan Gilbert continues to bring innovation to the forefront without losing sight of the orchestra's past.

With its three concert spaces and diverse programming, venerable Carnegie Hall (see p126) continues to set the standard for classical music in New York. The Brooklyn Academy of Music (30 Lafayette Avenue, between Ashland Place & St Felix Street; 1-718 636 4100, www.bam.org) has also become a major player, hosting the touring production of Philip Glass's *Einstein On the Beach* in September 2012, as well as its perennially popular Next Wave Festival and two 2013 productions from the New York City Opera, which left its home at Lincoln center after a major restructuring led by new general manager George Steel.

But if you want to catch this new generation at its most inventive, head to one of many small, genre-mixing venues, such as Le Poisson Rouge (see p96) and experimental-music mecca Roulette (509 Atlantic Avenue, at Third Avenue, Boerum Hill, Brooklyn; 1-917 267 0363, www.roulette.org), which are playing an increasingly important role in bringing classical music and opera to a hipper audience.

Dance

Depending on what part of town you're in, New York is home to both tradition and innovation in dance, an art form that continues to stretch its boundaries. Lately, the art-world crowd has embraced it – at 2012's Whitney Biennial, for instance, dance was prominently

SHORTLIST

Best new/revamped
- Film Society of Lincoln Center (see p157)
- Lincoln Center Theater's Claire Tow Theater (see p124)
- Pershing Square Signature Center (see p129)

Most experimental
- Anthology Film Archives (see p91)
- The Kitchen (see p110)
- The Stone (see p93)

Best for unwinding
- Great Jones Spa (see p93)
- Juvenex (see p119)

Best long-running shows
- Book of Mormon (see p126)
- Sleep No More (see p110)
- War Horse (see p157)

Best Off Broadway
- New York Theatre Workshop (see p93)
- Playwrights Horizons (see p129)
- Public Theater (see p93)

Best free outdoor arts
- River to River Festival (see p41)
- Shakespeare in the Park (see p41)
- SummerStage (see 41)

Essential high culture
- Carnegie Hall (see p126)
- Metropolitan Opera House (see p156)
- New York City Center (see p126)

Best cheap tickets
- Pershing Square Signature Center (see p129)
- Soho Rep (see p73)
- TKTS (see p122)

DON'T MISS: 2013

featured, including works by Sarah Michelson and Michael Clark. The Museum of Modern Art (see p130) is just as ambitious: from mid October to early November 2012, the choreographer and visual artist Ralph Lemon will organise a three-week program highlighting performances by contemporary choreographers. And keep an eye out for more experimental, intimate offerings at MoMA PS1 (see p165), where new performance practices are revered. Throughout New York, but especially in parts of Brooklyn and Queens, choreographers are intent on exploring the more complex notions of performance and the body; the internationally admired laboratory Movement Research (www.movementresearch.org) is devoted to the investigation of dance and movement-based forms and throughout much of the year showcases works-in-progress evenings at Greenwich Village's historic Judson Church.

But that's not to suggest that New York is lacking in more established quarters. For ballet fans, there is no greater place to bask in the world of George Balanchine and Jerome Robbins than the New York City Ballet (at the David H Koch Theater, see p156). The American Ballet Theatre – joined in 2009 by extraordinary Russian choreographer Alexei Ratmansky as its resident choreographer – presents a mix of full-length classics with one-act ballets by Twyla Tharp, Antony Tudor, Christopher Wheeldon and, of course, Ratmansky. His *Nutcracker* is in residence each holiday season at the Brooklyn Academy of Music (see p31), while the company has other seasons at the Metropolitan Opera House (see p156) and New York City Center (see p126).

Film

Every corner of NYC has been immortalised in celluloid, and it's quite common to stumble upon an actual scene being shot. So it's not surprising that the city has a special relationship with the movies. The calendar is packed with festivals, including Tribeca, the New York Film Festival and several others organised by the excellent Film Society of Lincoln Center (see p157), which recently premiered its new Elinor Bunin Monroe Film Center. Summer brings the wonderful tradition of free outdoor screenings in Midtown's Bryant Park (www.bryantpark.org) and other green spaces. Cinephiles

Alice Tully Hall p29

Time Out
New York

Check us out
online to book:

→Hotels

→Theater and live
entertainment
tickets

→Restaurants

→Tours and
attractions

YOUR
ULTIMATE
TRAVEL
GUIDE

**To book your itinerary, go to
timeout.com/newyork**

love Film Forum (see p101) for its wide range of revivals and new indie features, while Anthology Film Archives (see p91) specialises in experimental programming.

Sports

The professional sports scene has been marked by an edifice complex in the past few years, as several teams have built brand-new stadia. First it was baseball's turn with the 2009 openings of Citi Field in Queens and Yankee Stadium in the Bronx, the respective homes of the hapless Mets (newyork.mets.mlb.com) and the mighty Yankees (newyork.yankees.mlb.com).

Next came American football, when the Giants and Jets kicked off their 2010 seasons in the MetLife Stadium (www.metlifestadium.com) across the river in New Jersey.

Now gritty Madison Square Garden (see p120), home to basketball's Knicks and hockey's Rangers, is in the midst of a multi-million-dollar rolling revamp, and the brand-new Barclays Center (www.barclayscenter.com) in Brooklyn, welcomes basketball's Nets in autumn 2012.

Theatre

For most visitors, seeing a show means a trip to Broadway. Amid the winking lights of Times Square you'll find the biggest and starriest productions, often staged in beautiful venues dating from the early decades of the 20th century.

The crowning jewels of Broadway continue to be musicals. Megahits like *Wicked* and *The Lion King* are still selling out, but every season brings new sensations. Recent breakouts include the outrageously funny *The Book of Mormon* and the bittersweetly romantic *Once*; the bizarre but

colourful *Spider-Man: Turn Off the Dark* offers a huger sense of spectacle. Keep an eye out, too, for fresh stagings of older shows, such as a revival of the beloved *Annie* in autumn 2012.

Plays have shorter runs but can also generate considerable buzz, especially if they have big stars attached. It can be tough to score tickets for these shows, so check www.theatermania.com and www.playbill.com for advance information. Serious theatre fans, however, will want to visit the more intimate world of Off Broadway. You don't have leave midtown to find Playwrights Horizons (see p129) or Signature Theatre Company (see p129), which recently moved into a brand-new complex designed by Frank Gehry.

You can also find strong Off Broadway work at East Village institutions like New York Theatre Workshop (see p93) and the renovated Public Theater (see p93), which mounts two free Shakespeare in the Park (see p41) shows each summer. And Brooklyn Academy of Music's Harvey Theater (651 Fulton Street, between Ashland & Rockwell Places, Fort Greene, 1-718 636 4100, www.bam.org) stages first-rate productions from around the world. Nearly all Broadway and Off Broadway shows are served by big ticketing agencies, but for cheap seats, your best bet remains the TKTS Discount Booth (see p122).

For theatre that is weirder and more adventurous – and less expensive – explore the Off-Off Broadway scene downtown and in Brooklyn, where the experimental impulse is alive and well. Look for troupes like Elevator Repair Service (www.elevator.org), Radiohole (www.radiohole.com) and the Civilians (www.thecivilians.org), as well as venues such as Soho Rep (see p73).

DON'T MISS: 2013

Calendar

New Year's Eve p38

The following is our selection of annual events, plus the best one-offs confirmed when this guide went to press. For the latest information, check the listings in *Time Out New York* magazine or www.timeout.com/newyork, and always confirm dates before making any travel plans. Dates highlighted in **bold** indicate public holidays.

September 2012

1-3, 8, 9 **Washington Square Outdoor Art Exhibit**
Greenwich Village, p93
www.washingtonsquareoutdoorart exhibit.org
See art in streets around the park.

3 Labor Day

5 Sept-19 Jan **Next Wave Festival**
Brooklyn Academy of Music
www.bam.org
Showcasing the very best in avant-garde music, dance, theatre and opera.

9 **Broadway on Broadway**
Times Square, see p122
www.broadwayonbroadway.com
Stars perform their Broadway hits for free in Times Square.

13-23 **Feast of San Gennaro**
Little Italy, p73
www.sangennaro.org
Eleven-day street fair with a marching band and plenty of Italian eats.

18 Sept-31 Dec **Regarding Warhol: Sixty Artists, Fifty Years**
Metropolitan Museum of Art, p143
www.metmuseum.org

27-30 **New York Burlesque Festival**
Various venues
www.thenewyorkburlesquefestival.com
Catch more than 120 tassel-twirling, shimmying performances in this annual burlesque blowout. See box p39.

28-30 **Dumbo Arts Festival**
Various locations in Dumbo, Brooklyn.
www.dumboartsfestival.com

Concerts, forums, a short-film series, open studios and installations.

28 Sept-14 Oct **New York Film Festival**
Lincoln Center, p156
www.filmlinc.com

October 2012

Ongoing Next Wave Festival (see Sept); Regarding Warhol: Sixty Artists, Fifty Years (see Sept); New York Film Festival (see Sept)

6-7 **Open House New York**
Various locations
www.ohny.org
Architectural sites that are normally off-limits open their doors to the public.

8 **Columbus Day**

11-14 **New York City Wine & Food Festival**
Various locations
www.nycwff.org
Four belt-busting days of tasting events and celebrity chef demos.

12, 13 **Manhattan Vintage Clothing Show**
Metropolitan Pavilion, Chelsea
www.manhattanvintage.com
Around 90 exhibitors sell garb from the 1800s through to the 1980s.

16-20 **CMJ Music Marathon & Film Festival**
Various locations
www.cmj.com
Showcase for new musical acts.

31 **Village Halloween Parade**
Sixth Avenue, from Spring to 21st Streets
www.halloween-nyc.com

November 2012

Ongoing Next Wave Festival (see Sept); Regarding Warhol: Sixty Artists, Fifty Years (see Sept)

4 **ING New York City Marathon**
Various locations
www.ingnycmarathon.org
Starting on Staten Island, the runners hotfoot it through all five boroughs, finishing in Central Park.

7-11 **New York Comedy Festival**
Various locations
www.nycomedyfestival.com
Presented in association with Comedy Central, this five-day laugh fest features some big names, along with up-and-comers.

9 Nov-30 Dec **Radio City Christmas Spectacular**
Radio City Music Hall, p132
www.radiocity.com

Halloween

Precision dance troupe the Rockettes star in this annual festive show, a New York Christmas tradition.

11 Veterans' Day

12 Madonna
Madison Square Garden, p120
www.thegarden.com
The Material Girl takes to the stage.

18 Nov-25 Feb Tokyo 1955-1970
Museum of Modern Art, p130
www.moma.org
Exhibition focusing on the network of artists who helped transform post-war Tokyo into an international centre of arts, culture and commerce.

Macy's Thanksgiving Day Parade

22 Thanksgiving Day

22 Macy's Thanksgiving Day Parade
Central Park West, at 77th Street, to Broadway, at 34th Street
www.macys.com/parade
Gigantic balloons and elaborate floats at this annual parade.

28 Nov Rockefeller Center Tree-Lighting
Rockefeller Center, p131
www.rockefellercenter.com
The giant evergreen is illumintated following a star-studded line-up.

December 2012

Ongoing Next Wave Festival (see Sept); Regarding Warhol: Sixty Artists, Fifty Years (see Sept); Radio City Christmas Spectacular (see Nov); Tokyo 1955-1970 (see Nov)

11 Dec-17 Mar Matisse: In Search of True Painting
Metropolitan Museum of Art, p143
www.metmuseum.org

18, 20 Leonard Cohen
Madison Square Garden, p120;
Barclays Center, Brooklyn
www.thegarden.com,
www.barclayscenter.com
The septuagenarian singer-songwriter plays two rare NYC gigs.

25 Christmas Day

31 Emerald Nuts Midnight Run
Naumburg Bandshell, middle of Central Park
www.nyrrc.org
See in the new year with a four-mile jog through Central Park.

31 New Year's Eve in Times Square
Times Square, p122
www.timessquarenyc.org
See the giant illuminated ball descend as the midnight hour strikes; there are celebrity performers too.

Q&A: Angie Pontani

We grill a New York Burlesque Festival mover and shaker.

Before the first festival in 2002, what made you think you could pull it off?
I was pretty confident that we could do this, but like most things that I did back then, I didn't really know enough not to be confident. And the minute we announced that we were gonna do this, we got a tremendous response.

The festival always features plenty of local talent, but every year you seem to attract more performers from around the world.
There are lots of New York performers, of course; honestly, I think New York has more burlesque performers than any other city. But we do try to bring people in from all over. And when you put all these performers together, you can see how they're stylistically influenced by where they come from, which is really cool.

So there are regional burlesque differences?
Oh, yeah. New Orleans has its own style, for example; it's very traditional, very bluesy. Chicago is very theatrical, and Los Angeles is over-the-top glamorous. That's even truer of people that come in

from other countries. Cherry Typhoon – who's from Japan – will usually come in wearing a kimono and do something with silk fans or something.

Back in the early days of the festival, a lot of people looked at the burlesque scene as a novelty, but now it seems like an accepted part of nightlife.
It's just grown and grown. I've talked to a lot of the older ladies who were performing in the '50s and the '60s – people like Dixie Evans and Tempest Storm – and they all say things like 'Burlesque is an original form of American theatre, and it deserves its place in the annals of theatrical history'. And I feel that burlesque is getting to that point again.

That might even be truer now than it was then. Burlesque used to be run by male impresarios who, I assume, were mainly out to make a buck. Now it seems like the performers themselves are in charge.
Burlesque is 97 per cent lady land nowadays. It's run by the ladies, for the ladies. But the men enjoy it too!

January 2013

Ongoing Next Wave Festival (see Sept); Tokyo 1955-1970 (see Nov); Matisse: In Search of True Painting (see Dec)

1 New Year's Day

1 New Year's Day Marathon Benefit Reading
Poetry Project, St Mark's Church-in-the-Bowery, East Village
www.poetryproject.org
Big-name bohos step up to the mic in this spoken-word spectacle.

21 Martin Luther King, Jr Day

late Jan-early Feb **Winter Restaurant Week**
Various locations
www.nycgo.com/restaurantweek
Sample delicious gourmet food at highly palatable prices.

February 2013

Ongoing Winter Restaurant Week (see Jan)

1, 2 Manhattan Vintage Clothing Show
Metropolitan Pavilion, Chelsea
www.manhattanvintage.com
Around 90 exhibitors sell garb from the 1800s through to the 1980s.

3, 10 Chinese New Year
Around Mott Street, Chinatown
www.betterchinatown.com
The firecracker ceremony (3 Feb) and parade (10 Feb) are key events.

18 Presidents' Day

March 2013

Ongoing Matisse: In Search of True Painting (see Dec)

7-10 **Armory Show**
Piers 92 & 94, Hell's Kitchen
www.thearmoryshow.com
A huge contemporary art mart.

17 **St Patrick's Day Parade**
Fifth Avenue, from 44th to 86th Streets
www.nycstpatricksparade.org
March of green-clad merrymakers.

31 **Easter Parade**
Fifth Avenue, from 49th to 57th Streets
Admire the myriad creative Easter bonnets on show at this one-day event.

April 2013

6 Apr-11 May **Der Ring des Nibelungen**
Metropolitan Opera House, p156
www.metoperafamily.org
Three operas of Robert Lepage's flashy Ring Cycle return for Wagner's 200th birthday.

14 Apr-5 Aug **Claes Oldenburg: the 60s**
Museum of Modern Art, p130
www.moma.org

mid-late Apr **SOFA New York**
Seventh Regiment Armory, Upper East Side
www.sofaexpo.com
Giant show of Sculptural Objects and Functional Art.

late Apr-early May **Sakura Matsuri (Cherry Blossom Festival)**
Brooklyn Botanic Garden, p162
www.bbg.org
The climax to the cherry blossom season celebrates Japanese culture with a weekend of events, with music, manga exhibitions and tea ceremonies.

late Apr **Tribeca Film Festival**
Various locations
www.tribecafilm.com/festival
Robert De Niro's two-week downtown showcase of indie flicks.

May 2013

Ongoing Der Ring des Nibelungen (see April); Sakura Matsuri (see April); Claes Oldenburg: The 60s (see April)

Sakura Matsuri

5 **TD Five Boro Bike Tour**
Battery Park to Staten Island
www.bikenewyork.org
A 42-mile Tour de New York.

25-27, 1, 2 June **Washington
Square Outdoor Art Exhibit**
See Sept.

late May **Lower East Side
Festival of the Arts**
Theater for the New City, 155 First
Avenue, between 9th & 10th Streets
www.theaterforthenewcity.net
Three days of theatre, poetry readings,
and family-friendly programming.

27 **Memorial Day**

31 May, 1, 2 June **Howl! Festival**
East Village, p84
www.howlfestival.com
A reading of Allen Ginsberg's seminal
poem kicks off this three-day arts fest.

June 2013

Ongoing Claes Oldenburg: The 60s
(see April); Washington Square
Outdoor Art Exhibit (see May
and Sept); Howl! Festival (see May)

June-Aug **SummerStage**
Rumsey Playfield, Central Park
& parks across the city
www.summerstage.org
Rockers, orchestras, authors and dance
companies take to the stage.

June-Aug **Shakespeare in the Park**
Delacorte Theater, Central Park
www.publictheater.org
Join the queue for free alfresco theatre.

late June-late July **River to River
Festival**
Various Downtown venues
www.rivertorivernyc.org
Catch hundreds of free outdoor arts
events at waterside venues.

early June **National Puerto
Rican Day Parade**
Fifth Avenue, from 44th to 86th
Streets
www.nationalpuertoricandayparade.org
Celebrate the city's largest Hispanic
community, and its culture.

early June **Egg Rolls & Egg
Creams Festival**
Eldridge Street Synagogue, p77
www.eldridgestreet.org
The nabe's Jewish and Chinese tradi-
tions converge, with klezmer music, tea
ceremonies and more.

mid June **Museum Mile Festival**
Fifth Avenue, from 82nd to 110th
Streets, Upper East Side

Flea season

Shop and nosh outdoors throughout the year.

Smorgasburg

Rummaging in the city's outdoor flea markets has long been a favourite New York weekend pastime, but the past few years have seen the emergence of a more sophisticated breed of seasonal bazaar, offering high-quality crafts and gourmet snacks alongside vintage clothing, furniture and bric-a-brac. The popular **Brooklyn Flea** (www.brooklynflea.com) was launched in 2008 by Jonathan Butler, founder of Brooklyn real-estate blog Brownstoner.com, and Eric Demby, former PR man for the Brooklyn borough president, who identified Brooklyn as being ripe for a destination market. The original location (176 Lafayette Avenue, between Clermont & Vanderbilt Avenues, Fort Greene) is open from April through November on Saturdays, and includes around 150 vendors, selling a mix of vintage clothing, records, furnishings, locally designed fashion and crafts. A second location runs on Sundays in Williamsburg, along the waterfront between North 6th and 7th Streets, which is also the site of a nosh-only Saturday spin-off, **Smorgasburg**; in winter, the market moves indoors, occupying a majestic old bank (Skylight One Hanson, at Ashland Place, Fort Greene) on Saturday and Sunday through March.

On Saturdays from May until October, you can sample everything from New York State-made ice-cream to gourmet meatballs as you browse vintage fashion, handmade jewellery and skincare at **Hester Street Fair** (Hester Street, at Essex Street, www.hesterstreetfair.com). Located on the site of a former Lower East Side pushcart market, it has around 65 vendors. In winter, several holiday markets set up shop. From late October until early January, 125 glassed-in shoplets operate in Bryant Park (between Fifth & Sixth Avenues and 40th & 42nd Streets), forming a festive microcosm, the **Holiday Shops at Bryant Park** (1-212 661 6640, www.theholidayshopsatbryantpark.com), clustered around a seasonal skating rink. Although some of the wares here skirt tourist-craft-shop territory, there are always plenty of unusual finds, including jewellery and accessories, toys, foodstuffs and household devices. You'll find a similar mix of giftable wares at the **Union Square Holiday Market** at the south-west corner of Union Square, at 14th Street (1-212 529 9262, www.urbanspacenyc.com), open late November to late December.

www.museummilefestival.org
Ten major museums are free of charge
for one day every year.

mid June-Aug **Celebrate Brooklyn!**
Prospect Park Bandshell, Brooklyn
www.bricartsmedia.org
Brooklyn's premier summer fête offers
music, dance, film and spoken word.

mid June **Broadway Bares**
Roseland Ballroom, Theater District
www.broadwaycares.org/broadwaybares
Some of Broadway's hottest bodies *sans*
costumes feature in this fundraiser.

22 **Mermaid Parade**
Coney Island, Brooklyn
www.coneyisland.com
Decked-out mermaids, mermen and
elaborate, kitschy floats.

late June **NYC LGBT Pride March**
From Fifth Avenue, at 36th Street, to
Christopher Street
www.nycpride.org
Downtown's annual Pride event.

late June-mid July **Midsummer
Night Swing**
Lincoln Center Plaza, p156
www.lincolncenter.org
Dance under the stars to salsa, Cajun,
swing and other music for three weeks.

July 2013

Ongoing Claes Oldenburg: The 60s
(see April); SummerStage (see June);
Shakespeare in the Park (see June);
River to River Festival (see June);
Celebrate Brooklyn! (see June);
Midsummer Night Swing (see June)

4 **Independence Day**

4 **Macy's Fourth of July Fireworks**
Waterfront locations
www.macys.com/fireworks

4 **Nathan's Famous International
Hot Dog Eating Contest**
Nathan's Famous, 1310 Surf
Avenue, at Stillwell Avenue,
Coney Island, Brooklyn

www.nathansfamous.com
Eaters gather from all over the world for
the granddaddy of all pig-out contests.

early July-early Sept **Warm Up**
MoMA PS1, p165
www.ps1.org
Thousands make the pilgrimage to
Long Island City on summer Saturdays
for this underground clubbing event.

mid July **New York Philharmonic
Concerts in the Parks**
Various locations
www.nyphil.org

mid July-Aug **Harlem Week**
Various Harlem locations
www.harlemweek.com
'Week' is a misnomer: in addition to a
weekend street fair, events are spread
over more than a month.

late July/early Aug **Summer
Restaurant Week**
Various locations
www.nycgo.com/restaurantweek
See Jan Winter Restaurant Week.

late July-mid Aug **Lincoln Center
Out of Doors**
Lincoln Center, Upper West Side
www.lincolncenter.org
Several weeks of free family-friendly
classical and contemporary works outside at the Lincoln Center.

August 2013

Ongoing Claes Oldenburg: The 60s
(see April); SummerStage (see
June); Shakespeare in the Park (see
June); River to River Festival (see
June), Celebrate Brooklyn! (see
June); Warm Up (see July); Harlem
Week (see July)

mid-late Aug **New York
International Fringe Festival**
Various locations
www.fringenyc.org
Wacky, weird and sometimes wonderful, the Fringe Festival – inspired by
the Edinburgh original – crams hundreds of shows into 16 days.

31 Aug-2 Sept; 7, 8 Sept
Washington Square Outdoor Art Exhibit
See above Sept 2012.

September 2013

Ongoing Washington Square Outdoor Art Exhibit (see Sept)

2 Labor Day

early Sept-late Jan **Next Wave Festival**
See above Sept 2012.

early Sept **Broadway on Broadway**
See above Sept 2012.

mid Sept **Feast of San Gennaro**
See above Sept 2012.

late Sept **New York Burlesque Festival**
See above Sept 2012.

late Sept **Dumbo Arts Festival**
See above Sept 2012.

late Sept-mid Oct **New York Film Festival**
See above Sept 2012.

October 2013

Ongoing Next Wave Festival (see Sept); New York Film Festival (see Sept)

early Oct **Open House New York**
See above Oct 2012.

early-mid Oct **New York City Wine & Food Festival**
See above Oct 2012.

early-mid Oct **Manhattan Vintage Clothing Show**
See above Oct 2012.

14 Columbus Day

mid-late Oct **CMJ Music Marathon & FilmFest**
See above Oct 2012.

22 Oct-21 Jan 2014
Vermeer, Rembrandt & Hals: Masterpieces from the Mauritshuis
Frick Collection, p143
www.frick.org

31 **Village Halloween Parade**
See above Oct 2012.

November 2013

Ongoing Next Wave Festival (see Sept); Vermeer, Rembrandt and Hals: Masterpieces from the Mauritshuis (see Oct)

early Nov **New York Comedy Festival**
See above Nov 2012.

early Nov **ING New York City Marathon**
See above Nov 2012.

11 **Veterans' Day**

early Nov-late Dec **Radio City Christmas Spectacular**
See above Nov 2012.

28 **Thanksgiving Day**

28 **Macy's Thanksgiving Day Parade**
See above Nov 2012.

late Nov **Rockefeller Center Tree-Lighting**
See above Dec 2012.

December 2013

Ongoing Next Wave Festival (see Sept); Radio City Christmas Spectacular (see Nov)

25 **Christmas Day**

31 **Emerald Nuts Midnight Run**
See above Dec 2012.

31 **New Year's Eve in Times Square**
See above Dec 2012.

Itineraries

Skyscraper Museum

High Points

In *Here is New York*, EB White wrote that the city 'is to the nation what the white church spire is to the village – the visible symbol of aspiration and faith, the white plume saying that the way is up.' Despite the irrevocable damage to the skyline from the 9/11 attacks, that comment still resonates – New York is constantly rebuilding itself and adding to its cache of cloudbusters.

The logical starting point for an afternoon-into-evening architectural tour is a visit to the **Skyscraper Museum** (see p62) in the Financial District. Here you can see large-scale photographs of lower Manhattan's skyscrapers from 1956, 1976 and 2004, and a 1931 silent film documenting the construction of the Empire State Building; from January 2013 a temporary exhibition celebrates the centennial of the Woolworth Building (see p47).

Head out the door, make a left and follow Battery Place across West Street and along the northern edge

of Battery Park. Turn left up Greenwich Street, and at Morris Street walk along Trinity Place to make a brief stop at **Trinity Church** (see p65). In stark contrast to the skyscrapers that surround it, Trinity – the third church to stand on this spot – remains frozen in Gothic Revival style designed by Richard Upjohn, but it was the island's tallest structure when it was completed in 1846, thanks to its 281-foot-tall spire. The churchyard, which dates back to 1697, is one of New York's oldest cemeteries. Alexander Hamilton (the nation's first secretary of the treasury – you can check out his mug on the $10 bill) is buried here.

Afterwards, it's time to visit one of the most powerfully moving sites in recent history: Ground Zero, the spot where the mighty Twin Towers once stood. From the church, continue to walk up Trinity Place for two more blocks and cross over Liberty Street. The World

Trade Center site is to your left. The awe-inspiring **National September 11 Memorial**, comprising two 30-foot-deep waterfalls in the footprints of the towers, opened on the ten-year anniversary of the attacks, but until construction is completed on the site, you'll need to reserve a timed entry pass on the website or at the 9/11 **Memorial Preview Site** (see box p62) on Vesey Street, where you can also view architectural models of the entire development. When complete, it will include a museum, a striking transport hub designed by Santiago Calatrava, and five towers including **1 World Trade Center**; already the city's tallest building, it will reach 1,776 feet when it's finished in 2013.

From the place where New York's tallest towers fell, it's onwards and upwards to the spot where the race to the heavens began. Walk up Vesey Street, then north on Broadway to the **Woolworth Building** (No. 233, at Barclay Street). Note the flamboyant Gothic terracotta cladding designed by Cass Gilbert in 1913. The 55-storey, 793-foot 'Cathedral of Commerce' was the world's tallest structure for 16 years until it was topped by 40 Wall Street. The Woolworth Building overlooks City Hall Park. Walk through the park and aim for the foot of the **Brooklyn Bridge** (see p162). On the way, admire the curled and warped stainless-steel façade of the audaciously

Chrysler Building

named, 870-foot **New York by Gehry** (8 Spruce Street, between Gold & Nassau Streets). Our sojourn is about buildings, not bridges – but we wouldn't mind if you made a detour here; it takes about half an hour to walk out to the middle of the bridge and back, but you'll want to allow plenty of time to gaze at the East River, the web of steel cables – and, of course, the panoramic view of the Manhattan skyline.

Back to the current plan: once you've passed through the park (bordered to the east by Park Row), look for a subway entrance to your left. Board the Uptown 4 or 5 train to Grand Central-42nd Street. On the subway, consider this: it took ten years of unflagging effort for Jacqueline Kennedy Onassis and others to save **Grand Central Terminal** (see p135), your next destination. After the original Pennsylvania Station was demolished in 1963, developers unveiled plans to wreck the magnificent Beaux Arts edifice and erect an office tower in its place. Jackie O rallied politicians and celebritics to her cause. In 1978, her committee won a Supreme Court decision affirming landmark status for the beloved building – which celebrates its 100th birthday in February 2013. See also box p134.

By now you'll likely be famished. Head back downstairs to one of Manhattan's most famous eateries, the **Grand Central Oyster Bar & Restaurant** (Lower Concourse; see p136), for a late lunch. Before heading inside, linger a moment under the low ceramic arches, dubbed the 'whispering gallery'. Instruct a friend to stand in an opposite, diagonal corner from you and whisper sweet nothings to each other – they'll sound as clear as if you were face to face.

Revitalised, you're ready for the next stop: **Columbus Circle**.

ITINERARIES

Either hop back on the subway (S to Times Square, transfer to the Uptown 1 train and get off at 59th Street-Columbus Circle) or, preferably, you can hoof it there in about 30 minutes. Exit Grand Central on 42nd Street and head west. At Fifth Avenue, you'll pass by another Beaux Arts treasure from the city's grand metropolitan era, the **New York Public Library** (see p130); the sumptuous white-marble façade recently underwent a restoration for its centennial in 2011. Built on a former Revolutionary War battleground, the library now sits on the greensward known as Bryant Park. When you get to Broadway, make a right and head north into Times Square. Imposing, sentinel-like skyscrapers mark the southern entry to the electric carnival here; the 2000 **Condé Nast Building** (4 Times Square) and the 2001 **Reuters Building** (No.3), both by Fox & Fowle, complement Kohn Pedersen Fox's 2002 postmodern **5 Times Square** and the David Childs' 2004 **Times Square Tower** (No.7). Originally Longacre Square, the 'Crossroads of the World' was renamed after *The New York Times* moved here in the early 1900s; beneath its sheath of billboards and snaking news zipper, the broadsheet's old HQ, 1 Times Square, is an elegant 1904 structure. Take a detour if you want to see the paper's current home base, Renzo Piano's 2007 **New York Times Building** (620 Eighth Avenue, between W 40th & 41st Streets), one block west and a couple of blocks south. The glass-walled design is a representation of the newspaper's desire for transparency in reporting the news.

Back on Broadway, walk north on the pedestrian-packed sidewalks until you spot Christopher gazing out from his perch in the centre of Columbus Circle at 59th Street. The renovated traffic circle, with its ring of fountains and benches, is the perfect place to contemplate another set of twin towers, the 2003 **Time Warner Center**, also designed by David Childs.

Increasingly, skyscrapers are incorporating green design. Lord Norman Foster's extraordinary 2006 **Hearst Magazine Building** (959 Eighth Avenue, at W 57th Street) is a shining example. Look south-west and you can't miss it; it's the one that resembles a giant greenhouse.

At this point you have two options. The first is to end the day at the Time Warner Center and enjoy the staggering view from a leather chair in the **Mandarin Oriental Hotel**'s Lobby Lounge, perched 35 floors in the air. The drinks prices here are equally staggering, but the Fifth Avenue and Central Park South skylines make it worth the splurge. Alternatively, you can hail a cab and top off a day of skyscraper gazing with a panoramic view from either New York's tallest tower, the **Empire State Building** (see p129), or the **Top of the Rock** observation deck at **Rockefeller Center** (see p131). The latter has an edge as it affords a great view of the former. Also look out for William Van Alen's silver-hooded **Chrysler Building** (see p135). The acme of art deco design, it was part of a madcap three-way race to become the world's tallest building just before the Depression. The competitors were **40 Wall Street** (now the Trump Building) and the Empire State Building. Van Alen waited for the first to top out at 927 feet before unveiling his secret weapon – a spire assembled inside the Chrysler's dome and raised from within to bring the height to 1,046 feet. At 102 storeys and 1,250 feet, the Empire State Building surpassed it only 11 months later.

ITINERARIES

Brooklyn Bridge p162

Woody's Manhattan

You've seen the movies, now experience the city through the lens of quintessential New Yorker – and longtime Upper East Sider – Woody Allen. This full-day tour takes in locations from the director's 1970s masterpieces *Annie Hall* and *Manhattan*.

Alvy Singer and Annie Hall first meet at the now-defunct Wall Street Racquet Club on Pier 13, so start your voyage into Woody's world downtown – if you're feeling energetic you can even book a squash court at the nearby New York Health & Racquet Club (39 Whitehall Street, between Pearl & Water Streets, 1-212 269 9800). A day pass to the club costs $25 per person, plus $26 per hour to rent the court and $5 per racquet.

After your game, head for the waterfront. Walk south on Whitehall Street, left on Water Street and right on Old Slip, which will take you to the river. Stroll north along the East River

Esplanade; before you reach South Street Seaport's touristy Pier 17, you'll come to the recently developed Pier 15, which has a cool bi-level lawned viewing platform and deck chairs. Stop here to soak up a panorama of the Brooklyn Bridge, the gorgeous (or, as Annie might say, 'neat') backdrop for the scene in which Alvy and Annie profess their love to each other and kiss at dusk. Just a little foreshadowing for a certain other iconic bridge scene you may be familiar with…

You've probably worked up an appetite after your morning exertions, so it's time to stop for a cinematic bite. Walk up Wall Street to the subway stop of the same name – deep in the Financial District, you're sure to run into a few 'analysts', but not the kind Woody's neurotic characters typically rely on. Catch the 2 or 3 train, then change to the 1 at Chambers Street and get off at

Central Park p137

Christopher Street-Sheridan Square. From here it's a two minute walk south to John's of Bleecker Street (278 Bleecker Street, at Jones Street, 1-212 243 1680, www.johnsbrick ovenpizza.com), where Isaac Davis takes his 17-year-old girlfriend Tracy in *Manhattan* and learns she has won a place to study in London. There may be newer pizza places with more impressive foodie pedigrees, but John's, with its well-worn booths and divey vibe, has been a Village fixture since 1929.

Hop back on the subway and zip up to 59th Street-Columbus Circle to access Central Park, where Tracy and Isaac take a horse-and-buggy ride for their 'corny' date (their last before they break up). Since horse-drawn carriages are a controversial subject these days, you may prefer to hire one of the prolific human-powered pedicabs; Manhattan Rickshaw Company (1-212 604 4729, www.manhattanrickshaw.com) is a good bet.

Diehard location spotters will want to take a detour to 63rd Street and Columbus Avenue, across the street from Lincoln Center – the spot where Annie and Alvy part ways in *Annie Hall*'s final moments.

Ditch your ride at 81st Street and Central Park West and pay a visit to the Rose Center for Earth and Space at the American Museum of Natural History (see p151), the updated version of the Hayden Planetarium, where, in *Manhattan*, Isaac and Mary take shelter during an electrical storm. Use your brain (that most overrated organ) to count Saturn's moons and maybe, if you're travelling with a partner, indulge in some interstellar canoodling.

But to really experience the character of the classic Upper West Side, head west to grab a snack at quintessential Jewish food store Zabar's (see p155), which Isaac and Tracy pass in another scene. Order a sandwich of hand-sliced corned beef on fresh rye, and remember Isaac's comment: 'Corned beef hould not be blue.'

Your next destination is Woody's home patch – the Upper East Side. Catch the crosstown bus at the corner of 79th and Broadway and get off at Fifth Avenue. Walk north for the Solomon R Guggenheim Museum, site of Isaac's first,

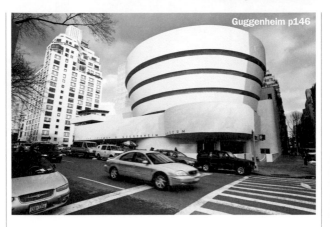

Guggenheim p146

unpromising, meeting with Mary, whose views on art he finds pretentious. Even if you don't venture inside, admire Frank Lloyd Wright's dramatic 1959 spiral building – the architect's only NYC structure apart from a private house on Staten Island. The pair's second, more successful, meeting takes place at the Museum of Modern Art (see p130) – but you won't be able to fit that into your schedule today.

If you fancy a stroll, explore Annie Hall's neighbourhood – her apartment was on East 70th Street, near Madison Avenue. And, coincidentally, the director's townhouse is on the same street.

Make your way southeast to the new location of the Beekman Theatre (1271 Second Avenue, between 66th and 67th Streets, 1-212 585 4141, www.beekman theatre.com), which featured in *Annie Hall*. At the original cinema, which was across the street (1254 Second Avenue) but has since been torn down, two pushy fans pester Alvy for an autograph before Annie shows up for their date. 'Hey, dis is Alvy Singah!' (Since Annie is late for the start of Ingmar Bergman's

Face to Face, Alvy insists on heading across town to the New Yorker Theater at Broadway and 88th, which has since closed. There, Alvy famously addresses the audience while arguing with a moviegoer about Marshall McLuhan – and happens to have Mr McLuhan on hand to prove his point. As Alvy says, 'Boy, if life were only like this'.

To recreate one of *Manhattan*'s most iconic scenes, continue southeast to Riverview Terrace at Sutton Square (E 58th Street, at the East River), where you can gaze at the view of the Queensboro Bridge that capped Isaac and Mary's unofficial first date, which lasted until dawn.

You'll have to drag yourself away from the stunning vista, though, for the grand finale of your itinerary – catch a cab to the Carlyle Hotel's swanky cabaret room, Café Carlyle (see p28), at 76th Street and Madison Avenue, to see the man himself. Woody Allen plays clarinet with the Eddy Davis New Orleans Jazz Band, which has an ongoing Monday-night slot ($95-$185 per person, plus $25 minimum).

White Horse Tavern

Literary Greenwich Village

Although its genteel townhouses and upscale restaurants might seem at odds with its bohemian reputation, Greenwich Village was once the city's answer to Paris' Left Bank. As the rich moved uptown following World War I, free thinkers and artists – most notably writers – from all over the world began to move in, taking advantage of the cheap rents and large apartments. In the 1950s the Beat poets made the area their own. You'd need a lot more than a struggling writer's salary to inhabit its leafy streets today, but many of the literary landmarks remain.

We suggest taking this half-day outing in the afternoon. Start with an espresso at the oldest coffeehouse in the village, **Caffe Reggio** (119 MacDougal Street, between Bleecker & W 3rd Streets, 1-212 475 9557), open since 1927. The carved wooden chairs and relaxed vibe maintain the cosy feel that appealed to Jack Kerouac, native Villager Gregory Corso and other Beat poets.

Sadly, the **San Remo Café** has not survived. Formerly located on the northwest corner of Bleecker and MacDougal Streets, it was one of literary bohemia's hotspots during the 1950s and '60s. Tennessee Williams, James Baldwin, Dylan Thomas and assorted Beats were habitués at the bar, which Dawn Powell, novelist and satirist of Village life, regarded as one of four bars that marked the boundaries of 'the cultural and social hub of New York City'. Kerouac is rumoured to have picked up Gore Vidal there.

Heading north, you'll pass the recently renovated **Provincetown Playhouse** (133 MacDougal Street, between W 3rd & 4th Streets), former home to the Provincetown Players (1916-29), a seminal group that introduced the works of leading members Eugene O'Neill, Djuna Barnes and Edna St Vincent Millay, among others. Although the Players didn't survive the Crash of 1929, the Playhouse continued as one of America's foremost independent theatres, premiering the works of David Mamet and John Guare, as well as the first NYC production of Edward Albee's *Zoo Story*, the city's quintessential drama.

Just across the street, at **Nos. 130-132**, Louisa May Alcott lived from 1867 to 1870. It was here, while convalescing from typhoid she contracted as a nurse during the Civil War, that she finished her masterpiece *Little Women*.

If the stately townhouses along the northern fringe of **Washington Square** still evoke Henry James' novel of that name, it's no small tribute to their preservation. Although the actual inspiration for the novel (James' grandmother's home at No.18) has not survived, the townhouses along Washington Square North provide a good indication of its august world. Edith Wharton lived at No.7 in 1882, while John Dos Passos commenced work on his *Manhattan Transfer* while briefly living in No.3 in 1925. At No.38 Washington Square South, Eugene O'Neill consecrated his first New York residence by having an affair with journalist Louise Bryant, while her husband, John Reed (author of *Ten Days That Shook the World*) was in hospital.

Leave the square via Fifth Avenue and head north, turning left on 10th Street, which brings you to Sixth Avenue and the Jefferson Market Library. Just behind it, off 10th, lies **Patchin Place**, former home to some of the leading luminaries of New York's literary pantheon. This cul-de-sac lined with brick houses built during the mid-19th century is off-limits to the public, but through the gate you can make out No.1,

which Reed and Bryant made their home; No.4, where the poet and foe of capitalisation e.e. Cummings resided from 1923 to 1962; and No.5, where Djuna Barnes, author of *Nightwood*, lived from 1940 to 1982. Ezra Pound, Theodore Dreiser and John Cowper Powys also lived here briefly.

Dylan Thomas, the self-destructive Welsh poet whose final years living in the Chelsea Hotel were marked by prodigious bouts of drinking, found liquid solace in the Village. His favourite watering hole – the **White Horse Tavern** (567 Hudson Street, at 11th Street, 1-212 989 3956) – was also beloved of Kerouac, Anaïs Nin, Baldwin and Norman Mailer. Thomas made the place his own, and a portrait of the poet hangs over his favourite table – although the story of him drinking 18 straight whiskies and expiring on the premises is a myth. He gave his mistress that highly unlikely figure upon returning from the White Horse on 4 November 1953, then slept it off before heading back to the bar for two glasses of beer. Returning to the Chelsea, he collapsed and later died.

The next stop requires a bit of forethought, since you'll need to make reservations in advance. Head straight down Bleecker Street, taking a left at Carmine Street, on to Minetta Lane and back to MacDougal. Here, revived hotspot the **Minetta Tavern** (see p94) was once a haunt for literati of the calibre of Ernest Hemingway and F Scott Fitzgerald, as well as the famously blocked – like Joe Gould, whose dry spell was recounted in Joseph Mitchell's *Joe Gould's Secret*. If you can't secure a table, or if the celebrated $26 Black Label burger seems a tad steep, head north to the **Corner Bistro** (see p97) at the junction of W 4th and Jane Streets, where the burgers are consistently rated among the city's best.

New York by Area

Washington Square Park p94

Downtown

The southern tip of Manhattan has always been the city's financial, legal and political powerhouse. It's where New York began as a Dutch colony, and where the 19th-century influx of immigrants infused the city with new energy. Yet with much of it off the Big Apple's orderly grid, Downtown doesn't conform to the standard. Here, the landscape shifts from block to block. In the Financial District, gleaming skyscrapers rub shoulders with 18th-century landmarks; Tribeca's top dining spots are only a short hop from Chinatown's frenetic food markets; and around the corner from the flashy nightspots of the Meatpacking District, affluent West Villagers reside in stately brownstones.

Financial District

Commerce has been the backbone of New York's prosperity since its earliest days. The southern point of Manhattan quickly evolved into the Financial District because, in the days before telecommunications, banks established their headquarters near the port. Wall Street, which took its name from a defensive wooden wall built in 1653 to mark the northern limit of Nieuw Amsterdam, is synonymous with the world's greatest den of capitalism. On the eastern shore of lower Manhattan, old buildings in the disused South Street Seaport area were redeveloped in the mid 1980s into restaurants, bars and stores. Also check out the views of Brooklyn Bridge (see p162).

Sights & museums

City Hall
City Hall Park, from Vesey to Chambers Streets, between Broadway & Park Row (1-212 788 2656, www. nyc.gov/designcommission). Subway J,

Z to Chambers Street; R to City Hall; 2, 3 to Park Place; 4, 5, 6 to Brooklyn Bridge-City Hall. **Open** *Tours* (individuals) noon Wed, 10am Thur; (groups) 10am Mon-Wed, Fri. **Admission** free. **Map** p58 C2 ❶
Designed by French émigré Joseph François Mangin and native New Yorker John McComb Jr, the fine, Federal-style City Hall was completed in 1812. Tours take in the rotunda, with its splendid coffered dome; the City Council Chamber; and the Governor's Room, which houses a collection of 19th-century American political portraits as well as historic furnishings (including George Washington's desk). Individuals can book for the Thursday-morning tour (two days in advance); alternatively, sign up before 11.45am on Wednesday at the NYC tourism kiosk at the southern end of City Hall Park on the east side of Broadway, at Barclay Street, for the first-come, first-served tour at noon. Group tours should be booked a week in advance.

Fraunces Tavern Museum

2nd & 3rd Floors, 54 Pearl Street, at Broad Street (1-212 425 1778, www. frauncestavernmuseum.org). Subway J, Z to Broad Street; 4, 5 to Bowling Green. **Open** noon-5pm daily.
Admission $7; free-$4 reductions.
Map p58 C4 ❷
True, George Washington slept here, but there's little left of the original 18th-century tavern that was favoured by Washington during the Revolution. Fire-damaged and rebuilt in the 19th century, it was reconstructed in its current Colonial Revival style in 1907. The museum itself features a collection of flags, paintings devoted to events of the Revolutionary War, and such Washington relics as one of his false teeth. It was here, after the British had finally been defeated, that Washington took tearful farewell of his troops and vowed to retire from public life. Luckily, he had a change of heart six years later and became the country's

first president. You can still raise a pint in the bar, now run by Dublin's Porterhouse Brewing Company.

Governors Island

1-212 440 2202, www.govisland.com. Subway R to Whitehall Street-South Ferry; 1 to South Ferry; 4, 5 to Bowling Green; then take ferry from Battery Maritime Building at Slip no.7. **Open** late May-late Sept (see website for hours and ferry schedule).
Admission free. **Map** p58 C5 ❸
A seven-minute ride on a free ferry takes you to this seasonal island sanctuary, a scant 800 yards from lower Manhattan. Thanks to its strategic position in the middle of New York Harbor, Governors Island was a military outpost and off-limits to the public for 200 years. It finally opened to summer visitors in 2006. The verdant, 172-acre isle still retains a significant chunk of its military-era architecture, including Fort Jay, started in 1776, and Castle Williams, completed in 1812 and for years used as a prison. Today, as well as providing a peaceful setting for cycling (bring a bike on the ferry, or rent from Bike & Roll once there), the island hosts a programme of events (see website for schedule). In spring 2012 construction began on a new park, which will feature 30 acres of lawns and gardens and a Hammock Grove for shady reclining, scheduled for completion in autumn 2013.

Museum of American Finance

48 Wall Street, at William Street (1-212 908 4110, www.financialhistory. org). Subway 2, 3, 4, 5 to Wall Street, R, 1 to Rector Street. **Open** 10am-4pm Tue-Sat. **Admission** $8; free-$5 reductions. **Map** p58 C4 ❹
Situated in the old headquarters of the Bank of New York, the Museum of American Finance's permanent collection traces the history of Wall Street and America's financial markets. Displays in the august banking hall

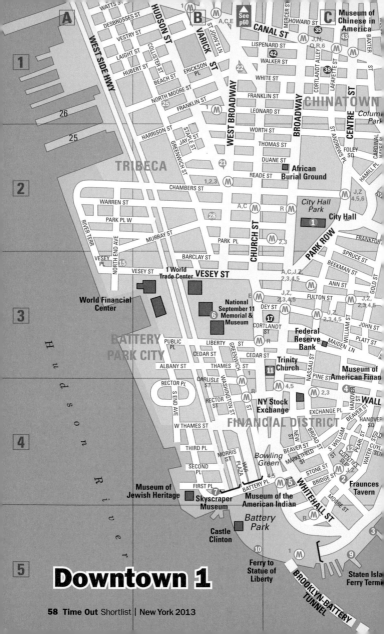

Downtown 1

THE BOWERY

D

E

EAST BROADWAY

F

East
River
Park

1

Eldridge St
Synagogue

Confucius
Plaza

See
p61
Seward
Park

Rutgers
Park

First Shearith
Israel Graveyard

ROOSEVELT DR

MANHATTAN BRIDGE

2

ARK ROW

BROOKLYN BRIDGE

FRANKLIN

South Street
Seaport

South St
Seaport
Museum

3

BROOKLYN

New York City
Police Museum

4

0   200 m

0   200 yds

© Copyright Time Out Group 2012

5

❶ Sights & museums
❶ Eating & drinking
❶ Shopping
❶ Nightlife
❶ Arts & leisure

Downtown 2

A   **B**   **C**

Museum at FIT

1

High Line

W 26TH ST

W 22ND ST

Madison Square

Flatiron Building

CHELSEA

FLATIRON DISTRICT

General Theological Seminary of the Episcopal Church

W 20TH ST

W 18TH ST

Theodore Roosevelt Birthplace

Joyce Theater

W 16TH ST

MIDTOWN (pp102-136)

Union Square

TENTH AVE

W 14TH ST   A,C,E,L   1,2,3   F,L,M   L,N,Q,R, 4,5,6

2

143

W 13TH ST

LITTLE W 12TH ST   145   HORATIO ST

MEATPACKING DISTRICT

131   JANE ST   134

GANSEVOORT ST

W 12TH ST

122   107

W 11TH ST

120

W 10TH ST

WEST VILLAGE

149

W 9TH ST

BETHUNE ST

135

W 8TH ST

125

GREENWICH

E 8TH ST

147

148

BANK ST

140

WAVERLY PL

119

New York University

GREENWICH

HUDSON ST

142

WASHINGTON PL

Washington Square

118

PERRY ST

139

124

WASH SQ EAST

3

50

CHARLES ST

144

133

B.D.F.M

138

126

123 121

127

AIA Center for Architecture

VILLAGE

46

CHRISTOPHER ST

130

129

45

BARROW ST

146

137

128

BLEECKER ST

42

MORTON ST

LEROY ST

CLARKSON ST

150

W HOUSTON ST

B.D.F.M

4

40

39

PRINCE ST

23

SOHO

34

KING ST

CHARLTON ST

33

VANDAM ST

40

SPRING ST

20

19

SPRING ST

New York City Fire Museum

WATTS ST

36

30

5

34

CANAL ST

DESBROSSES ST

29

35

HOLLAND TUNNEL

37

A,C,E

CANAL ST

WEST SIDE HWY

VESTRY ST

42

WALKER ST

J,Z,N, Q,R,6

LAIGHT ST

WHITE ST

26

HUBERT ST

BEACH ST

22

FRANKLIN ST

CHINA

NORTH MOORE ST

LEONARD ST

0   300 m

0   300 yds

FRANKLIN ST

WORTH ST

© Copyright Time Out Group 2012

See p58

THOMAS ST

TRIBECA

Manhattan Marina

Legend:
- ❶ Sights & museums
- ❶ Eating & drinking
- ❶ Shopping
- ❶ Nightlife
- ❶ Arts & leisure

THIRD AVE
E 26TH ST
E 24TH ST
E 23RD ST
ASSER LEVY PL
FRANKLIN D ROOSEVELT DR

GRAMERCY PARK

Peter Cooper Village

mercy Park ational s Club

22ND ST

E 20TH ST

SECOND AVE
FIRST AVE
RUTHERFORD PL
NATHAN D PERLMAN PL

E 18TH ST
E 16TH ST

Stuyvesant Town

Stuyvesant Square

16TH ST
E 16TH ST
E 15TH ST

E 14TH ST

105
93 110
97 94
80
St Mark's Church in-the-Bowery
111
ace rch
91
102
84 87
95
84 87
90 83 82 81
96
86
92

Tompkins Square

108

E 13TH ST
E 12TH ST
E 11TH ST
E 10TH ST
E 9TH ST
E 8TH ST
E 7TH ST
E 6TH ST

AVENUE A
AVENUE B
AVENUE C
AVENUE D

SZOLD PL
E 12TH ST

STUYVESANT ST
ST MARKS PL

EAST VILLAGE

E 5TH ST
E 4TH ST
E 3RD ST
E 2ND ST

FOURTH AVE
109
116
100 115
114
GT JONES ST
101
98 103 98
BONI
99 104
112
113
85
117

E HOUSTON ST

73
70
67
72
61
78
71
75 77
66
64
59
NORFOLK ST
ATTORNEY ST
RIDGE ST
PITT ST
COLUMBIA ST

East River Park

New Museum of Contemporary Art
51
44
STANTON ST
57 60
FREEMAN ALLEY
76
MOTT ST
ELIZABETH ST
RIVINGTON ST

65
63 58 63
SUFFOLK ST
CLINTON ST

WILLIAMSBURG BRIDGE

DELANCEY ST NORTH

F.J.M.Z.
55
LOWER EAST SIDE
DELANCEY ST SOUTH
BIALYSTOKER PL
ABRAHAM E KAZAN ST
LEWIS ST

52
54
KENMARE ST
Lower East Side Tenement Museum
68
74
BROOME ST
GRAND ST

72
B, D
THE BOWERY
CHRYSTIE ST
FORSYTH ST
ALLEN ST
ORCHARD ST
ELDRIDGE ST
LUDLOW ST
ESSEX ST
78 79
ATTORNEY ST
HENRY ST
MADISON ST
JACKSON ST
CHERRY CT

LITTLE ITALY
BAXTER ST
CENTRAL MARKET PL

Museum of Chinese in America
HESTER ST

Seward Park
EAST BROADWAY
JEFFERSON ST
CLINTON ST
MONTGOMERY ST
GOUVERNEUR ST
WATER ST

CANAL ST
56
Eldridge St Synagogue
FORSYTH ST
RUTGERS ST
CHERRY ST

FRANKLIN D ROOSEVELT DR

Confucius Plaza
BAYARD ST
PELL ST
49
DIVISION ST
See p59

OWN
Columbus Park
PARK ROW
CARDINAL HAYES PL
MOSCO ST
CHATHAM SQ
45
BOWERY
HENRY ST
MARKET ST
MADISON ST
MONROE ST

include a bearer bond made out to President George Washington and ticker tape from the morning of the stock market crash of 1929. A timeline, 'Tracking the Credit Crisis' helps to clarify the current global predicament, while themed temporary exhibitions bring the world of money to life.

National Museum of the American Indian

George Gustav Heye Center, Alexander Hamilton US Custom House, 1 Bowling Green, between State & Whitehall Streets (1-212 514 3700, www.nmai. si.edu). Subway R to Whitehall Street-South Ferry; 1 to South Ferry; 4, 5 to Bowling Green. **Admission** free. **Map** p58 C4 ⑤

The National Museum of the American Indian's George Gustav Heye Center, a branch of the Smithsonian, displays its collection on the first two floors of Cass Gilbert's grand 1907 Custom House, one of the finest Beaux-Arts buildings in the city. On the second level, the life and culture of Native Americans is illuminated in three galleries radiating out from the rotunda. A new permanent exhibition, 'Infinity of Nations', displays 700 of the museum's wide-ranging collection of Native American art and objects, from decorated baskets to elaborate ceremonial headdresses, organised by region. On the ground floor, the Diker Pavilion for Native Arts & Culture is the city's only dedicated showcase for Native American performing arts.

National September 11 Memorial & Museum

NEW *Enter on Albany Street, at Greenwich Street (1-212 266 5211, www.911memorial.org). Subway A, C, J, Z, 2, 3, 4, 5 to Fulton Street; E to World Trade Center; N, R, 1 to Rector Street.* **Open** *Mar-Sept* 10am-8pm daily. *Oct-Feb* 10am-6pm daily (see website for updates and extended holiday hours). **Map** p58 B3 ⑥

Until construction is completed on the World Trade Center site, visitors must reserve timed entry passes to the memorial online or at the 9/11 Memorial Preview Site (20 Vesey Street, at Church Street), where you can also see an architectural model of the plans and other displays; there are further exhibits at the visitor centre (90 West Street, at Albany Street). See box right.

Skyscraper Museum

39 Battery Place, between Little West Street & 1st Place (1-212 968 1961, www.skyscraper.org). Subway 4, 5 to Bowling Green. **Open** noon-6pm Wed-Sun. **Admission** $5; $2.50 reductions. **Map** p58 B4 ⑦

The only institution of its kind in the world, this modest space explores high-rise buildings as objects of design, products of technology, real-estate investments and places of work and residence. A large portion of the single gallery (a mirrored ceiling gives the illusion of verticality) is devoted to temporary exhibitions, such as one celebrating the Woolworth Building's centennial, opening in January 2013. Among the permanent collection are photographs documenting the reconstruction of the World Trade Center and scale models of international cloudbusters Burj Khalifa, Taipei 101, and Shanghai World Financial Center.

South Street Seaport Museum

12 Fulton Street, at South Street (1-212 748 8786, www.southstreet seaportmuseum.org). Subway A, C to Broadway-Nassau Street; J, Z, 2, 3, 4, 5 to Fulton Street. **Open** 10am-6pm daily. **Admission** $10; free-$6 reductions. **Map** p59 D3 ⑧

Founded in 1967, the South Street Seaport Museum closed to the public in 2011 due to financial difficulties, but has since reopened under the auspices of the Museum of the City of New York. New programming includes *Timescapes,* a 22-minute multimedia presentation that illuminates the history of NYC. In addition to three floors of galleries devoted

Rising from the ashes

The new World Trade Center moves closer to completion.

For most of the decade following 9/11, visitors who made the pilgrimage to Ground Zero were confronted by an impenetrable fence, and although plans for the World Trade Center site's redevelopment were announced in 2003, there wasn't much evidence of progress. Yet, as the tenth anniversary of the attacks loomed, construction surged, and the 9/11 Memorial opened to visitors on 11 September 2011. In spring 2012, the site's centrepiece tower, 1 World Trade Center, surpassed the Empire State Building as the city's tallest skyscraper; it's expected to reach its full height of 1,776 feet in late 2013.

The **National September 11 Memorial & Museum** (see left) occupies half of the WTC site's 16 acres. The memorial itself, Reflecting Absence, designed by architects Michael Arad and Peter Walker, comprises two one-acre 'footprints' of the destroyed towers, with 30-foot man-made waterfalls – the country's largest – cascading down their sides. Bronze parapets around the edges are inscribed with the names of those who died. As the title makes clear, the intention is to convey a powerful sense of loss.

Budget overruns have delayed completion of museum, currently under construction beneath the plaza (originally scheduled for autumn 2012), though you can see the museum pavilion, designed by Snøhetta – the Oslo-based firm behind its home city's New Norwegian National Opera & Ballet building (2008) – between the waterfalls. Its web-like glass atrium houses two steel trident-shaped columns salvaged from the base of the Twin Towers. Once it opens, visitors will be able to descend to the vast spaces of the original foundations alongside a remnant of the Vesey Street staircase known as the 'Survivors' Stairs', as it was used by hundreds escaping the carnage. The collection, which is expanding daily, commemorates the victims of both the 1993 and 2001 attacks on the World Trade Center. Survivors and victims' families have donated items from the attacks and helped weave personal tales of people who died in the towers. One gallery will be devoted to artists' responses to the events, and items like the East Village's Ladder Company 3 fire truck, which was dispatched to the towers with 11 firefighters who died during the rescue, will be on display.

North End Grill p66

to changing exhibitions illuminating aspects of the city and its relationship with the sea, the museum also encompasses historic ships and Bowne & Co Stationers (see p67).

Staten Island Ferry

Battery Park, South Street, at Whitehall Street (1-718 727 2508, www.siferry. com). Subway R to Whitehall Street-South Ferry; 1 to South Ferry; 4, 5 to Bowling Green. **Open** ferry runs 24hrs daily. **Tickets** free. **Map** p58 C5 ⑨
During this commuter ferry's 25-minute crossing, you'll see superb panoramas of lower Manhattan and the Statue of Liberty.

Statue of Liberty & Ellis Island Immigration Museum

Liberty Island & Ellis Island (1-212 363 3200, www.nps.gov/stli, www.ellisisland. org). Subway R to Whitehall Street-South Ferry; 1 to South Ferry; 4, 5 to Bowling Green; then take Statue of Liberty ferry (1-201 604 2800, www.statuecruises.com), departing roughly every 30mins from gangway 4 or 5 in southernmost Battery Park. **Open** ferry runs 8.30am-4.30pm daily. Purchase tickets online, by phone or at Castle Clinton in Battery Park. **Admission** $17; free-$14 reductions. **Map** p58 B5 ⑩
The sole occupant of Liberty Island, *Liberty Enlightening the World* stands 305ft tall from the bottom of her base to the tip of her gold-leaf torch. Intended as a gift from France on America's 100th birthday, the statue was designed by Frédéric Auguste Bartholdi (1834-1904). Construction began in Paris in 1874, her skeletal iron framework crafted by Gustave Eiffel (the man behind the Tower), but only the arm with the torch was finished in time for the centennial. In 1884, the statue was finally completed – only to be taken apart to be shipped to New York, where it was unveiled in 1886. It served as a lighthouse until 1902 and as a welcom-

ing beacon for millions of immigrants. These 'tired…poor…huddled masses' were evoked in Emma Lazarus's poem 'The New Colossus', written in 1883 to raise funds for the pedestal and engraved inside the statue in 1903. Following a year-long renovation, the statue's interior is scheduled to reopen to visitors by late autumn 2012. With a free Monument Pass, only available with ferry tickets reserved in advance, you can enter the pedestal and view the interior through a glass ceiling. Access to the crown costs an extra $3 and must be reserved in advance.

A half-mile across the harbour from Liberty Island is 32-acre Ellis Island, gateway to the country for over 12 million people who arrived between 1892 and 1954. In the Immigration Museum, photos and exhibits pay tribute to the hopeful souls who made the voyage, and the nation they helped transform. Visitors can also search the archives for an ancestor's records.

Trinity Wall Street & St Paul's Chapel

Trinity Wall Street *89 Broadway, at Wall Street (1-212 602 0800, www.trinitywallstreet.org). Subway R, 1 to Rector Street; 2, 3, 4, 5 to Wall Street.* **Open** 7am-6pm Mon-Fri; 8am-4pm Sat; 7am-4pm Sun.
St Paul's Chapel *209 Broadway, between Fulton & Vesey Streets (1-212 233 4164, www.saintpaulschapel.org). Subway A, C to Broadway-Nassau Street; J, Z, 2, 3, 4, 5 to Fulton Street.* **Open** 10am-6pm Mon-Fri; 10am-4pm Sat; 7am-9pm Sun. **Both Admission** free. **Map** p58 B3 ⑪
Trinity Church was the island's tallest structure when it was completed in 1846 (the original burned down in 1776; a second was demolished in 1839). A set of gates north of the church on Broadway allows access to the adjacent cemetery, where tombstones mark the final resting places of dozens of past city dwellers, including such notable New Yorkers as Founding

Father Alexander Hamilton, business tycoon John Jacob Astor and steamboat inventor Robert Fulton. The church museum displays an assortment of historic diaries, photographs, sermons and burial records. Trinity Church also hosts the inexpensive lunchtime Concerts at One series (see website for details).

Six blocks north, Trinity's satellite, St Paul's Chapel (1766), is more important architecturally. The oldest building in New York still in continuous use, it is one of the nation's most valued Georgian structures.

Eating & drinking

Adrienne's Pizzabar

54 Stone Street, between Coenties Alley and Mill Lane (1-212 248 3838, www. adriennespizzabar.com). Subway R to Whitehall Street-South Ferry; 2, 3 to Wall Street. **Open** 11.30am-midnight Mon-Sat; 11.30am-10pm Sun. **$. Café.** Map p58 C4 ⑫

Good, non-chain eateries are scarce in the Financial District, but this bright, modern pizzeria on quaint Stone Street provides a pleasant break from the crowded thoroughfares and skyscrapers – there are outside tables from April through November. The kitchen prepares nicely charred pies with delectable toppings such as the rich quattro formaggi. If you're in a hurry, you can eat at the 12-seat bar, or opt for the sleek, wood-accented dining room to savour small plates and main courses such as baked sea scallops and ravioli al formaggio.

Bin No. 220

220 Front Street, between Beekman Street & Peck Slip (1-212 374 9463, www.binno220.com). Subway A, C to Broadway-Nassau; J, Z, 2, 3, 4, 5 to Fulton Street. **Open** 4pm-4am daily. **$$. Wine bar.** Map p59 D3 ⑬

This sleek Italian-style wine bar, decked out with cast-iron columns and a polished walnut bar, offers refuge from the South Street Seaport tourist scene. Of the selection of 60 wines, 20 are available by the glass, and you can pair them with cured meats, mozzarella and house-made olive oil.

Jack's Stir Brew Coffee

222 Front Street, between Beekman Street & Peck Slip (1-212 227 7631, www.jacksstirbrew.com). Subway A, C to Broadway-Nassau; J, Z, 2, 3, 4, 5 to Fulton Street. **Open** Apr-Sept 7am-7pm Mon-Sat; 8am-7pm Sun. Oct-Mar 7am-6pm. **$. Café.** Map p59 D3 ⑭

Java fiends convene at this award-winning caffeine spot that offers organic, shade-grown beans and a homely vibe. Coffee is served by espresso artisans with a knack for oddball concoctions, such as the super-silky Mountie latte, infused with maple syrup.

North End Grill

NEW *104 North End Avenue, at Murray Street (1-646 747 1600, www.northendgrillnyc.com). Subway A, C to Chambers Street; E to World Trade Center; 2, 3 to Park Place.* **Open** 11.30am-2pm, 5.30-10pm Mon-Thur; 11.30am-2pm, 5.30-11pm Fri; 11am-2pm, 5.30-11pm Sat; 11am-2pm, 5.30-10pm Sun. **$$$. American.** Map p58 A3 ⑮

Danny Meyer brings his Midas touch to Battery Park City for this instant classic. The place has all the hallmarks of a Meyer joint: effortless, affable service; a warm, buzzy space with top-notch acoustics; and Continental cooking that's easy, accessible and tasty, too. Former Tabla toque Floyd Cardoz leaves his stamp on the menu, devoting an entire section to eggs and adding generous doses of fire and spice. You might start with evanescent cod throats meunière before moving on to excellent composed plates such as wood-fired lamb loin shingled on a bed of stewed chickpeas seasoned with mint. Desserts are crowd-pleasing, but not predictably so – the sticky toffee pudding is elevated by a shot of Glenlivet.

Shopping

Bowne & Co Stationers

South Street Seaport Museum, 211 Water Street, at Fulton Street (1-212 748 8651). Subway ubway A, C to Broadway-Nassau; J, Z, 2, 3, 4, 5 to Fulton Street. **Open** 11am-6pm Wed-Sun. **Map** p59 D3 ⑯

South Street Seaport Museum's re-creation of an 1870s print shop, Bowne & Co Stationers, doesn't just look the part: the 19th-century platen presses – hand-set using antique type and powered by a treadle – turn out beautiful art prints and cards. The shop also stocks journals and other gifts.

Century 21

22 Cortlandt Street, between Broadway & Church Street (1-212 227 9092, www.c21stores.com). Subway A, C to Broadway-Nassau Street; E to World Trade Center; J, Z, 2, 3, 4, 5 to Fulton Street; R to Cortlandt Street.. **Open** 7.45am-9pm Mon-Wed; 7.45am-9.30pm Thur, Fri; 10am-9pm Sat; 11am-8pm Sun. **Map** p58 C3 ⑰

A Gucci men's suit for $300? A Marc Jacobs cashmere sweater for less than $200? No, you're not dreaming – you're shopping at Century 21. You may have to rummage around to unearth a treasure, but with savings of up to 65% off regular store prices, this is a gold mine for less-minted fashion addicts.

Tribeca & Soho

A former industrial wasteland, Tribeca (the Triangle Below Canal Street) is now one of the city's most expensive areas. Likewise, Soho (the area South of Houston Street) was once a hardscrabble manufacturing zone with the derisive nickname Hell's Hundred Acres. Earmarked for destruction in the 1960s by over-zealous urban planner Robert Moses, its signature cast-iron warehouses were saved by the artists who inhabited them as cheap live-work spaces. Although the large chain stores and sidewalk-encroaching street vendors along Broadway create a crush at weekends, there are some fabulous shops, galleries and eateries in the locale.

Sights & museums

Museum of Comic & Cartoon Art

594 Broadway, Suite 401, between Houston & Prince Streets (1-212 254 3511, www.moccany.org). Subway B, D, F, M to Broadway-Lafayette Street; N, R to Prince Street; 6 to Bleecker Street. **Open** noon-5pm Tue-Sun. **Admission** suggested donation $6; free under-10s. **Map** p60 C4 ⑬

Founded in 2001, MoCCA embraces every genre of comic and cartoon art and hosts regular lectures and events with creators and experts. In July 2012 the museum announced it was closing its galleries to the public, so check before visiting. Each spring, the museum organises the two-day MoCCA Festival, a celebration of comic art bringing together established and emerging artists and fans.

Eating & drinking

508 GastroBrewery

NEW *508 Greenwich Street, at Spring Street (1-212 219 2444, www.508nyc.com). Subway C, E to Spring Street.* Open 11am-midnight Mon-Wed, Sun; 11am-2am Thur, Fri; 5pm-2am Sat; 11am-11pm Sun. **Bar/eclectic.** **Map** p60 B4 ⑲
See box p68.

Balthazar

80 Spring Street, between Broadway & Crosby Street (1-212 965 1414, www.balthazarny.com). Subway N, R to Prince Street; 6 to Spring Street. **Open** 7.30-11.30am, noon-5pm, 6pm-midnight Mon-Thur; 7.30-11.15am,

The underground brewpub

A suds-loving chef debuts a basement mini brewery.

508 GastroBrewery

Though craft-beer bars and bottle shops are now ubiquitous in NYC, brewpubs remain a rare breed. While these industrious public houses – throwbacks to the days when local taverns made all their own suds – are a point of pride for trailblazing beer towns like Portland, Oregon, and Chicago, they don't make as much sense in space-strapped Gotham. Thankfully, tight quarters couldn't contain the ingenuity of chef Anderson Sant'anna De Lima. His out-of-control home-brewing hobby led him and his wife, Jennifer Sant'anna Hill, to transform their Mediterranean-leaning restaurant and bar, into what they've dubbed a 'gastrobrewery'. It wasn't an easy route: The pair spent more than a year navigating red tape to retrofit the eaterie's cramped basement into a makeshift brew house, with a one-barrel system – each batch yields 31 gallons, or two kegs –and two refrigerated walk-in closets for fermentation and conditioning. Now the tattooed chef pulls double duty

as a brewer, masterminding a steady rotation of proprietary beers (most are $7-$8 per pint) to pump through six dedicated draft lines, each graced with a house-designed tap handle.

Curious guests at **508 GastroBrewery** (see p67) can start with a flight of six four-ounce pours ($16), working through creations like the chocolaty Montezuma imperial stout and the ginger-and-citrus-spiced Neve's Winter Ale. With a better hold on his jury-rigged setup, Sant'anna De Lima has also begun experimenting with more boundary-pushing brews, such as Brazil Nut Brown Ale (a shout-out to his native São Paulo) and a sour, bottle-conditioned Flanders red ale. He's also got serious about designing beers around the plates coming out of the kitchen: his citrusy 508 IPA is tailor-made for the tender, lemon-spritzed grilled octopus, while the caramel-driven 508 Red Ale is superb with a hearty dish of homemade gnocchi and braised lamb.

noon-5pm, 6pm-1am Fri; 8am-4pm, 6pm-1am Sat; 8am-4pm, 5.30pm-midnight Sun. **$$. French. Map** p60 C4 ⑳
At dinner, this iconic eaterie is perennially packed with rail-thin lookers dressed to the nines. But it's not only fashionable – the kitchen rarely makes a false step and the service is surprisingly friendly. The $125 three-tiered seafood platter casts an impressive shadow, and the roast chicken on mashed potatoes for two is *délicieux*.

Brushstroke

NEW *30 Hudson Street, at Duane Street (1-212 791 3771). Subway 1, 2, 3 to Chambers Street.* **Open** 5.30pm-midnight Mon-Sat. **$$$. Japanese. Map** p58 B2 ㉑
Prominent local chef David Bouley's name may be behind this venture, but he's not in the kitchen. Instead, he has handed the reins to talented import Isao Yamada, who turns out some of the most accomplished Japanese food in the city. The ever-changing seasonal menu is best experienced as an intricate multicourse feast inspired by the Japanese *kaiseki*. (A small à la carte selection is also available.) A meal might start with muted petals of raw kombu-wrapped sea bass, before building slowly toward a subtle climax. In keeping with the basic tenets of this culinary art form, the savoury procession concludes with a rice dish – such as seafood and rice cooked in a clay casserole – and delicate sweets such as creamy soy-milk panna cotta.

Corton

239 West Broadway, between Walker & White Streets (1-212 219 2777, www.cortonnyc.com). Subway A, C, E to Canal Street; 1 to Franklin Street. **Open** 5.30-10.30pm Tue-Thur; 5.30-11pm Fri, Sat. **$$$. French. Map** p58 B1 ㉒
When it opened in 2008, Corton was given the highest possible star rating by *Time Out New York* magazine's critics. A meal here is an extraordinary

experience. Restaurateur Drew Nieporent's white-on-white sanctuary focuses all attention on chef Paul Liebrandt's finely wrought food. The presentations, in the style of the most esteemed modern kitchens of Europe, are Photoshop flawless: sweet bay scallops, for example, anchor a visual masterpiece featuring wisps of radish, marcona almonds and sea urchin.

The Dutch

NEW *131 Sullivan Street, at Prince Street (1-212 677 6200, www.thedutchnyc.com). Subway C, E to Spring Street.* **Open** 11.30am-3pm, 5.30pm-midnight Mon-Thur; 11.30am-3pm, 5.30pm-1am Fri; 10am-3pm, 5.30pm-1am Sat; 10am-3pm, 5.30pm-midnight Sun. **$$. American. Map** p60 C4 ㉓
Andrew Carmellini, Josh Pickard and Luke Ostrom – the white-hot team behind Italian hit Locanda Verde – turned to American eats for their sophomore effort. The Dutch boasts late-night hours and a freewheeling menu, completing Carmellini's progression from haute golden boy (Café Boulud, Lespinasse) to champion of lusty plates and raucous settings. Carmellini plays off the country's diverse influences with a broad spectrum of dishes. Rabbit pot pie, dry-aged steaks and peel 'n' eat prawns all get their due. Guests can drop by the airy oak bar or adjacent oyster room to order from the full menu or sip cocktails such as the Dutch Courage, a mix of gin, kumquat marmalade and grapefruit with a citrus salt rim.

Jack's Wife Freda

NEW *224 Lafayette Street, between Kenmare & Spring Streets (1-212 510 8550, jackswifefreda.com). Subway 6 to Spring Street.* **Open** 10am-midnight Mon-Sat; 10am-10pm Sun. **$$. Café. Map** p61 D4 ㉔
Keith McNally protégé Dean Jankelowitz is behind this café. The 40-seat spot –

sporting dark-green leather banquettes, brass railings and marble counters – serves homey fare, like Jankelowitz's grandmother's matzo ball soup made with duck fat or a skirt steak sandwich served alongside hand-cut fries. See box p92.

Locanda Verde

377 Greenwich Street, at North Moore Street (1-212 925 3797, www.locandaverdenyc.com). Subway 1 to Franklin Street. **Open** 8-11am, 11.30am-3pm, 5.30-11pm Mon-Fri; 8am-3pm, 5.30-11pm Sat, Sun. $$.
Italian. Map p60 B5 ㉕
This buzzy eaterie in Robert Di Niro's Greenwich Hotel is co-owned by the actor and Daniel Boulud protegé Andrew Carmellini. The bold family-style fare is best enjoyed as a bacchanalian banquet. Steak tartara piedmontese with hazelnuts, truffles and crispy guanciale (pork jowl bacon) won't last long in the middle of the table. Nor will the chef's ravioli – as delicate as silk and oozing pungent robiola. Locanda is the rare Italian restaurant with desserts worth saving room for, courtesy of ace pastry chef Karen DeMasco.

Osteria Morini

218 Lafeyette Street, between Broome & Spring Streets (1-212 965 8777, www.osteriamorini.com). Subway 6 to Spring Street. **Open** 11.30am-11pm Mon-Wed; 11.30am-midnight Thur, Fri; 11.30am-3.30pm, 5pm-midnight Sat; 11.30am-3.30pm, 5-11pm Sun. $$.
Italian. Map p61 D4 ㉖
Michael White (Alto, Marea) is one of New York's most prolific and successful Italian-American chefs, and this terrific downtown homage to a classic Bolognese tavern is the most accessible restaurant in his stable. The toque spent seven years cooking in Italy's Emilia-Romagna region, and his connection to the area surfaces in the rustic food. Handmade pastas – frail ricotta gnocchi in light tomato cream,

fat *tortelli* bundles oozing an absurdly rich mix of braised meats – are fantastic across the board. Superb meats, meanwhile, include porchetta with crisp, crackling skin and potatoes bathed in pan drippings.

Pegu Club

77 W Houston Street, between West Broadway & Wooster Street (1-212 473 7348, www.peguclub.com). Subway B, D, F, M to Broadway-Lafayette Street; N, R to Prince Street. **Open** 5pm-2am Mon-Wed, Sun; 5pm-4am Thur-Sat. **Bar**. Map p60 C4 ㉗
Audrey Saunders, the drinks maven who turned Bemelmans Bar (see p148) into one of the city's most respected cocktail lounges, is behind this sleek liquid destination. It has just the right element of secrecy without any awkward faux-speakeasy trickery. Tucked away on the second floor, it was inspired by a British officers' club in Burma (now Myanmar). The cocktail list features classics culled from decades-old booze bibles. Gin is the key ingredient, and these are serious drinks for grown-up tastes.

Silver Lining

75 Murray Street, between West Broadway & Greenwich Street (1-212 513 1234). Subway A, C, 1, 2, 3 to Chambers Street. **Open** 5pm-1am Mon-Thur; 5pm-2am Fri; 6pm-2am Sat. **Bar**. Map p58 B2 ㉓
New York is lousy with venues offering craft cocktails and ones that spotlight live jazz. But enjoying these two noble pursuits in the same place has been nigh impossible. At this well-heeled Tribeca drinkery, the sound of piano keys and shaking jiggers find a common stage inside a majestic 154-year-old townhouse. Little Branch vets Joseph Schwartz and Vito Dieterle, along with bar guru Sasha Petraske, have transported their studied classic cocktails to Tribeca, and Dieterle – who moonlights on the tenor sax – curates the talent.

Shopping

(3x1)

NEW *15 Mercer Street, between Canal & Grand Streets (1-212 391 6969, www.3x1.us). Subway A, C, E, J, N, Q, R, Z, 6, 1 to Canal Street.* **Open** 11am-7pm Mon-Sat; noon-6pm Sun. **Map** p60 C5 ㉙

Denim obsessives who are always looking for the next It jeans have another place to splurge: (3x1) creates entirely limited-edition styles sewn in the store. Designer Scott Morrison, who previously launched Paper Denim & Cloth and Earnest Sewn, fills the large, gallery-like space with a variety of jeans for men and women (prices start at $235) and other denim pieces such as shorts or miniskirts. Watch the construction process take place in a glass-walled design studio, positioned in the middle of the boutique. You can even go bespoke and design your own jeans from scratch (starting at $1,200).

Alexis Bittar

465 Broome Street, between Greene & Mercer Streets (1-212 625 8340, www.alexisbittar.com). Subway N, R to Prince Street; 6 to Spring Street. **Open** 11am-7pm Mon-Sat; noon-6pm Sun. **Map** p60 C4 ㉚

Alexis Bittar, the jewellery designer who started out selling his designs from a humble Soho street stall now has three shops in which to show off his art-object designs. His trademark sculptural Lucite cuffs and oversized crystal-encrusted earrings are all hand-crafted in his Brooklyn atelier.

Housing Works Bookstore Café

126 Crosby Street, between Houston & Prince Streets, Soho (1-212 334 3324, www.housingworksbookstore.org). Subway B, D, F, M to Broadway-Lafayette Street; N, R to Prince Street; 6 to Bleecker Street. **Open** 10am-9pm Mon-Fri; 10am-5pm Sat, Sun. **Map** p60 C4 ㉛

This endearing two-level space – which stocks literary fiction, non-fiction, rare books and collectibles – is a peaceful spot to relax over coffee or wine. All proceeds go to providing support services for people living with HIV/AIDS.

In God We Trust

NEW *265 Lafayette Street, between Prince & Spring Streets (1-212 966 9010, www.ingodwetrustnyc.com). Subway N, R to Prince Street; 6 to Spring Street.* **Open** noon-8pm Mon-Sat; noon-7pm Sun. **Map** p61 D4 ㉜

Designer Shana Tabor's cosy antique-furnished store caters to that ever-appealing vintage-intellectual aesthetic, offering locally crafted collections for men and women. The line of well-priced, cheeky accessories is a highlight – for example, gold heart-shaped pendants engraved with blunt sayings like 'Talk to the hand', rifle-shaped tie bars, and a wide selection of retro sunglasses for only $15 a pair.

Kiki de Montparnasse

79 Greene Street, between Broome & Spring Streets (1-212 965 8150, www.kikidm.com). Subway N, R to Prince Street; 6 to Spring Street. **Open** 11am-7pm Mon, Sun; 11am-8pm Tue-Sat. **Map** p60 C4 ㉝

This erotic boutique channels the spirit of its namesake, a 1920s sexual icon and Man Ray muse, with a posh array of tastefully provocative contemporary lingerie in satin and French lace. Bedroom accoutrements, including molten crystal 'dilettos' and tastefully packaged 'intimacy kits', give new meaning to the expression 'satisfied customer'.

Kiosk

95 Spring Street, between Broadway & Mercer Street (1-212 226 8601, www.kioskkiosk.com). Subway 6 to Spring Street. **Open** noon-7pm Mon-Sat. **Map** p60 C4 ㉞

Don't be put off by the unprepossessing, graffiti-covered stairway that leads up to this gem of a shop. Alisa Grifo has collected an array of inexpensive items – mostly simple and functional but with a strong design aesthetic – from around the world, such as cool Japanese can openers, colourful net bags from Germany and Shaker onion baskets handmade in New Hampshire.

Opening Ceremony

35 Howard Street, between Broadway & Lafayette Street (1-212 219 2688, www.openingceremony.us). Subway J, N, Q, R, Z, 6 to Canal Street. **Open** 11am-8pm Mon-Sat; noon-7pm Sun. **Map** p60 C5 ⑮
The name references the Olympic Games; each year Opening Ceremony assembles wares from hip US designers (Band of Outsiders, Alexander Wang, Patrik Ervell, Rodarte) and pits them against the competition from abroad. The store has been so popular it recently expanded upwards, adding another floor that houses a book and music shop; next door is its Part Deux annex. There's also an outpost in the hip Ace Hotel (see p179).

What Goes Around Comes Around

351 West Broadway, between Broome & Grand Streets (1-212 343 1225, www.whatgoesaroundnyc.com. Subway A, C, E, 1 to Canal Street. **Open** 11am-8pm Mon-Sat; noon-7pm Sun. **Map** p60 C4 ⑯
A favourite among the New York fashion cognoscenti, this Downtown vintage destination sells highly curated stock alongside its own retro label. Style mavens particularly recommend it for '60s, '70s and '80s rock T-shirts, pristine Alaïa clothing and vintage furs.

Nightlife

92YTribeca

200 Hudson Street, between Desbrosses & Vestry Streets (1-212 601 1000, www.92ytribeca.org). Subway A, C, E, 1 to Canal Street. **Map** p60 B5 ⑰

Ostensibly a cultural centre for hip young Jews, 92YTribeca houses a performance space, screening room, art gallery and café – has become one of the most daring music venues in Manhattan. Its breadth is impressive, featuring obscure indie-rock, world music, country and mixed-media shows. It also hosts an energising slate of comedy that takes in stand-up, storytelling and singalong musical film screenings.

Santos Party House

96 Lafayette Street, between Walker & White Streets (1-212 584 5492, www.santospartyhouse.com). Subway J, N, Q, R, Z, 6 to Canal Street. **Open** varies Mon-Thur; 11pm-4am Fri-Sun. **Map** p58 C1 ⑱
Launched by a team that includes rocker Andrew WK, Santos Party House – two black, square rooms done out in a bare-bones, generic club style – was initially hailed as a scene gamechanger. While those high expectations didn't exactly pan out, it's still a solid choice, featuring everything from hip hop to underground house.

SOB's

204 Varick Street, at Houston Street (1-212 243 4940, www.sobs.com). Subway 1 to Houston Street. **Map** p60 B4 ⑲
The titular Sounds of Brazil (SOB, geddit?) are just some of the many global genres that keep this spot hopping. Hip hop, soul, reggae and Latin beats all figure in the mix, with Raphael Saadiq, Maceo Parker and Eddie Palmieri each appearing of late. The drinks are expensive, but the sharp-looking clientele doesn't seem to mind.

Arts & leisure

HERE

145 Sixth Avenue, between Broome & Spring Streets (1-212 647 0202, Theatremania 1-212 352 3101, www. here.org). Subway C, E to Spring Street. **Map** p60 C4 ⑳

This recently renovated Soho arts complex, dedicated to not-for-profit arts enterprises, has been the launch pad for such well-known shows as Eve Ensler's *The Vagina Monologues*. More recently, HERE has showcased the talents of the brilliantly freaky play-wright-performer Taylor Mac.

Jazz Gallery

290 Hudson Street, between Dominick & Spring Streets (1-212 242 1063, www.jazzgallery.org). Subway C, E to Spring Street. **Map** p60 B4 ❹
The fact that there's no bar here should be a tip-off: the Jazz Gallery is a place to witness true works of art, from the sometimes obscure but always interesting jazzers who play the club (Henry Threadgill and Vijay Iyer, to name a couple) to the photos and artefacts displayed on the walls. The diminutive room's acoustics are sublime.

Soho Rep

46 Walker Street, between Broadway & Church Street (Smarttix 1-212 868 4444, www.sohorep.org). Subway A, C, E, N, R, 6 to Canal Street; 1 to Franklin Street. **Map** p58 C1/p60 C5 ❹
A couple of years ago, this Off-Off mainstay moved to an Off Broadway contract, but tickets for most shows have remained cheap for Off Broadway. Artistic director Sarah Benson's programming is diverse and audacious: recent productions include works by Young Jean Lee, Sarah Kane and the Nature Theater of Oklahoma.

Chinatown, Little Italy & Nolita

Take a walk around the area south of Broome Street and east of Broadway, and you'll feel as though you've entered a different continent. New York's Chinatown is one of the largest Chinese communities outside Asia. Here, crowded Mott and Grand Streets

are lined with fish-, fruit- and vegetable-stocked stands, and Canal Street glitters with cheap jewellery and gift shops, but beware furtive vendors of (undoubtedly fake) designer goods. The main attraction is the food: Mott Street, between Kenmare and Worth Streets, is packed with restaurants.

Little Italy once stretched from Canal to Houston Streets, between Lafayette Street and the Bowery, but these days a strong Italian presence can only truly be observed on the blocks immediately surrounding Mulberry Street. Ethnic pride remains, though: Italian-Americans flood in from across the city during the 11-day Feast of San Gennaro (see p36).

Nolita (North of Little Italy) became a magnet for pricey boutiques and trendy eateries in the 1990s. Elizabeth, Mott and Mulberry Streets, between Houston and Spring Streets, in particular, are home to hip designer shops.

Sights & museums

Museum of Chinese in America

215 Centre Street, between Grand & Howard Streets (1-212 619 4785, www.mocanyc.org). Subway J, N, Q, R, Z, 6 to Canal Street. **Open** 11am-6pm Tue, Wed, Fri-Sun; 11am-9pm Thur (check website for hours). **Admission** $7; free-$4 reductions; free Thur. **Map** p59 D1/p61 D5 ❹
Designed by prominent Chinese-American architect Maya Lin, MoCA reopened in an airy former machine shop in 2009. Its interior is loosely inspired by a traditional Chinese house, with rooms radiating off a central courtyard and areas defined by screens. The core exhibition traces the development of Chinese communities in the US from the 1850s to the present through objects, images and video. Innovative displays

cover the development of industries such as laundries and restaurants in New York, Chinese stereotypes in pop culture, and the suspicion and humiliation Chinese-Americans endured during World War II and the McCarthy era. A mocked-up Chinese general store evokes the feel of the multipurpose spaces that served as vital community lifelines for men severed from their families under the 1882 Exclusion Act, which restricted immigration. A gallery is devoted to temporary exhibitions.

Eating & drinking

Café Habana

17 Prince Street, at Elizabeth Street (1-212 625 2001, www.ecoeatery.com). Subway N, R to Prince Street; 6 to Spring Street. Open 9am-midnight daily. **$. Cuban. Map** p61 D4 ㊹
Trendy Nolita types storm this chrome corner fixture for the addictive grilled corn: golden ears doused in fresh mayo, chargrilled, and generously sprinkled with chilli powder and grated *cotija* cheese. Staples include a Cuban sandwich of roasted pork, ham, melted swiss and pickles, and beer-battered catfish with spicy mayo. At the takeout annexe next door, you can get that corn-on-a-stick to go.

Dim Sum Go Go

5 East Broadway, between Catherine Street & Chatham Square (1-212 732 0797). Subway F to East Broadway. Open 10am-10.30pm daily. **$. Chinese. Map** p59 D2 ㊺
A red and white colour scheme spruces up this Chinatown dim sum restaurant, where dumplings (more than 24 types) are the focus. A neophyte-friendly menu is divided into categories that include 'fried', 'baked' and 'steamed'. To avoid tough decisions, order the dim sum platter, whose artful array of ten items includes juicy steamed duck and mushroom dumplings, and the offbeat, slightly sweet pan-fried dumplings filled with pumpkin.

Ed's Lobster Bar

222 Lafayette Street, between Kenmare & Spring Streets (1-212 343 3236, www.lobsterbarnyc.com). Subway B, D, F, M to Broadway-Lafayette Street. **Open** noon-3pm, 5-11pm Mon-Thur; noon-3pm, 5pm-midnight Fri; noon-midnight Sat; noon-9pm Sun. **$$. Seafood. Map** p61 D4 ㊻
Chef Ed McFarland (formerly of Pearl Oyster Bar) is behind this tiny seafood joint. If you secure a place at the 25-seat marble bar or one of the few tables in the whitewashed eaterie, expect superlative raw-bar eats, delicately fried clams and lobster served every which way: steamed, grilled, broiled, chilled, stuffed into a pie and – the crowd favourite – the lobster roll. Here, it's a buttered bun stuffed with premium chunks of meat and just a light coating of mayo.

Mother's Ruin

18 Spring Street, between Elizabeth & Mott Streets (1-212 219 0942). Subway J, Z to Bowery; 6 to Spring Street. **Open** 5pm-4am Mon-Fri; noon-4am Sat, Sun. **Bar. Map** p61 D4 ㊼
See box p92.

Parm & Torrisi Italian Specialties

NEW **Parm** *248 Mulberry Street, between Prince and Spring Streets f (1-212 993 7189, www.parmnyc.com).* **Open** 11am-midnight Mon-Wed, Sun; 11am-1am Thur-Sat. **$.**
Torrisi Italian Specialties *250 Mulberry Street, between Prince & Spring Streets (1-212 965 0955, www.piginahat.com).* **Open** 5.30-11pm Mon-Thur; noon-2.30pm, 5.30-11pm Fri-Sun. **$$. Both** *Subway N, R to Prince Street; 6 to Spring Street* **Italian. Map** p61 D4 ㊽
Young guns Mario Carbone and Rich Torrisi, two fine-dining vets, brought a cool-kid sheen to red-sauce plates in 2010, when they debuted Torrisi Italian Specialties, a deli by day and haute eatery by night. People lined up for their

Deal makers

Discount shopping is chic at two new Nolita boutiques.

AvaMaria

The past few years have been challenging for retailers, but one sector has seen a boom – in autumn 2011, legendary downtown cut-price emporium **Century 21** (see p67) debuted its second Manhattan location in a five-floor former bookstore on the Upper West Side. But if the idea of elbowing crowds and sifting through messy racks fills you with dread, you'll be pleased to hear that there has also been a rise of independent discount boutiques, offering more closely edited collections and, sometimes, steeper reductions.

Former competitive ballroom dancer and costume designer Katherine Virketlene opened **AvaMaria** (see p76) with a dual purview. In addition to reasonably priced clothing by emerging designers, the small space is a goldmine of never-been-worn big-name deadstock, including threads by Miu Miu, Alberta Ferretti and Stella McCartney, and shoes by Manolo Blahnik, Brian Atwood and Jimmy Choo – all slashed by 15-80 per cent. Items may be from past seasons, but many of these styles have staying power. As Virketiene stresses, 'If you're going to buy Manolos, hopefully you're going to wear them for more than three months.'

At **Bit+Piece** (see p76), two blocks away, owner and seasoned bargain hunter Cynthia Solis Yi aims to create a calm discount-shopping experience in her tiny, but precisely organised shop. 'I wanted to create an environment where the shopper doesn't have to dig through horribly crowded racks of damaged and often unfashionable merchandise, or wait on long lines as you often do at a sample sale,' she says. Choice pieces from Marc Jacobs, Jean Paul Gaultier and Helmut Lang are up to 80 per cent off and, to help you create your perfect look, the shop also offers an on-site wardrobe stylist. You won't find that at a chain discount store.

NEW YORK BY AREA

buzzworthy sandwiches (outstanding herb-rubbed roasted turkey, classic cold cuts or chicken parmesan) and hard-to-score dinner seats, packing the joint until it outgrew the space. The pair smartly split the operations, devoting their original flagship to tasting menus and transplanting the sandwich offerings to fetching diner digs next door.

Peking Duck House

28 Mott Street, between Mosco & Pell Streets (1-212 227 1810, www.pekingduckhousenyc.com). Subway J, N, Z, Q, R, 6 to Canal Street. **Open** 11.30am-10.30pm Mon-Thur, Sun; 11.30am-11.30pm Fri, Sat. **$$. Chinese.** **Map** p61 D5 ㊾

Unlike some establishments, Peking Duck House doesn't require you to order the namesake speciality in advance; a chef will slice the aromatic, crisp-skinned, succulent meat at your table. Select the 'three-way' and your duck will yield the main course, a vegetable stir-fry with leftover bits of meat, and a cabbage soup made with the remaining bone.

Shopping

AvaMaria

NEW *107 Crosby Street, between E Houston & Prince Streets (1-212 966-0909, www.virketyne. com). Subway B, D, F, M to Broadway-Lafayette Street.* **Open** noon-7pm Mon-Sat; noon-6pm Sun. **Map** p60 C4 ㊿

See box p75.

Bit+Piece

NEW *246 Mott Street, between E Houston & Prince Streets (1-212 343-2268, www.bit-piece.com). Subway B, D, F, M to Broadway-Lafayette Street.* **Open** 11am-7pm Mon-Wed, Sun; 11am-8pm Thur-Sat. **Map** p61 D4 (51)

See box p75.

Creatures of Comfort

205 Mulberry Street, between Kenmare & Spring Streets (1-212 925 1005, www.creaturesofcomfort.us). Subway 6 to Spring Street; N, R to Prince Street. **Open** 11am-7pm Mon-Sat; noon-7pm Sun. **Map** p61 D4 (52)

Jade Lai opened Creatures of Comfort in Los Angeles in 2005 and brought her cool-girl aesthetic east five years later. Occupying the former home of the 12th police precinct, the New York offshoot offers a similar mix of pricey but oh-so-cool pieces from avant-garde lines such as MM6 Maison Martin Margiela, Acne and Isabel Marant's Etoile, plus the store's own-label bohemian basics and shoes and accessories.

Downtown Music Gallery

13 Monroe Street, between Catherine & Market Streets (1-212 473 0043, www.downtownmusicgallery.com). Subway J, Z to Chambers Street; 4, 5, 6 to Brooklyn Bridge-City Hall. **Open** noon-6pm Mon-Wed; noon-8pm Thur-Sun. **Map** p59 D2 (53)

Many landmarks of the so-called Downtown music scene have closed, but as long as DMG exists, the community will have a sturdy anchor. The shop, which moved from a plum Bowery spot to a Chinatown basement in 2009, stocks the city's finest selection of avant-garde jazz, contemporary classical, progressive rock and related styles.

Erica Weiner

173 Elizabeth Street, between Kenmare & Spring Streets (1-212 334 6383, www.ericaweiner.com). Subway C, E, 6 to Spring Street. Open noon-8pm Tue-Sun. **Map** p61 D4 (54)

Seamstress-turned-jewellery-designer Erica Weiner sells her own bronze, brass, silver and gold creations – many under $100 – alongside vintage and reworked baubles. Old wooden cabinets and stacked crates showcase rings and charm-laden necklaces, such as those bearing a tiny dangling harmonica and steel penknife. Other favourites include brass ginkgo-leaf earrings, and moveable-type-letter necklaces for your favourite wordsmith.

Lower East Side

Once better known for bagels and bargains, this area – formerly an immigrant enclave – is now brimming with vintage and indie-designer boutiques, fashionable bars and, since the New Museum of Contemporary Art opened a $50 million building on the Bowery in late 2007, dozens of storefront galleries.

Sights & museums

Lower East Side Tenement Museum

Visitors' centre: 103 Orchard Street at Delancey Street (1-212 982 8420, www.tenement.org). Subway F to Delancey Street; J, Z to Delancey-Essex Streets. **Open** *Museum shop & ticketing* 10am-6pm daily. *Tours* 10.30am-5pm Mon-Fri; 10.30am-5pm Sat, Sun (see website for schedule). **Admission** $22; $17 reductions. **Map** p61 E4 ⑮

This fascinating museum – actually a series of restored tenement apartments at 97 Orchard Street – is accessible only by guided tour. Tickets can be purchased at the visitors' centre at 103 Orchard Street or online, and tours often sell out, so it's a good idea to book ahead.

'Getting By' visits the homes of an Italian and a German-Jewish clan; 'Piecing It Together' explores the apartments of two Eastern European Jewish families as well as a garment shop where many of the locals would have found employment; 'The Moores' unfurls the life of an Irish family coping with the loss of their child; and the 'Confino Family Living History Program' takes visitors to the homes of Sephardic Jewish occupants with the help of an interpreter in period costume. From April to December, the museum also conducts themed daily 90-minute walking tours of the Lower East Side.

Museum at Eldridge Street (Eldridge Street Synagogue)

12 Eldridge Street, between Canal & Division Streets (1-212 219 0302, www.eldridgestreet.org). Subway F to East Broadway. **Open** 10am-5pm Mon-Thur, Sun; 10am-3pm Fri. **Admission** $10; free-$8 reductions. **Map** p59 D1/63 E5 ⑯

With an impressive façade that combines Moorish, Gothic and Romanesque elements, the first grand synagogue on the Lower East Side is now surrounded by dumpling shops and Chinese herb stores. As Jews left the area the building fell into disrepair. However, the 20-year, $18.5 million facelift has restored its splendour; the soaring main sanctuary features hand-stencilled walls and a resplendent stained-glass rose window incorporating Star of David motifs. The renovations were completed in autumn 2010, with the installation of a new stained-glass window designed by artist Kiki Smith and architect Deborah Gans. The admission price includes a guided tour (see website for schedule). Downstairs, touch-screen displays highlight the synagogue's architecture, aspects of worship and local history, including other Jewish landmarks.

New Museum of Contemporary Art

235 Bowery, between Prince & Stanton Streets (1-212 219 1222, www.newmuseum.org). Subway F to Lower East Side-Second Avenue; J, Z to Bowery; N, R to Prince Street; 6 to Spring Street. Open 11am-6pm Wed, Fri-Sun; 11am-9pm Thur. **Admission** $14; free-$12 reductions, free 7-9pm Thur. **Map** p61 D4 ⑰

Having occupied various sites for 30 years, New York City's only contemporary art museum finally got its own purpose-built space in late 2007. Dedicated to emerging media and under-recognised artists, the seven-floor space is worth a look for the architecture alone – a striking, off-centre stack of aluminium-mesh-clad boxes designed by the cutting-edge Tokyo architectural firm Sejima + Nishizawa/SANAA. On weekends, don't miss the fabulous views from the minimalist, seventh-floor Sky Room, and be sure to wander across the street to the recently launched Studio 231, which features exhibitions and performance by emerging artists. Event highlights Rosemarie Trockel: A Cosmos (24 Oct 2012-Feb 2013).

Eating & drinking

Back Room

102 Norfolk Street, between Delancey & Rivington Streets (1-212 228 5098). Subway F to Delancey Street; J, Z to Delancey-Essex Streets. **Open** 7.30pm-3am Tue-Thur, Sun; 7.30pm-4am Fri, Sat. **Bar**. **Map** p61 E4 ❸

For access to this ersatz speakeasy, look for a sign that reads 'The Lower East Side Toy Company'. Pass through the gate, walk down an alleyway, up a metal staircase and open an unmarked door to find a convincing replica of a 1920s watering hole. Cocktails are poured into teacups, and bottled beer is brown-bagged before being served. Patrons must be 25 or older on Fridays and Saturdays.

Clinton Street Baking Company

4 Clinton Street, between Houston & Stanton Streets (1-646 602 6263, www.clintonstreetbaking.com). Subway F to Delancey Street; J, Z to Delancey-Essex Streets. **Open** 8am-4pm, 6-11pm Mon-Fri; 9am-4pm, 6-11pm Sat; 9am-6pm Sun. **$**. **Café**. **Map** p61 E4 ❺

The warm buttermilk biscuits and fluffy pancakes at this pioneering little eaterie give you reason enough to face the guaranteed brunch-time crowds. If you want to avoid the onslaught, however, the homely spot is just as reliable at both lunch and dinner; drop in for the $14 beer-and-burger special (6-8pm Mon-Thur): 8oz of Black Angus

topped with cheese and caramelised onions, and served with a beer.

Freemans

2 Freeman Alley, off Rivington Street, between Bowery & Chrystie Street (1-212 420 0012, www.freemans restaurant.com). Subway F to Lower East Side-Second Avenue; J, Z to Bowery. **Open** 11am-4pm, 6-11.30pm Mon-Fri; 10am-4pm, 6-11.30pm Sat, Sun. **$$**. **American**. **Map** p61 D4 ❻

Up at the end of a graffiti-marked alley, Freemans' appealing colonial-tavern-meets-hunting-lodge style is still a hit with retro-loving New Yorkers. Garage-sale oil paintings and moose antlers serve as backdrops to a curved zinc bar, while the menu recalls a simpler time – devils on horseback (prunes stuffed with stilton and wrapped in bacon); rum-soaked ribs, the meat falling off the bone with a gentle nudge of the fork; and stiff cocktails that'll get you good and sauced.

Katz's Delicatessen

205 E Houston Street, at Ludlow Street (1-212 254 2246, www.katz delicatessen.com). Subway F to Lower East Side-Second Avenue. **Open** 8am-10.45pm Mon-Wed; 8am-2.45am Thur; 24hrs Fri (from 8am), Sat; closes 10.45pm Sun. **$-$$**. **American**. **Map** p61 E4 ❻

A visit to Gotham isn't complete without a stop at a quintessential New York deli, and this Lower East Side survivor is the real deal. You might get a kick out of the famous faces (from Bill Clinton to Ben Stiller) plastered on the panelled walls, or the spot where Meg Ryan faked it in *When Harry Met Sally…*, but the real stars of this cafeteria are the thick-cut pastrami sandwiches and the crisp-skinned all-beef hot dogs – the latter are a mere $3.35.

PKNY

NEW *49 Essex Street, between Grand & Hester Streets (1-212 777 8454, www.pk-ny.com). Subway B, D to Grand Street; F to Delancey Street; J, Z to*

Delancey-Essex Streets. **Open** 6pm-2am Mon-Thur, Sun; 6pm-4am Fri, Sat. **Bar**. **Map** p61 E4 ⑫

This (tastefully restrained) tiki-style bar is a refreshing sign that a new age of mixology has arrived – one in which bitters and paper umbrellas can peacefully coexist. PKNY (AKA Painkiller) takes a studied approach to tropical drinks, offering tiki archetypes (frozens, swizzles, zombie punches) tailored to your preferences. A passion fruit-spiked piña colada arrives as a thick, fruity slush served in a hollowed-out pineapple. A classic mai tai, balances the acid notes of lime with the round sweetness of aged rum and the bitter edge of house-made curaçao.

Schiller's Liquor Bar

131 Rivington Street, at Norfolk Street (1-212 260 4555, www.schillersny.com). Subway F to Delancey Street; J, Z to Delancey-Essex Streets. **Open** 11am-1am Mon-Thur; 11am-2am Thur; 10am-3am Fri-Sun. **$$. Eclectic. Map** p61 E4 ⑬

The menu at Schiller's is a mix of French bistro (steak-frites), British pub (fish and chips) and good ol' American (cheeseburger), while the wine menu famously hawks a down-to-earth hierarchy: Good, Decent, Cheap. As at Keith McNally's other establishments, Balthazar (see p67) and Minetta Tavern (see p94), folks pack in for the scene, triple-parking at the bar for cocktails and star sightings.

Spitzer's Corner

101 Rivington Street, at Ludlow Street (1-212 228 0027, www.spitzerscorner. com). Subway F to Delancey Street; J, Z to Delancey-Essex Streets. **Open** noon-4am Mon-Fri; 10am-4am Sat, Sun. **Bar**. **Map** p61 E4 ⑭

Referencing the Lower East Side's pickle-making heritage, the walls at this rustic gastropub are made from salvaged wooden barrels. The formidable beer list – 40 rotating draughts – includes Bear Republic's fragrant Racer 5 IPA. Mull over your selection, with the help of appetising tasting notes, at one of the wide communal tables. The gastro end of things is manifest in the menu of quality pub grub – pan-seared sea scallops or a lamb burger.

Shopping

Alife Rivington Club

158 Rivington Street, between Clinton & Suffolk Streets (1-212 432 7200, www.alifenyc.com). Subway F to Delancey Street; J, Z to Delancey-Essex Streets. **Open** noon-7pm Mon-Sat; noon-6pm Sun. **Map** p61 E4 ⑮

Whether you're looking for a simple white trainer or a trendy graphic style, you'll want to gain entry to this 'club', which stocks a wide range of major brands including Nike, Adidas and New Balance, along with less mainstream names including its own label. Shoes that get sneaker freaks salivating include retro styles such as Warrior Footwear (which originated in China in the 1930s) and the Nike Air Jordan 1.

Dear: Rivington

95 Rivington Street, between Ludlow & Orchard Streets (1-212 673 3494, www.dearrivington.com). Subway F to Delancey Street; J, Z to Delancey-Essex Streets. **Open** noon-8pm daily. **Map** p61 E4 ⑯

The glass storefront is a stage for Moon Rhee and Hey Ja Do's art installation-like displays; inside the white bi-level space, head downstairs for their own Victorian-inspired line and select pieces by avant-garde Japanese labels such as Comme des Garçons and Yohji Yamamoto. Upstairs is a fascinating archive of vintage homewares, objects and contemporary art, including framed antique silhouettes, old globes and tins.

Doyle & Doyle

189 Orchard Street, between E Houston & Stanton Streets (1-212 677 9991, www.doyledoyle.com). Subway F to

Lower East Side-Second Avenue.
Open 1-7pm Tue, Wed, Fri; 1-8pm
Thur; noon-7pm Sat, Sun. **Map**
p61 D4 67
Whether your taste is art deco or nouveau, Victorian or Edwardian, gemol-
ogist sisters Pam and Elizabeth Doyle,
who specialise in estate and antique
jewellery, will have that one-of-a-kind
item you're looking for, including
engagement and eternity rings. The
artfully displayed pieces within wall-
mounted wood-frame cases are just a
fraction of what they have in stock.

Dressing Room

*75A Orchard Street, between Broome
& Grand Streets (1-212 966 7330,
www.thedressingroomnyc.com). Subway
B, D to Grand Street; F to Delancey
Street; J, Z to Delancey-Essex Streets*
Open 1pm-midnight Tue, Wed, Sun;
1pm-2am Thur-Sat. **Map** p61 E4 68
At first glance, the Dressing Room may
look like any Lower East Side lounge,
thanks to a handsome wood bar, but
this quirky co-op cum watering hole
rewards the curious. The adjoining
room displays lines by indie designers
alongside select vintage pieces, and
there's a second-hand clothing
exchange downstairs.

Honey in the Rough

*161 Rivington Street, between Clinton
& Suffolk Streets (1-212 228 6415,
www.honeyintherough.com). Subway F
to Delancey Street; J, Z to Delancey-
Essex Streets.* **Open** noon-8pm Mon-
Sat; noon-7pm Sun. **Map** p61 E4 69
Looking for something sweet and
charming? Hit this cosy, ultra-femme
boutique. Owner Ashley Hanosh fills
the well-worn spot with an excellent
line-up of local indie labels, including
Samantha Pleet, Thread Social and
Nomia, alongside carefully selected
accessories, some of which are exclusive to the shop. In the downstairs
beauty studio, Rosie Rodriguez offers
eyebrow sculpting, make-up applica-
tion and more.

The Hoodie Shop

NEW *181 Orchard Street, between E
Houston & Stanton Streets (1-646 559
2716, www.thehoodieshop.com). Subway
1 to Houston Street.* **Open** 11am-8pm
Mon-Wed, Sun; noon-10pm Thur-Sat.
Map p61 D4 70
More than 50 different brands of
hooded apparel for men and women are
showcased in this '70s-inspired boutique, from retro zip-ups to army-print
utility jackets. The shop has a DJ booth
and movie screen for late-night shopping parties and other in-store events.

Obsessive Compulsive Cosmetics

NEW *174 Ludlow Street, between E
Houston & Stanton Streets (1-212 675
2404, www.occmakeup.com). Subway F
to Lower East Side-Second Avenue.*
Open 11am-7pm Mon-Sat; noon-6pm
Sun. **Map** p61 E4 71
Creator David Klasfeld founded OCC
in the kitchen of his Lower East Side
apartment in 2004. The makeup artist
has since expanded his 100% vegan
and cruelty-free cosmetics line from
just two shades of lip balm to an extensive assortment of bang-for-your-buck
beauty products. In the downtown flagship, you can browse more than 30
shades of nail polish and nearly 40
loose eye-shadow powders, among
other products, but we especially fancy
the Lip Tars, which glide on like a gloss
but have the matte finish and saturated
pigmentation of a lipstick.

Reed Space

*151 Orchard Street, between Rivington
& Stanton Streets (1-212 253 0588,
www.thereedspace.com). Subway F to
Delancey Street; J, Z to Delancey-Essex
Streets.* **Open** 1-7pm Mon-Fri; noon-
7pm Sat, Sun. **Map** p61 D4 72
Reed Space is the brainchild of Jeff Ng
(AKA Jeff Staple), who has worked on
product design and branding with the
likes of Nike and Timberland. It stocks
local and international urban menswear
brands (10.Deep, Crooks & Castle),

NEW YORK BY AREA

Lower East Side

footwear (including exclusive Staple collaborations), and hard-to-get accessories, such as Japanese Head Porter nylon bags and pouches. Art books and culture mags are shelved on an eye-popping installation of four stacked rows of white chairs fixed to one wall.

Russ & Daughters

179 E Houston Street, between Allen & Orchard Streets (1-212 475 4880, www.russanddaughters.com). Subway F to Lower East Side-Second Avenue. **Open** 8am-8pm Mon-Fri; 9am-7pm Sat; 8am-5.30pm Sun. **Map** p61 D4 **73**
The daughters in the name have given way to great-grandchildren, but this Lower East Side survivor, established in 1914, is still run by the same family. Specialising in smoked and cured fish and caviar, it sells about ten varieties of smoked salmon, eight types of herring and many other Jewish-inflected Eastern European delectables. Filled bagels are available to take away.

Thecast

71 Orchard Street, between Broome & Grand Streets (1-212 228 2020, www.thecast.com). Subway F to Lower East Side-Second Avenue. **Open** noon-8pm Tue-Sat; noon-6pm Sun. **Map** p61 E4 **74**
Owner Chuck Guarino traded his (literally) underground location for a sliver of a storefront on Orchard Street, but the shop maintains the neo-gothic vibe with ghoulish knickknacks, such as a human skull. At the core of the unabashedly masculine collection is the trinity of well-cut denim, superior leather jackets based on classic motorcycle styles, and the artful T shirts that launched the label in 2004. The ladies have their own line, Bitch Club, covering similar ground.

Victor Osborne

160 Orchard Street, between Rivington & Stanton Streets (1-212 677 6254, www.victorosborne.com). Subway F to Lower East Side-Second Avenue. **Open** noon-7pm Tue-Sun. **Map** p61 E4 **75**

Victor Osborne, who moved his shop-atelier from Williamsburg, Brooklyn, to the Lower East Side in 2009, displays an ample selection of handmade hats for men and women. The look for non-custom hats is stylishly understated, encompassing funky patterned fabric hats, vintage-inspired cloches and smart fedoras, which range in price from $100 for caps to around the $200 mark for a structured felt style.

Nightlife

Bowery Ballroom

6 Delancey Street, between Bowery & Chrystie Street (1-212 533 2111, www.boweryballroom.com). Subway B, D to Grand Street; J, Z to Bowery; 6 to Spring Street. **Map** p61 D4 **76**
It's probably the best venue in the city for seeing indie bands, either on the way up or holding their own. Still, the Bowery also manages to bring in a diverse range of artists from home and abroad. Expect a clear view and bright sound from any spot. The spacious downstairs lounge is a great place to hang out between sets.

Cake Shop

152 Ludlow Street, between Rivington & Stanton Streets (1-212 253 0036, www.cake-shop.com). Subway F to Lower East Side-Second Avenue. **Open** 5pm-2am Mon-Fri; 5pm-4am Sat, Sun. **Map** p61 E4 **77**
It can be hard to see the stage in this narrow, stuffy basement, but Cake Shop gets big points for its keen indie and underground-rock bookings, among the most adventurous in town. True to its name, the venue sells vegan pastries and coffee upstairs, and record-store ephemera in the street-level back room.

Mercury Lounge

217 E Houston Street, between Essex & Ludlow Streets (1-212 260 4700, www.mercuryloungenyc.com). Subway F to Lower East Side-Second Avenue. **Map** p61 E4 **78**

The unassuming, boxy Mercury Lounge is an old standby, with solid sound and sight lines (and a cramped bar in the front room). There are four-band bills most nights, though they can seem stylistically haphazard and set times are often later than advertised. It's a good idea to book bigger shows in advance.

Arts & leisure

Abrons Arts Center
466 Grand Street, at Pitt Street (1-212 598 0400, www.henrystreet.org/arts). Subway B, D to Grand Street; F to Delancey Street; J, Z to Delancey-Essex Streets. **Map p61 E4** ⓴
Once the headquarters of the Alwin Nikolais Dance Theater, this multidiscipline arts venue, which features a beautiful proscenium theatre, focuses on a wealth of contemporary dance, courtesy of artistic director Jay Wegman. It's worth a look, especially in January when the American Realness festival fills the space's three theatres with experimental work.

East Village

The area east of Broadway between Houston and 14th Streets has a long history as a countercultural hotbed. From the 1950s to the '70s, St Marks Place (8th Street, between Lafayette Street & Avenue A) was a hangout for artists, writers, radicals and musicians. It's still packed until the wee hours, but these days it's with crowds of college students and tourists browsing for bargain T-shirts, used CDs and pot paraphernalia. While legendary music venues such as CBGB are no more, a few bohemian hangouts endure, and the East Village has also evolved into a superior cheap-eats hotspot. In the neighbourhood's renovated green space, Tompkins Square Park,

bongo beaters, guitarists, yuppies and the homeless all mingle.

Eating & drinking

Back Forty
190 Avenue B, between 11th & 12th Streets (1-212 388 1990, www.back fortynyc.com). Subway L to First Avenue. **Open** 6-10.30pm Mon-Wed; 6-11pm Thur; 6pm-midnight Fri; 11am-3pm, 6pm-midnight Sat; 11.30am-3.30pm, 6-10.30pm Sun. **$$. American. Map p61 E2** ⓴
Peter Hoffman (the pioneering chef who launched the now-defunct, market-driven restaurant Savoy) is behind this East Village seasonal-eats tavern, where pared-down farmhouse chic prevails in the decor and on the menu. House specialities include juicy grass-fed burgers, stout floats made with beer from New York-area breweries, and golden pork-jowl nuggets. The spacious back garden is a bonus during the warmer months.

Big Gay Ice Cream Shop
NEW *125 E 7th Street, between First Avenue & Avenue A (1-212 533 9333, www.biggayicecream.com). Subway L to First Avenue.* **Open** 1pm-midnight daily. **$. Ice-cream. Map p61 E3** ⓴
Ice-cream truckers Doug Quint and Bryan Petroff now offer their quirky soft-serve creations in this small shop, decorated with a giant unicorn mural bedazzled with 6,000 Swarovski crystals. Toppings run the gamut from Trix cereal to cayenne pepper and the menu also includes sweet treats from flea-market friends including La Newyorkina (ice pops), Melt Bakery (ice-cream sandwiches) and Danny Macaroons.

Bourgeois Pig
111 E 7th Street, between First Avenue & Avenue A (1-212 475 2246, www.bourgeoispigny.com). Subway F to Lower East Side-Second Avenue; 6 to Astor Place. **Open** 6pm-2am daily. **Wine bar. Map p61 E3** ⓴

Ornate mirrors and antique chairs give this small, red-lit wine and fondue joint a decidedly decadent feel. The wine list is well chosen, and although the hard stuff is verboten here, mixed concoctions based on wine, champagne or beer – such as the thick Le Marin Port Flip, featuring tawny port, espresso, chocolate, egg yolk and cream – cater to cocktail aficionados.

Caracas Arepa Bar

93½ E 7th Street, between First Avenue & Avenue A (1-212 529 2314, www.caracasarepabar.com). Subway F to Lower East Side-Second Avenue; 6 to Astor Place. **Open** noon-11pm daily. **$**. **Venezuelan**. Map p61 D3 ⑬

This endearing spot, with floral vinyl-covered tables and bare-brick walls, zaps you straight from New York to Caracas. Each *arepa* is made from scratch daily; the pitta-like pockets are stuffed with a choice of a dozen fillings, such as the classic beef with black beans, cheese and plaintain, or chicken and avocado. Top off your snack with a *cocada*, a thick and creamy milkshake made with freshly grated coconut and cinnamon.

Crif Dogs

113 St Marks Place, between First Avenue & Avenue A (1-212 614 2728). Subway L to First Avenue; 6 to Astor Place. **Open** noon-2am Mon-Thur, Sun; noon-4am Fri, Sat. **$**. **American**. Map p61 D3 ㉞

You'll recognise this place by the giant hot dog outside, bearing the come-on 'Eat me'. Crif offers the best Jersey-style dogs this side of the Hudson: handmade smoked-pork tube-steaks that are deep-fried until they're bursting out of their skins. While they're served in various guises, among them the Spicy Redneck (wrapped in bacon and covered in chilli, coleslaw and jalapeños), we're partial to the classic with mustard and kraut. If you're wondering why there are so many people hanging around near the public phone booth at night, it's because there's a trendy cocktail bar, PDT (see p87), concealed behind it.

DBGB Kitchen & Bar

299 Bowery, at Houston Street (1-212 933 5300, www.danielnyc.com). Subway B, D, F, M to Broadway-Lafayette Street; 6 to Bleecker Street. **Open** noon-11pm Mon; noon-midnight Tue-Thur; noon-1am Fri; 11am-1am Sat; 11am-11pm Sun. **$$**. **French**. Map p61 D3 ㉟

This big, buzzy brasserie – chef Daniel Boulud's most populist venture – stands out for its kitchen-sink scope. More than a dozen kinds of sausage, from Thai-accented to Tunisienne, are served alongside burgers, offal and haute bistro fare. The best way to get your head around the schizophrenic enterprise is to bring a large group and try to sample as much of the range as possible, including ice-cream sundaes or sumptuous cakes for dessert.

Death & Company

433 E 6th Street, between First Avenue & Avenue A (1-212 388 0882, www. deathandcompany.com). Subway F to Lower East Side-Second Avenue; 6 to Astor Place. **Open** 6pm-1am Mon-Thur, Sun; 6pm-2am Fri, Sat. **Bar**. Map p61 E3 ㊱

The nattily attired mixologists are deadly serious about drinks at this pseudo speakeasy with Gothic flair (don't be intimidated by the imposing wooden door). Black walls and cushy booths combine with chandeliers to set the luxuriously sombre mood. The inventive cocktails are matched by top-notch grub including goat's cheese profiteroles.

Dirt Candy

430 E 9th Street, between First Avenue & Avenue A (1-212 228 7732, www.dirtcandynyc.com). Subway L to First Avenue; 6 to Astor Place. **Open** 5.30-11pm Tue-Sat. **$$**. **Vegetarian**. Map p61 E2 ㊲

The shiny, futuristic surroundings here look more like a chic nail salon than a restaurant. Chef-owner Amanda Cohen has created an unlikely space to execute her less-likely ambition: to make people crave vegetables. She mostly succeeds. Elaborate dishes might include a a pungent portobello mousse accompanied by shiitake mushrooms and fennel-peach compote or stone-ground grits served with corn cream, pickled shiitake mushrooms, *huitlacoche* (Mexican truffle) and a tempura poached egg.

Dos Toros

137 Fourth Avenue, between 13th & 14th Streets (1-212 677 7300, www.dostorosnyc.com). Subway L to Third Avenue; N, Q, R, 4, 5, 6 to 14th Street-Union Square. **Open** 11.30am-10.30pm Mon; 11.30am-11pm Tue-Fri; noon-11pm Sat; noon-10.30pm Sun. **$. Mexican**. **Map** p60 C2 ⑤⑨

This bright little Cal-Mex taqueria just off Union Square won a 2010 *Time Out New York* Eat Out Award for its bangin' burritos and has not lost a step. The fillings – juicy flap steak, moist grilled chicken, smooth guacamole – are among the best in town.

Il Buco Alimentari & Vineria

NEW *53 Great Jones Street, between Bowery and Lafayette Street (1-212 837 2622, www.ilbucovineria.com). Subway B, D, F, M to Broadway-Lafayette Street; 6 to Bleecker Street.* **Open** 7am-midnight Mon-Fri midnight Sat, Sun. **$$. Italian**. **Map** p61 D3 ⑥⑨

Il Buco has been a mainstay of the downtown dining scene since the '90s and a pioneer in the sort of rustic Italian food now consuming the city. Owner Donna Leonard took her sweet time (18 years, to be exact) to unveil her first offshoot, Il Buco Alimentari & Vineria. It was worth the wait: the new hybrid bakery, food shop, café and trattoria is as confident as its decades-old

sibling with sure-footed service, the familial bustle of a neighborhood pillar, and heady aromas of wood-fired short ribs and salt-crusted fish drifting from an open kitchen.

Other locations Il Buco, 47 Bond Street, between Bowery & Lafayette Street (1-212 533 1932).

International Bar

120½ First Avenue, between St Marks Place & E 7th Street (1-212 777 1643). Subway F to Lower East Side-Second Avenue; L to First Avenue. **Open** 8am-4am Mon-Sat; 8am-midnight Sun. **Bar**. **Map** p61 D3 ⑨⓪

The walls have been cleared of graffiti, but the second coming of this legendary saloon stays true to its dive bar roots (the original closed in 2005 after more than 40 years of business). A scuffed mahogany bar and vintage film posters make up the decor, and the jukebox is still killer (Black Flag, Nina Simone). The cheap booze and grimy vibe foster the feeling that I-Bar never left.

Ippudo New York

65 Fourth Avenue, between 9th & 10th Streets (1-212 388 0088, www.ippudony.com). Subway 6 to Astor Place. **Open** 11am-3.30pm, 5-11.30pm Mon-Thur; 11.30am-3.30pm, 5pm-12.30am Fri; 11am-3.30pm, 5pm-12.30am Sat; 11am-10.30pm Sun. **$-$$**. **Japanese**. **Map** p61 D2 ⑨①

This sleek outpost of a Japanese ramen chain is packed mostly with Nippon natives who queue up for a taste of 'Ramen King' Shigemi Kawahara's *tonkotsu* – a pork-based broth. About half a dozen varieties include the Akamaru Modern, a smooth, buttery soup topped with scallions, cabbage, a slice of roasted pork and pleasantly elastic noodles.

Jimmy's No. 43

43 E 7th Street, between Second & Third Avenues (1-212 982 3006, www.jimmysno43.com). Subway F to

*Lower East Side-Second Avenue; 6
to Astor Place.* **Open** noon-2am Mon-
Thur; noon-4am Fri; 10am-4am Sat;
10am-2am Sun. No credit cards. **Bar**.
Map p61 D3 ⓷⓶
You could easily miss this worthy subterranean spot if it weren't for the sign
painted on a doorway over an incon-
spicuous set of stairs. Descend them
and you'll encounter burnt-yellow
walls displaying taxidermy, mismatched wood tables and medieval-
style arched passageways that lead to
different rooms. Beer is a star here,
with 14 quality selections on tap (23 in
the bottle), many of which also make it
into the slow-food dishes filled with
organic ingredients.

Momofuku Ssäm Bar

*207 Second Avenue, at 13th Street
(1-212 254 3500, www.momofuku.com).
Subway L to First or Third Avenue;
L, N, Q, R, 4, 5, 6 to 14th Street-Union
Square.* **Open** 11.30am-3.30pm, 5pm-
midnight Mon-Thur, Sun; 11.30am-
3.30pm, 5pm-1am Fri, Sat. **$$. Korean.**
Map p61 D2 ⓷⓷
At chef David Chang's second restau-
rant, waiters hustle to noisy rock
music in the 50 seat space, which feels
expansive compared with its Noodle
Bar predecessor's crowded counter
dining. Try the wonderfully fatty
pork-belly steamed bun with hoisin
sauce and cucumbers or one of the
ham platters, but you'll need to come
with a crowd to sample the house spe-
ciality, *bo ssäm* (a slow-roasted hog
butt that is consumed wrapped in let-
tuce leaves, with a dozen oysters and
other accompaniments); it serves six
to eight people and must be ordered in
advance. Chang has further expanded
his E Vill empire with a bar at this
location and a sweet annexe, Milk Bar
(one of several in the city), across the
street (251 E 13th Street, at Second
Avenue). Other Momofuku branches
are at 163 First Avenue, at 10th Street;
and 171 First Avenue, between 10th
and 11th Streets.

Northern Spy Food Co

*511 E 12th Street, between Avenues A
& B (1-212 228 5100; www.northern
spyfoodco.com). Subway L to First
Avenue.* **Open** 10am-4pm, 5.30-11pm
Mon-Fri; 10am-3.30pm, 5.30-11pm Sat,
Sun. **$. American.** Map p61 E2 ⓷⓸
Named after an apple indigenous to the
Northeast, Northern Spy serves locally
sourced meals at reasonable prices.
The frequently changing menu is
based almost entirely on what's in sea-
son. The food isn't fancy, but it satis-
fies. A 'chicken and egg' sandwich
memorably combined pan-crisped
dark meat, zingy chimichurri, arugula
and a poached egg on Sullivan Street
bread. Toothsome pastured pork loin
shared the plate with rich pork jus and
sautéed leeks, green cabbage and brus-
sels-sprout leaves.

PDT

*113 St Marks Place, between First
Avenue & Avenue A (1-212 614 0386).
Subway L to First Avenue; 6 to Astor
Place.* **Open** 6pm-2am Mon-Thur, Sun;
6pm-4am Fri, Sat. **Cocktail bar**.
Map p61 D3 ⓷⓹
Word has got out about 'Please Don't
Tell', the faux speakeasy inside gour-
met hot dog joint Crif Dogs (see p85),
so it's a good idea to reserve a booth
in advance. Once you arrive, you'll
notice people lingering outside an old
wooden phonebooth near the front.
Slip inside, pick up the receiver and
the host opens a secret panel to the
dark, narrow space. The cocktails sur-
pass the gimmicky entry: try the
house old-fashioned, made with
bacon-infused bourbon, which leaves
a smoky aftertaste.

Porchetta

*110 E 7th Street, between First Avenue
& Avenue A (1-212-777-2151, www.
porchettanyc.com). Subway F to Lower
East Side-Second Avenue; L to First
Avenue; 6 to Astor Place.* **Open**
11.30am-10pm Mon-Thur, Sun; 11.30am-
11pm Fri, Sat. **Italian.** Map p61 E3 ⓷⓺

This small, subway-tiled space has a narrow focus: central Italy's classic boneless roasted pork. The meat – available as a sandwich or a platter – is amazingly moist and tender, having been slowly roasted with rendered pork fat, seasoned with fennel pollen, herbs and spices, and flecked with brittle shards of skin. The other menu items (a mozzarella sandwich, humdrum sides) seem incidental; the pig is the point.

Terroir

413 E 12th Street, between First Avenue & Avenue A (no phone, www. wineisterroir.com). Subway L to First Avenue; L, N, Q, R, 4, 5, 6 to 14th Street-Union Square. **Open** 5pm-2am Mon-Sat; 5pm-midnight Sun. **Bar**. **Map** p61 D2 ⑰

The surroundings are stripped-back basic at this wine-bar offspring of nearby restaurant Hearth – the focus is squarely on the drinks. Co-owner and oenoevangelist Paul Grieco preaches the powers of *terroir* – grapes that express a sense of place – and the knowledgeable waitstaff deftly help patrons to navigate about 45 by-the-glass options. Pair the stellar sips with their restaurant-calibre small plates.

The Wren

344 Bowery at Great Jones Street (1-212 388 0148, thewrennyc.com). Subway B, D, F, M to Broadway-Lafayette Street; 6 to Bleecker Street. **Open** 4pm-2am Mon-Wed; 4pm-4am Thur, Fri; noon-4am Sat; noon-2am Sun. **Gastropub**. **Map** p61 D3 ⑱
See box p92.

Shopping

Bond No.9

9 Bond Street, between Broadway & Lafayette Street (1-212 228 1732, www.bondno9.com). Subway B, D, F, M to Broadway-Lafayette Street; 6 to Bleecker Street. **Open** 10am-8pm Mon-Sat; 10am-7pm Sun. **Map** p61 D3 ⑲

The collection of scents here pays olfactory homage to New York City. Choose from 44 'neighbourhoods' and 'sensibilities', including Wall Street, Park Avenue, Eau de Noho, the High Line, even Chinatown (but don't worry, it smells of peach blossom, gardenia and patchouli, not fish stands). The arty bottles and the neat, colourful packaging are highly gift-friendly.

Bond Street Chocolate

63 E 4th Street, between Bowery & Second Avenue (1-212 677 5103, www.bondstchocolate.com). Subway 6 to Bleecker Street. **Open** noon-8pm Tue-Sat; 1-6pm Sun. **Map** p61 D3 ⑩

Former pastry chef Lynda Stern's East Village spot is a grown-up's candy store, with quirky chocolate confections in shapes ranging from gilded Buddhas (and other religious figures) to skulls, and flavours from elderflower to bourbon and absinthe.

Dave's Quality Meat

7 E 3rd Street, between Bowery & Second Avenue (1-212 505 7551, www.dqmnewyork.com). Subway F to Lower East Side-Second Avenue. **Open** 11.30am-7.30pm Mon-Sat; noon-6pm Sun. **Map** p61 D3 ⑩

Dave Ortiz – formerly of urban threads label Zoo York – and professional skateboarder Chris Keefe stock a range of top-shelf streetwear in their wittily designed shop, complete with butcher-block counter. In addition to a line-up of the latest sneakers by Adidas, Nike and Vans, DQM sells its own-label T-shirts, chinos and button-downs.

Fabulous Fanny's

335 E 9th Street, between First & Second Avenues (1-212 533 0637, www.fabulousfannys.com). Subway L to First Avenue; 6 to Astor Place. **Open** noon-8pm daily. **Map** p61 D2 ⑩

Formerly a Chelsea flea market booth, this two-room shop is the city's best source of period glasses, stocking more than 30,000 pairs of spectacles, from

EXIT

Il Buco Alimentari & Vineria p86

Jules Verne-esque wire rims to 1970s rhinestone-encrusted Versace shades.

The Future Perfect

55 Great Jones Street, between Bowery & Lafayette Street (1-212 473 2500, www.thefutureperfect.com). Subway 6 to Bleecker Street. **Open** 10am-7pm Mon-Fri; noon-7pm Sat; noon-6pm Sun. **Map** p61 D3 **103**

Championing avant-garde interior design, this innovative design store showcases international and local talent – it's the exclusive US stockist of Dutch designer Piet Hein Eek's furniture and pottery. Look out for Kiel Mead's quirky gold and silver jewellery and colourful driftwood wall hooks, crafted from wood found on New York State beaches.

INA

15 Bleecker Street, between Bowery & Lafayette Street (1-212 228 8511, www.inanyc.com). Subway B, D, F, M to Broadway-Lafayette Street, 6 to Bleecker Street. **Open** noon-8pm Mon-Sat; noon-7pm Sun. **Map** p61 D3 **104**

For more than 20 years, INA has been a leading light of the designer-resale scene. A string of six consignment shops offers immaculate, bang-on-trend items (Christian Louboutin and Manolo Blahnik shoes, Louis Vuitton and Marc Jacobs bags, clothing by Alexander McQueen and Marni) at a fraction of their original prices. This branch caters to both sexes.

Kiehl's

109 Third Avenue, between 13th & 14th Streets (1-212 677 3171, www.kiehls.com). Subway L to Third Avenue; L, N, Q, R, 4, 5, 6 to 14th Street-Union Square. **Open** 10am-8pm Mon-Sat; 11am-6pm Sun. **Map** p61 D2 **105**

The apothecary founded on this East Village site in 1851 has morphed into a major skincare brand, but the products, in their minimal packaging, are still good value and give pretty good results. Lip balms and the thick-as-custard Creme de Corps have become cult classics.

Other Music

15 E 4th Street, between Broadway & Lafayette Street (1-212 477 8150, www.othermusic.com). Subway B, D, F, M to Broadway-Lafayette Street; 6 to Bleecker Street. **Open** 11am-9pm Mon-Fri; noon-8pm Sat; noon-7pm Sun. **Map** p60 C3 **106**

Other Music opened in the shadow of Tower Records in the mid '90s, a pocket of resistance to chain-store tedium. All these years later, the Goliath across the street is gone, but tiny Other Music carries on. Whereas the shop's mishmash of indie rock, experimental music and stray slabs of rock's past once seemed adventurous, the curatorial foundation has proved prescient, amid the emergence of mixed-genre venues in the city.

Strand Book Store

828 Broadway, at 12th Street (1-212 473 1452, www.strandbooks.com). Subway L, N, Q, R, 4, 5, 6 to 14th Street-Union Square. **Open** 9.30am-10.30pm Mon-Sat; 11am-10.30pm Sun. **Map** p60 C1 **107**

Boasting 18 miles of books, the Strand has a mammoth collection of more than two million discount volumes, and the store is made all the more daunting by its chaotic, towering shelves and sometimes crotchety staff. Reviewer discounts are in the basement, while rare volumes lurk upstairs. If you spend enough time here you can find just about anything, from that out-of-print Victorian book on manners to the kitschiest of sci-fi pulp.

Voz

618 E 9th Street, between Avenues B & C (1-646 845 9618, www.voznewyork.com). Subway L to First Avenue. **Open** noon-7pm Mon-Sat; noon-6pm Sun. **Map** p61 E3 **108**

This shop is a pleasure to browse – pages from a 1950s Webster's dictionary are sealed into the floors, and the stock spans fashion, mid-century Danish and modern furniture, paintings and pottery. Owners Alex de Laxalt and Naoko Ito believe a woman's wardrobe should be equally eclectic, so they offer a mix of new labels – including up-and-coming Japanese designers 4 Corners of a Circle, Mew New York and Ayumi Moore – with vintage pieces by the likes of Yves Saint Laurent, Givenchy and Gucci. The duo hope to launch their own label, Ito de Laxalt, soon.

Nightlife

Joe's Pub
Public Theater, 425 Lafayette Street, between Astor Place & E 4th Street (1-212 539 8778, www.joespub.com). Subway N, R to 8th Street-NYU; 6 to Astor Place. **Map** p61 D3 **109**
One of the city's premier small spots for sit-down audiences, Joe's Pub brings in impeccable talent of all genres and origins. While some well-established names play here (Steve Martin's bluegrass crew, the Steep Canyon Rangers, for example), Joe's also lends its stage to up-and-comers (this is where Amy Winehouse made her debut in the United States), drag acts and comedy and cabaret performers (Justin Vivian Bond is a mainstay). A small but solid menu and deep bar selections seal the deal to make this a place for a great night out – but keep an eye on those drinks prices.

Nowhere
322 E 14th Street, between First & Second Avenues (1-212 477 4744). Subway L to First Avenue. **Open** 3pm-4am daily. **Map** p61 D2 **110**
Low ceilings and dim lighting help to create a speakeasy vibe at this subterranean gay bar. The place attracts everyone from cross-dressers to bears, thanks to an entertaining line-up of

theme nights. Tuesday nights are especially fun, when DJ Damian Cote's long-running Buddies party takes over. The pool table is also a big draw.

Webster Hall
125 E 11th Street, between Third & Fourth Avenues (1-212 353 1600, www.websterhall.com). Subway L to Third Avenue; L, N, Q, R, 4, 5, 6 to 14th Street-Union Square. **Map** p61 D2 **111**
Dinosaur venue Webster Hall is booked by Bowery Presents, the folks who run Bowery Ballroom and Mercury Lounge. Expect to find high-calibre indie acts (Animal Collective, Battles, Gossip), but be sure to show up early if you want a decent view. Friday night's Girls & Boys bash attracts music makers of the stature of Grandmaster Flash and dubstep duo Nero.

Arts & leisure

Anthology Film Archives
32 Second Avenue, at 2nd Street (1-212 505 5181, www.anthologyfilmarchives.org). Subway F to Lower East Side-Second Avenue; 6 to Bleecker Street. No credit cards. **Map** p61 D3 **112**
This red-brick building feels a little like a fortress – and in a sense, it is one, protecting the legacy of NYC's fiercest experimenters. Anthology is committed to screening the world's most adventurous fare, from 16mm found-footage works to digital video dreams. Dedicated to the preservation, study and exhibition of independent and avant-garde film, it houses a gallery and film museum, in addition to its two screens.

Bowery Poetry Club
308 Bowery, between Bleecker & Houston Streets (1-212 614 0505, www.bowerypoetry.com). Subway F to Lower East Side-Second Avenue. **Map** p61 D3 **113**

Bargain brunches

Fuel up downtown with an affordable weekend meal.

The Wren

Jack's Wife Freda

Why we love it: Brunch purists may balk at the globe-trotting offerings at this airy Soho café (see p69), but for the rest of us, the multiculti dishes are a welcome departure from standard bacon-and-eggs fare. **Why it's a deal**: Most of the creative brunch options clock in at $10 or less. We especially like the green shakshuka, a take on a traditional Middle Eastern baked-egg dish that's lavished with a salsa-like concoction of green tomatoes, tomatillos, garlic, cumin and serrano chilies, served with challah toast to mop it all up.

The Wren

Why we love it: This Irish-style gastropub (see p88) does a roaring trade with East Village night owls, but come brunch time, it's blissfully quiet – a windfall when you're nursing a hangover. The sparse crowd means you can easily score a seat by the front windows or in the cozier, candlelit back space. **Why it's a deal**: Bubble and squeak ($13) is traditionally a breakfast plate of leftover potato and brussels sprouts fried into patties. The Wren remixes the classic, using whole boiled spuds, plus two crispy-edged fried eggs, a plump Berkshire-pork sausage and a dollop of sharp, grainy mustard blended with charred onions. Pair the hearty fare with a brunch cocktail like the Back in Black: a bracing mix of La Colombe black coffee, burnt sugar, Black Bush whiskey and a shot of Guinness.

Mother's Ruin

Why we love it: A peaceful haven from Soho's shopping-bag-toting hordes, this light-filled Nolita bar (see p74) feels especially welcoming during daylight hours, when it's scarcely populated and offers a friendly neighborhood vibe. **Why it's a deal**: Cheap but filling dishes – try the salad of shaved brussels sprouts and bacon lardons topped with two perfectly poached eggs ($10) or the chicken and waffles ($13) – and don't forget to leave cash to spare for expertly crafted cocktails.

The BPC features a jam-packed programme of high-energy spoken word events, plus hip hop, burlesque, comedy, theatre and workshops. The Urbana Poetry Slam team leads an open mic on Tuesday nights.

Great Jones Spa

29 Great Jones Street, at Lafayette Street (1-212 505 3185, www.great jonesspa.com). Subway 6 to Astor Place. **Open** 9am-10pm daily. **Map** p61 D3 ⓬

Based on the theory that water brings health, Great Jones is outfitted with a popular water lounge complete with subterranean pools, saunas, steam rooms and a three-and-a-half-storey waterfall. Access is complimentary with services over $100 – treat yourself to a divinely scented body scrub, a massage or one of the many indulgent packages. Alternatively, a three-hour pass to the 15,000sq ft paradise costs $50.

New York Theatre Workshop

79 E 4th Street, between Bowery & Second Avenue (1-212 460 5475, www.nytw.org). Subway F to Lower East Side-Second Avenue; 6 to Astor Place. **Map** p61 D3 ⓭

Founded in 1979, the New York Theatre Workshop works with emerging directors eager to take on challenging pieces. Besides presenting plays by world-class artists such as Caryl Churchill and Tony Kushner, this company also premièred *Rent*, Jonathan Larson's seminal 1990s musical. The iconoclastic Flemish director Ivo van Hove has made the NYTW his New York pied à-terre.

Public Theater

425 Lafayette Street, between Astor Place & E 4th Street (1-212 539 8500, 1-212 967 7555, www.public theater.org). Subway N, R to 8th Street-NYU; 6 to Astor Place. **Map** p61 D3 ⓮

Under the guidance of the civic-minded Oskar Eustis, this local institution – dedicated to producing the work of new American playwrights, but also known for its Shakespeare productions (Shakespeare in the Park) – has retaken its place at the forefront of the Off Broadway world. The ambitious, multicultural programming ranges from new works by major playwrights to the annual Under the Radar festival for emerging artists. The company's home building, an Astor Place landmark, has five stages and has recently been extensively renovated.

The Stone

Avenue C, at 2nd Street (no phone, www.thestonenyc.com). Subway F to Lower East Side-Second Avenue. No credit cards. **Map** p61 E3 ⓱

Don't call sax star John Zorn's not-for-profit venture a 'club'. You'll find no food or drinks here, and there's no nonsense, either: the Stone is an art space dedicated to 'the experimental and the avant-garde'. And if you're down for some rigorously adventurous sounds (with intense improvisers such as Tim Berne and Okkyung Lee, or moonlighting rock mavericks like Thurston Moore), Zorn has made it easy: there are no advance sales, and all ages are admitted. The bookings are left to a different artist-curator each month.

Greenwich Village

Stretching from Houston Street to 14th Street, between Broadway and Sixth Avenue, the Village has been inspiring bohemians for almost a century. Now that it's one of the most expensive neighbourhoods in the city, you need a lot more than a struggling artist's income to inhabit its leafy streets, but it's still a fine place for idle wandering, candlelit dining and hopping between bars and cabaret venues.

NEW YORK BY AREA

Sights & museums

Washington Square Park

Subway A, B, C, D, E, F, M to W 4th Street. **Map** p60 C3 ⑱

The city's main burial ground until 1825, Washington Square Park has served ever since as the spiritual home, playground and meeting place for Greenwich Village. The Washington Square Arch at the northern end, was designed by Stanford White and dedicated in 1895. It marks the southern end of Fifth Avenue. The central fountain, completed in 1872, was recently shifted to align it with the arch, as part of extensive park renovations (the last phase should wrap up in 2013).

In the 1960s, the park was a frequent gathering spot for the Beat poets – Allen Ginsberg gave several impromptu readings here – and it retains its vitality, thanks to the numerous street performers, NYU students, chess players, political agitators and hustlers who congregate when the weather is fine.

Eating & drinking

Blue Hill

75 Washington Place, between Sixth Avenue & Washington Square West (1-212 539 1776, www.bluehillnyc.com). Subway A, B, C, D, E, F, M to W 4th Street. Open 5.30-11pm Mon-Sat; 5.30-10pm Sun. **$$$. American.** Map p60 C3 ⑲

More than a mere crusader for sustainability, Dan Barber is also one of the most talented cooks in town, building his menu around whatever's at its peak on his family farm in Great Barrington, Massachusetts, and the not-for-profit Stone Barns Center for Food and Agriculture in Westchester, NY (home to a sibling restaurant), among other suppliers. The evening may begin with a sophisticated seasonal spin on a pig-liver terrine and move on to a sweet slow-roasted parsnip 'steak' with creamed spinach and beet ketchup.

Kin Shop

NEW *469 Sixth Avenue, between 11th & 12th Streets (1-212 675 4295, www.kinshopnyc.com). Subway F, M to 14th Street; L to Sixth Avenue.* **Open** 11.30am-3pm, 5.30-11pm Mon-Thur; 11.30am-3pm, 5.30-11.30pm Fri, Sat; 11.30am-2.30pm, 5-10pm Sun. **$$.** **Thai.** Map p60 B2 ⑳

Top Chef champ Harold Dieterle channels his South-east Asian travels into the menu at this eatery, which serves classic Thai street food alongside more upmarket Thai-inspired dishes. The traditional fare seems extraneous, but Dieterle's auteur creations are often inspired. A salad of fried oysters, slivered celery and crispy pork belly was bright and refreshing, while a chefly riff on massaman curry featured long-braised goat neck with a silky sauce infused with coconut milk, duck fat and pineapple juice.

Minetta Tavern

113 MacDougal Street, between Bleecker & W 3rd Streets (1-212 475 3850, www.minettatavernny.com). Subway A, B, C, D, E, F, M to W 4th Street. **Open** 5.30pm-1am Mon, Tue; noon-2.30, 5.30pm-1am Wed-Fri; 11am-3pm, 5.30pm-1am Sat, Sun. **$$.** **Eclectic.** Map p60 C3 ㉑

Thanks to restaurateur extraordinaire Keith McNally's spot-on restoration, this former literati hangout, which was once frequented by Hemingway and Fitzgerald, is as buzzy now as it must have been in its mid-20th-century heyday. The big-flavoured bistro fare is as much of a draw as the scene and includes classics such as roasted bone marrow, trout meunière topped with crabmeat, and an airy Grand Marnier soufflé for dessert. But the most illustrious thing on the menu is the Black Label burger. You might find the $26 price tag a little hard to swallow, but the superbly tender sandwich – essentially chopped steak in a bun smothered with caramelised onions – is worth every penny.

Num Pang Sandwich Shop

21 E 12th Street, between Fifth Avenue & University Place (1-212 255 3271, www.numpangnyc.com). Subway L, N, Q, R, W, 4, 5, 6 to 14th Street-Union Square. **Open** 11am-10pm Mon-Sat; noon-9pm Sun. **$**. **Cambodian**. Map p60 C2 ⓬

At this small shop, the rotating varieties of *num pang* (Cambodia's answer to the Vietnamese *banh mi*) include pulled duroc pork with spiced honey, peppercorn catfish, and hoisin veal meatballs, all stuffed into crusty baguettes. There's counter seating upstairs, or get it to go and eat in nearby Washington Square Park.

Perla

NEW *24 Minetta Lane, between Sixth Avenue & MacDougal Street (1-212 933 1824, www.perlanyc.com). Subway A, B, C, D, E, F, M to W 4th Street.* **Open** 4.30-11pm Mon, Sun; 4.30pm-midnight Tue, Wed; 4.30pm-1am Thur-Sat. **$$**.

Italian. Map p60 C3 ⓬

For his latest Village hit, restaurateur Gabriel Stulman has teamed up with talented young chef Michael Toscano. The toque has wasted no time in embracing the spotlight here, turning out bold, playful food to match the electric vibe. Pop in early or late for cocktails and snacks at the bar, or settle in for a procession of small plates that tease freshness and excitement from humble Italian classics. You might start with cool pieces of lobster served with robiolina and a sprinkle of caviar, then move onto handmade pastas like translucent brown-buttered tortelli with Technicolor ricotta-beet filling. The generous entrées have self-confident swagger, all big, bold proteins under an assertive sear.

Vol de Nuit Bar (aka Belgian Beer Lounge)

148 W 4th Street, between Sixth Avenue & MacDougal Street (1-212 982 3388, www.voldenuitbar.com). Subway A, B, C, D, E, F, M to W 4th Street. **Open** 4pm-1am Mon-Thur, Sun; 4pm-3am Fri, Sat. **Bar**. Map p60 C3 ⓬

Duck through an unmarked doorway on a busy stretch of West 4th Street and find yourself in a red-walled Belgian bar that serves brews exclusively from the motherland. Clusters of European grad students knock back glasses of De Konick and La Chouffe – just two of 13 beers on tap and 22 by the bottle. Moules and frites, fittingly, are the only eats available.

Shopping

CO Bigelow Chemists

414 Sixth Avenue, between 8th & 9th Streets (1-212 473 7324, www.bigelowchemists.com). Subway A, B, C, D, F, M to W 4th Street; 1 to Christopher Street. **Open** 7.30am-9pm Mon-Fri; 8.30am-7pm Sat; 8.30am-5.30pm Sun. Map p60 C3 ⓬

Established in 1838, Bigelow is the oldest apothecary in America. Its simply packaged and appealingly old-school line of toiletries include such tried-and-trusted favourites as Mentha Lip Shine, Barber Cologne Elixirs and Lemon Body Cream. The spacious, chandelier lit store is packed with natural and homeopathic remedies, organic skincare products and drugstore essentials – and they still fill prescriptions.

Nightlife

Blue Note

131 W 3rd Street, between MacDougal Street & Sixth Avenue (1-212 475 8592, www.bluenote.net). Subway A, B, C, D, E, F, M to W 4th Street. Map p60 C3 ⓬

The Blue Note prides itself on being 'the jazz capital of the world'. Bona fide musical titans (Jimmy Heath, Lee Konitz) rub against contemporary heavyweights (The Bad Plus), while the close-set tables in the club get patrons rubbing up against each other. The Sunday brunch is the best bargain bet.

Comedy Cellar

*117 MacDougal Street, between
Bleecker & W 3rd Streets (1-212 254
3480, www.comedycellar.com). Subway
A, B, C, D, E, F, M to W 4th Street.*
Map p60 C3 **127**

Despite being named one of NYC's
best stand-up clubs year after year,
the Cellar maintains a hip, underground feel. It gets packed, but no-
nonsense comics such as Dave
Chapelle, Jim Norton and Marina
Franklin will distract you from your
bachelorette-party neighbours.

Le Poisson Rouge

*158 Bleecker Street, at Thompson
Street (1-212 505 3474, www.le
poissonrouge.com). Subway A, B,
C, D, E, F, M to W 4th Street.*
Map p60 C3 **128**

Tucked into the basement of the long-
gone Village Gate – a legendary performance space that hosted everyone
from Miles Davis to Jimi Hendrix – Le
Poisson Rouge was opened in 2008 by
a group of young music enthusiasts
with ties to both the classical and indie
rock worlds. The cabaret space's
booking policy reflects both camps,
often on a single bill. No other joint in
town books such a wide range of great
music, whether from a feverish Malian
band (Toumani Diabaté's Symmetric
Orchestra), rising indie stars (Zola
Jesus) or young classical stars (pianist
Simone Dinnerstein).

Sullivan Room

*218 Sullivan Street, between Bleecker
& W 3rd Streets (1-212 252 2151,
www.sullivanroom.com). Subway
A, B, C, D, E, F, M to W 4th Street.*
Open 10pm-5am Tue-Sun. **Map**
p60 C3 **129**

Where's the party? Look no further: it's
right here in this unmarked subterranean space, which hosts some of the
best deep-house, tech-house and breaks
bashes the city has to offer. It's an
utterly unpretentious place, but hell, all
you really need are some thumpin'

beats and a place to move your feet,
right? And keep a special lookout for
the nights hosted by local stalwarts
Sleepy and Boo, featuring top house
music stars such as Derrick Carter and
Mark Farina.

Arts & leisure

IFC Center

*323 Sixth Avenue, at 3rd Street (1-212
924 7771, www.ifccenter.com). Subway
A, B, C, D, E, F, M to W 4th Street.*
Map p60 B3 **130**

The long-darkened 1930s Waverly
cinema was reborn in 2005 as the
modern three-screen art house IFC
Center, showing the latest indie hits,
choice midnight cult items and foreign
classics. You may even see the directors or the actors on the screen in the
flesh, as many introduce their work on
opening night.

West Village &
Meatpacking District

The area west of Sixth Avenue to
the Hudson River, from 14th Street
to Houston Street, has held on to
much of its picturesque charm.
Bistros abound along Seventh
Avenue and Hudson Street and
high-rent shops proliferate on
this stretch of Bleecker Street,
including no fewer than three
Marc Jacobs boutiques. The
West Village is also a long-
standing gay mecca, although
the scene has largely moved
north to Chelsea and Hell's
Kitchen. The north-west corner
of the West Village is known as
the Meatpacking District, dating
to its origins as a wholesale meat
market in the 1930s. In recent
years designer flagships, self-
consciously hip eateries and
nightclubs have moved in, and
the area is the starting point
for the High Line.

Sights & museums

High Line

www.thehighline.org. **Open** usually
7am-10pm daily (hours vary; see
website for updates). **Map** p60 A2 ❶
Running from Gansevoort Street in the
Meatpacking District through
Chelsea's gallery district to 30th Street,
this slender, sinuous green strip – formerly an elevated freight train track –
has been designed by landscape architects James Corner Field Operations
and architects Diller Scofidio + Renfro.
Negotiations are underway to gain
access to the final section, from 30th to
34th Streets; skirting the West Side
Rail Yards, which is being developed
into a residential and commercial complex, this stretch is still privately
owned by a railroad company.

As well as lawns, trees and plant-
ings, the park-cum-walkway has several interesting features along the
way. Commanding an expansive river
view, the 'sun deck' between 14th and
15th Streets features wooden deck
chairs that can be rolled along the
original tracks, plus a water feature
with benches for cooling your feet. At
17th Street, steps descend into a
sunken amphitheatre with a glassed-
over 'window' in the steel structure
overlooking the avenue. Further
along, look out for the Empire State
Building rising above the skyline to
the east. Befitting the art-rich location,
there are changing installations dot-
ted along its length.

Eating & drinking

Blind Tiger Ale House

*281 Bleecker Street, at Jones Street
(1-212 462 4682, www.blindtigerale
house.com). Subway A, B, C, D, E, F, M
W to 4th Street; 1 to Christopher Sreet-
Sheridan Square.* **Open** 11.30am-4am
daily. **Bar**. **Map** p60 B3 ❷
Brew geeks descend upon this hops
heaven for boutique ales and 28 daily
rotating, hard-to-find drafts (like Dale's

Pale Ale and Allagash's Belgian-style
Double). The clubby room features windows that open onto bustling Bleecker
Street. Late afternoons and early
evenings are ideal for serious sippers
enjoying plates of Murray's Cheese,
while the after-dark set veers danger-
ously close to Phi Kappa territory.

Buvette

NEW *42 Grove Street, between Bedford
& Bleecker Streets (1-212 255 3590,
www.ilovebuvette.com). Subway 1 to
Christopher Street-Sheridan Square.*
Open 8am-2am Mon-Fri; 11am-2am Sat,
Sun. **$$. French**. **Map** p60 B3 ❸
Chef Jody Williams has filled every
nook of tiny, Gallic-themed Buvette with
old picnic baskets, teapots and silver
trays, among other vintage ephemera.
The food is just as thoughtfully
curated – Williams' immaculate rendi-
tions of coq au vin, goose-fat rillettes or
intense, lacquered wedges of tarte Tatin
arrive on tiny plates, in petite jars or in
miniature casseroles, her time-warp fla-
vors recalling an era when there were
still classic bistros on every corner.

Corner Bistro

*331 W 4th Street, at Jane Street
(1-212 242 9502). Subway A, C, E to
14th Street; L to Eighth Avenue.* **Open**
11.30am-3.30am daily. No credit cards.
Bar. **Map** p60 B3 ❹
There's only one reason to come to this
legendary pub: it serves what many
believe are the city's best burgers – and
beer is just $3 a mug (well, that makes
two reasons). The prime patties here
are no frills and served on a paper
plate. To get one, you may have to wait
for a good hour, especially on weekend
nights; if the wait is too long for a table,
try to slip into a space at the bar.

Fedora

*239 W 4th Street, between Charles
& W 10th Streets (1-646 449 9336,
www.fedoranyc.com). Subway A, B,
C, D, E, F, M to W 4th Street; 1 to
Christopher Street-Sheridan Square.*

NEW YORK BY AREA

Open 5.30pm-midnight Mon, Sun; 5.30pm-2am Tue-Sat. $$. **Canadian**. Map p60 B3 ⑬⑤

Part of restaurateur Gabriel Stulman's expanding Village mini-empire (which also includes nearby Joseph Leonard and Perla, see p95) with this clubby French-Canadian knockout. Mehdi Brunet-Benkritly produces some of the most exciting toe-to-tongue cooking in town, plying epicurean hipsters with Quebecois party food that's eccentric, excessive and fun – crisp duck breast with hazelnuts, for example, or scallops with bacon, tomatoes and polenta.

Kesté Pizza & Vino

271 Bleecker Street, between Cornelia & Jones Streets (1-212 243 1500, www.kestepizzeria.com). Subway 1 to Christopher Street-Sheridan Square. Open noon-3.30pm, 5-11pm Mon-Sat; noon-3.30pm, 5-10pm Sun. $. **Pizza**. Map p60 B3 ⑬⑥

If anyone can claim to be an expert on Neapolitan pizza, it's Kesté's Roberto Caporuscio: as president of the US branch of the Associazione Pizzaiuoli Napoletani, he's top dog for the training and certification of *pizzaioli*. At his intimate, 46-seat space pizzeria, it's all about the crust – blistered, salty and elastic, it could easily be eaten plain. Add fantastic toppings such as sweet-tart San Marzano tomato sauce, milky mozzarella and fresh basil, and you have one of New York's finest pies.

Little Branch

20 Seventh Avenue South, at Leroy Street (1-212 929 4360). Subway 1 to Houston Street. Open 7pm-3am daily. No credit cards. **Bar**. Map p60 B3 ⑬⑦

Sasha Petraske's members-only Lower East Side bar Milk & Honey (134 Eldridge Street, between Broome & Delancey Streets, www.mlkhny.com) may require a referral, but Little Branch, his clubby, low-ceilinged Village rathskeller, retains an open-door policy. The drinks – such as a velvety smooth and mildly spiced hot buttered rum – are nigh perfect.

Pearl Oyster Bar

18 Cornelia Street, between Bleecker & W 4th Streets (1-212 691 8211, www. pearloysterbar.com). Subway A, B, C, D, E, F, M to W 4th Street. Open noon-2.30pm, 6-11pm Mon-Fri; 6-11pm Sat. $$ **Seafood**. Map p60 B3 ⑬⑧

There's a good reason this convivial, no-reservations, New England-style fish joint always has a line – the food is outstanding. Signature dishes include the lobster roll – sweet lemon-scented meat laced with mayonnaise on a butter-enriched bun – and a contemporary take on bouillabaisse: a briny lobster broth packed with mussels, cod, scallops and clams, topped with an aïoli-smothered croûton.

RedFarm

NEW *529 Hudson Street, between Charles & W 10th Streets (1-212 792 9700, www.redfarmnyc.com). Subway 1 to Christopher Street-Sheridan Square.* Open 5-11.45pm Mon-Fri; 11am-2.30pm, 5-11.45pm Sat; 1am-2.30pm, 5-11pm Sun. $$ **Chinese**. Map p60 B3 ⑬⑨

The high-end ingredients and whimsical plating at Ed Schoenfeld's interpretive Chinese restaurant have helped pack the narrow contemporary dining room since opening night. Chef Joe Ng is known for his dim sum artistry: pork and shrimp shumai come skewered over shot glasses of warm carrot soup – designed to be eaten and gulped in rapid succession; other nouveau creations include pastrami-stuffed egg rolls and miso-glazed filet mignon in crispy tartlet shells.

Spotted Pig

314 W 11th Street, at Greenwich Street (1-212 620 0393, www. thespottedpig.com). Subway A, C, E to 14th Street; L to Eighth Avenue. Open noon-3pm, 5.30pm-2am Mon-Fri; 11am-3pm, 5.30pm-2am Sat, Sun. $$. **Eclectic**. Map p60 B3 ⑭⓪

Meatpacking District

With a creaky interior that recalls an ancient pub, this Anglo-Italian hybrid from Ken Friedman and chef April Bloomfield (formerly of London's River Café) is still hopping almost a decade after opening. The gastropub doesn't take reservations and a wait can always be expected. The burger is a must-order: a top-secret blend of ground beef, covered with gobs of pungent roquefort and served with a tower of rosemary-spiked shoestring fries. The indulgent desserts, like the flourless chocolate cake and banoffee pie, are worth loosening your belt for.

Sweet Revenge

62 Carmine Street, between Bedford Street & Seventh Avenue (1-212 242 2240, www.sweetrevengenyc.com). Subway A, B, C, D, E, F, -M to W 4th Street; 1 to Christopher Street-Sheridan Square. **Open** 7am-11pm Mon-Thur; 7am-12.30am Fri; 11am-12.30am Sat; 11am-10pm Sun. **$**.
Café/Bar. Map p60 B3 ❹❶
Baker Marlo Scott steamrollered over the Magnolia Bakery-model cupcake's innocent charms: at her café/bar, she pairs her confections with wine or beer; where there were pastel swirls of frosting, there are now anarchic spikes of peanut butter, cream cheese and milk-chocolate icing. In the process, she saved the ubiquitous treat from becoming a cloying cliché. Gourmet sandwiches and other plates means it's not strictly for sweet-tooths.

Shopping

Castor & Pollux

238 W 10th Street, between Bleecker & Hudson Streets (1-212 645 6572, www.castorandpolluxstore.com). Subway A, B, C, D, E, F, M to W 4th Street; 1 to Christopher Street-Sheridan Square. **Open** noon-7pm Tue-Sat; 1-6pm Sun. **Map** p60 B3 ❹❷
This beloved Brooklyn-born boutique unites European and New York labels in a stylish yet relaxed setting. Owner Kerrilynn Pamer sleuths out such breakout stars as Macedonian-born Risto Bimbiloski, the Louis Vuitton knitwear designer who launched his own womenswear label, and Katie Finn, who creates delicate gold and gem jewellery under her Elizabeth Street label. Pamer's own line of brass bracelets have become a cult hit.

Jeffrey New York

449 W 14th Street, between Ninth & Tenth Avenues (1-212 206 1272, www.jeffreynewyork.com). Subway A, C, E to 14th Street; L to Eighth Avenue. **Open** 10am-8pm Mon-Wed, Fri; 10am-9pm Thur; 10am-7pm Sat; 12.30-6pm Sun. **Map** p60 A2 ❹❸
Jeffrey Kalinsky, a former Barneys shoe buyer, was a Meatpacking District pioneer when he opened his store in 1999. Designer clothing abounds here – by Yves Saint Laurent, Céline, L'Wren Scott and young British star Christopher Kane, among others. But the centrepiece is the shoe salon, featuring Manolo Blahnik, Prada and Christian Louboutin, as well as newer names to watch.

Rag & Bone

100 & 104 Christopher Street, between Bedford & Bleecker Streets (1-212 727 2990, 2999, www.rag-bone.com). Subway 1 to Christopher Street-Sheridan Square. **Open** 11am-8pm Mon-Sat; noon-7pm Sun. **Map** p60 B3 ❹❹
Born out of its founders' frustration with mass-produced jeans, what began as a denim line back in 2002 has since expanded to cover clothing for both men and women, all put together with an emphasis on craftsmanship. The designs, in substantial, luxurious fabrics such as cashmere and tweed, make a nod towards tradition (riding jackets, granddad cardigans), while exuding an utterly contemporary vibe. This aesthetic is reflected in the brand's elegant, industrial-edged his 'n' hers stores.

Nightlife

Cielo

18 Little W 12th Street, between Ninth Avenue & Washington Street (1-212 645 5700, www.cieloclub.com). Subway A, C, E to 14th Street; L to Eighth Avenue. **Open** 10pm-4am Mon, Wed-Sat. **Map** p60 A2 ⓐ

You'd never guess from the Heidi Montag wannabes hanging out in the neighbourhood that the attitude inside this exclusive club is close to zero – at least once you get past the bouncers. On the sunken dancefloor, hip-to-hip crowds gyrate to deep beats from top DJs, including NYC old-schoolers François K, Tedd Patterson and Louie Vega. Cielo, which features a crystal-clear sound system, has won a bevy of 'best club' awards – and it deserves them all.

Henrietta Hudson

438 Hudson Street, at Morton Street (1-212 924 3347, www.henrietta hudson.com). Subway 1 to Christopher Street-Sheridan Square. **Open** 5pm-2am Mon, Tue; 4pm-4am Wed-Fri; 2pm-4am Sat, Sun. **Map** p60 B3 ⓐ

A much-loved lesbian nightspot, this glam lounge attracts young hottie girls from all over the New York area. Every night's a different party, with hip hop, pop and rock music and live shows among the musical pulls.

Smalls

183 W 10th Street, between Seventh Avenue South & W 4th Street (1-212 252 5091, www.smallsjazzclub.com). Subway 1 to Christopher Street-Sheridan Square. No credit cards. **Open** 4pm-4am daily. **Map** p60 B3 ⓐ

This cosy basement venue feels like one of those hole-in-the-wall NYC jazz haunts of yore over which fans routinely obsess. The line-up is solid, with a fun late-night jam session starting after midnight each evening (when admission drops to $10 at 12.30am), and there's a fully stocked bar. It's a great place to catch the best and brightest up-and-comers as well as the occasional moonlighting star.

Stonewall Inn

53 Christopher Street, between Seventh Avenue South & Waverly Place (1-212 488 2705, www.thestonewallinnnyc. com). Subway 1 to Christopher Street-Sheridan Square. **Open** 2pm-4am daily. **Map** p60 B3 ⓐ

This gay landmark is the site of the 1969 rebellion against police harassment (though back then it also included the building next door). Is it hip? Not really. But you have to give the Stonewall credit for being one of the few queer bars that caters equally to males and females. Special nights range from dance soirées and drag shows to bingo gatherings.

Village Vanguard

178 Seventh Avenue South, at Perry Street (1-212 255 4037, www.village vanguard.com). Subway A, C, E, 1, 2, 3 to 14th Street; L to Eighth Avenue. **Map** p60 B2 ⓐ

Still going strong for more than three-quarters of a century, the Village Vanguard is one of New York's legendary jazz centres. History surrounds you: John Coltrane, Miles Davis and Bill Evans have all grooved in this hallowed hall. Big names both old and new still fill the schedule, and the Grammy Award-winning Vanguard Jazz Orchestra has been the Monday-night regular for more than 40 years.

Arts & leisure

Film Forum

209 W Houston Street, between Sixth Avenue & Varick Street (1-212 727 8110, www.filmforum.org). Subway 1 to Houston Street. **Map** p60 B4 ⓐ

The city's leading revival and repertory cinema is programmed by fest-scouring staff who take their duties as seriously as a Kurosawa samurai. The print qualities are invariably excellent, and a recent renovation included comfy new seats.

NEW YORK BY AREA

Midtown

Soaring office towers, crowded pavements and taxi-choked streets – that's the image most people have of Midtown, the area roughly between 14th Street and 59th Street, from river to river. This part of town draws visitors to some of the city's best-known landmarks, including the electronic spectacle that is Times Square, the Empire State Building, the Chrysler Building and Rockefeller Center. But there's more to Midtown than iconic architecture and commerce. It contains the city's most concentrated contemporary gallery district (Chelsea), its hottest gay enclave (Hell's Kitchen), some of its swankiest shops (Fifth Avenue) and most of its big theatres on Broadway.

Chelsea

The corridor between 14th and 29th Streets west of Sixth Avenue emerged as the nexus of New York's queer life in the 1990s. While it's slowly being eclipsed by Hell's Kitchen to the north as a gay hotspot, it's still home to numerous bars, restaurants and shops catering to 'Chelsea boys'. The western edge of the neighbourhood is the city's major contemporary art-gallery zone.

Sights & museums

Museum at FIT

Building E, Seventh Avenue, at 27th Street (1-212 217 4558, www.fitnyc. edu/museum). Subway 1 to 28th Street. **Open** *noon-8pm Tue-Fri; 10am-5pm Sat.* **Admission** *free.* **Map** p104 C3 ❶
The Fashion Institute of Technology owns one of the largest and most impressive collections of clothing, textiles and accessories in the world, including some 50,000 costumes and fabrics dating from the fifth century to the present. Under the directorship of fashion historian

Times Square p122

Event highlights Modernist Art from India: Radical Terrain (opens 9 Nov 2012); Living Shrines of Uyghur China: Photography by Lisa Ross (8 Feb-8 July 2013).

Eating & drinking

Cookshop

156 Tenth Avenue, at 20th Street (1-212 924 4440, www.cookshopny.com). Subway C, E to 23rd Street. **Open** 8-11am, 11.30am-4pm, 5.30-11.30pm Mon-Fri; 10.30am-4pm, 5.30-11.30pm Sat; 10.30am-3pm, 5.30-10pm Sun. **$$.** **American.** Map p104 B4 ❸

Chef Marc Meyer and his wife/co-owner Vicki Freeman want Cookshop to be a platform for sustainable ingredients from independent farmers. True to the restaurant's mission, the ingredients are consistently top-notch, and the menu changes daily. While organic ingredients alone don't guarantee a great meal, Meyer knows how to let the natural flavours speak for themselves, and Cookshop scores points for getting the house-made ice-cream to taste as good as Ben & Jerry's.

Half King

505 W 23rd Street, between Tenth & Eleventh Avenues (1-212 462 4300, www.thehalfking.com). Subway C, E to 23rd Street. **Open** 11am-4am Mon-Fri; 9am-4am Sat, Sun. **Bar.** Map p104 B4 ❹

Don't let their blasé appearance fool you – the creative types gathered at the Half King's yellow pine bar are probably as excited as you are to catch a glimpse of the part-owner, author Sebastian Junger. While you're waiting, order one of the 15 draught beers – including several local brews or a seasonal cocktail.

Tillman's

165 W 26th Street, between Sixth & Seventh Avenues (1-212 627 8320, www.tillmansnyc.com). Subway F, M, 1 to 23rd Street. **Open** 5.30pm-midnight Mon-Wed; 5.30pm-3am Thur, Fri; 6pm-3am Sat. **Bar.** Map p104 C3 ❺

Valerie Steele, the museum showcases a selection from the permanent collection, as well as temporary exhibitions focusing on individual designers or the role fashion plays in society.

Rubin Museum of Art

150 W 17th Street, at Seventh Avenue (1-212 620 5000, www.rmanyc.org). Subway A, C, E to 14th Street; L to Eighth Avenue; 1 to 18th Street. **Open** 11am-5pm Mon, Thur; 11am-7pm Wed; 11am-10pm Fri; 11am-6pm Sat, Sun. **Admission** $10; free-$5 reductions; free 6-10pm Fri. Map p104 C4 ❷

Dedicated to Himalayan art, the Rubin is a very stylish museum – which falls into place when you learn the six-storey space was once occupied by famed fashion store Barneys. Rich-toned walls are classy foils for the serene statuary and intricate, multi-coloured painted textiles. The second level is dedicated to 'Gateway to Himalayan Art', a yearly rotating display of selections from the permanent collection of more than 2,000 pieces from the second century to the present day. The upper floors are devoted to temporary themed exhibitions.

NEW YORK BY AREA

THEATER DISTRICT

W 48TH ST

A

W 46TH ST

B

C

Times Square Visitor Center

Intrepid Sea, Air & Space Museum

W 44TH ST

1

Times Square

TKTS

W 42ND ST

A,C,E

N,Q,R,S, 1,2,3,7

Bryant Park

B,D,F

W 40TH ST

Port Authority Bus Terminal

Madame Tussaud's New York

GARMENT DISTRICT

W 38TH ST

Javits Center

W 36TH ST

2

W 34TH ST

A,C,E

1,2,3

Macy's

HERALD SQUARE

B,D,F,N,Q,R

James A Farley Post Office

Madison Square Garden

Penn Station

Manhattan Mall

3

Chelsea Park

High Line

Museum at FIT

W 30TH ST

W 28TH ST

W 26TH ST

W 23RD ST

C,E

Chelsea Piers Sports Complex

4

W 22ND ST

CHELSEA

FLATIRON DISTRICT

General Theological Seminary of the Episcopal Church

W 20TH ST

W 18TH ST

High Line

W 16TH ST

Midtown 1

W 14TH ST

A,C,E,L

1,2,3

F,L

W 13TH ST

5

MEATPACKING DISTRICT

LITTLE W 12TH ST

GANSEVOORT ST

HORATIO ST

JANE ST

W 12TH ST

GREENWICH AVE

WAVERLY PL

WEST VILLAGE

W 4TH ST

WEST SIDE HWY

ELEVENTH AVE

TENTH AVE

NINTH AVE

EIGHTH AVE

BROADWAY

SEVENTH AVE

SIXTH AVE

Sights & museums
Eating & drinking
Shopping
Nightlife
Arts & leisure

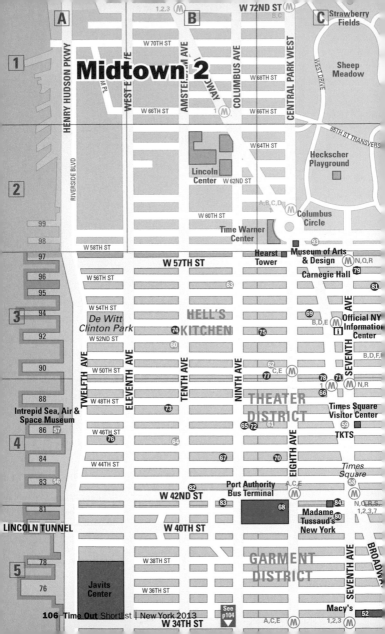

Midtown 2

A | **B** | **C** Strawberry Fields

W 72ND ST

Sheep Meadow

W 70TH ST

W 68TH ST

1

HENRY HUDSON PKWY

WEST END AVE

AMSTERDAM AVE

BROADWAY

COLUMBUS AVE

CENTRAL PARK WEST

WEST DRIVE

W 66TH ST

W 66TH ST

RIVERSIDE BLVD

W 64TH ST

65TH ST TRANSVERSE

Heckscher Playground

Lincoln Center

W 62ND ST

2

W 60TH ST

Columbus Circle

Time Warner Center

93

Hearst Tower

Museum of Arts & Design

W 58TH ST

99
98

W 57TH ST

N,Q,R

Carnegie Hall

79

97

W 56TH ST

63

81

96
95

W 54TH ST

HELL'S KITCHEN

69

B,D,E

Official NY Information Center

3

94

De Witt Clinton Park

74

75

i

92

W 52ND ST

60

B,D,F

TWELFTH AVE

ELEVENTH AVE

TENTH AVE

NINTH AVE

SEVENTH AVE

W 50TH ST

62

C,E

90

77

78

71

W 48TH ST

1

66

N,R

88

73

THEATER DISTRICT

Times Square Visitor Center

Intrepid Sea, Air & Space Museum

86 57

W 46TH ST

76

65 72

61

59

TKTS

4

84

64

W 44TH ST

67

70

EIGHTH AVE

Times Square

83 56

A,C,E

58

81

82

W 42ND ST

Port Authority Bus Terminal

84

N,Q,R,S,
1,2,3,7

LINCOLN TUNNEL

83

68

Madame Tussaud's New York

80

W 40TH ST

GARMENT DISTRICT

78

W 38TH ST

SEVENTH AVE

BROADWAY

5

76

W 36TH ST

Javits Center

See p104

Macy's

52

W 34TH ST

A,C,E

1,2,3

Bethesda Terrace
Naumburg Bandshell
D
Asia Society and Museum
E E 72ND ST
F

E 70TH ST
The Frick Collection
E 68TH ST

Sights & museums
Eating & drinking
Shopping
Nightlife
Arts & leisure

Tisch Children's Zoo
China Institute
E 66TH ST
FRANKLIN D ROOSEVELT DR
1

Delacorte Musical Clock
E 64TH ST
Rockefeller University
The Dairy
Zoo
E 62ND ST
YORK AVE
TRAMWA

Trump Wollman Rink
Scholars' Gate
UPTOWN (pp137-160)
E 60TH ST
ED KOCH QUEENSBO (59TH ST)BR
2

FIFTH AVE
MADISON AVE
PARK AVE
LEXINGTON AVE
THIRD AVE
SECOND AVE
FIRST AVE

Grand Army Plaza
98
94 95

E 58TH ST
E 57TH ST
E 56TH ST

SUTTON PL SOUTH
SUTTON

Trump Tower
96
E 54TH ST
104
E 52ND ST
Museum of Modern Art
87 92
E,M
103
3

89 Paley Center for Media
MIDTOWN EAST
E 50TH ST

BEEKMAN PL
MITCHELL PL

Radio City Music Hall
97
St Patrick's Cathedral
91
6
E 48TH ST
90
NBC
Rockefeller Center
Christie's
E 46TH ST
Japan Society
E 44TH ST
SECOND AVE
4

SIXTH AVE
B,D,F,M
Grand Central Terminal
100 102
Chrysler Building
99
105
United Nations Headquarters
101
E 42ND ST
FIRST AVE
TUDOR CITY PL
QUEENS-MIDTOWN TUNNEL

Bryant Park
88
NY Public Library
7
S,4,5,6,7
E 40TH ST

PARK AVE SOUTH
LEXINGTON AVE
THIRD AVE

Scandinavia House: The Nordic Center in America
E 38TH ST
300 m
300 yds
© Copyright Time Out Group 2012
5

41 Morgan Library
E 36TH ST

HERALD SQUARE
B,D,F,N,Q,R
Empire State Building
See p105
6
Time Out Shortlist | New York 2013 107
E 34TH ST

Sepia images of jazz, funk and soul legends line the walls at this warm, earth-toned cocktail emporium. Waitresses glide amid crescent-shaped leather booths, and you'll likely hear Coltrane oozing from the speakers. Given the old-fashioned aesthetic, a classic cocktail is the way to go: try a well-crafted negroni or a bracing dark & stormy (dark rum, ginger beer and lime juice).

Shopping

Antiques Garage

112 W 25th Street, between Sixth & Seventh Avenues (1-212 243 5343, www.annexmarkets.com). Subway F to 23rd Street. **Open** *9am-5pm Sat, Sun. No credit cards.* **Map** *p104 C3* ❻
Designers (and the occasional celebrity) hunt regularly at this flea market held in a vacant parking garage. Specialities include old prints, vintage clothing and household paraphernalia. The weekend outdoor Hell's Kitchen Flea Market (39th Street, between Ninth & Tenth Avenues), run by the same people, features a mix of vintage clothing and textiles, furniture and miscellaneous bric-a-brac.

Billy's Bakery

184 Ninth Avenue, between 21st & 22nd Streets (1-212 647 9956, www.billys bakerynyc.com). Subway C, E to 23rd Street. **Open** *8.30am-11pm Mon-Thur; 8.30am-midnight Fri, Sat; 9am-10pm Sun.* **Map** *p104 B4* ❼
Amid super-sweet retro delights such as coconut cream pie, cupcakes and Famous Chocolate Icebox Cake, you'll find friendly service in a setting that will remind you of grandma's kitchen – or at least, it will if your grandmother was Betty Crocker.

Loehmann's

101 Seventh Avenue, at 16th Street (1-212 352 0856, www.loehmanns.com). Subway A, C, E to 14th Street; L to Eighth Avenue; 1 to 18th Street. **Open** *9am-9pm Mon-Sat; 11am-7pm Sun.* **Map** *p104 C5* ❽

You'll find five floors of major markdowns on current and off-season clothes at this venerable discount emporium. Make a beeline upstairs to the 'Back Room' for big names such as Prada and Armani.

Mantiques Modern

146 W 22nd Street, between Sixth & Seventh Avenues (1-212 206 1494, www.mantiquesmodern.com). Subway 1 to 23rd Street. **Open** *10.30am-6.30pm Mon-Fri; 11am-7pm Sat, Sun.* **Map** *p104 C4* ❾
Specialising in industrial and modernist furnishings and art from the 1880s to the 1980s, Mantiques Modern is a fantastic repository of beautiful and bizarre items, from kinetic sculptures and early-20th-century wooden artists' mannequins to a Russian World War II telescope and a rattlesnake frozen in a slab of Lucite. Pieces by famous designers such as Hermès sit side by side with natural curiosities, and skulls (in metal or Lucite), crabs, animal horns and robots are all recurring themes.

Printed Matter

195 Tenth Avenue, between 21st & 22nd Streets (1-212 925 0325, www.printedmatter.org). Subway C, E to 23rd Street. **Open** *11am-7pm Mon-Wed, Sat; 11am-8pm Thur, Fri.* **Map** *p104 B4* ❿
This non-profit organisation is devoted to artists' books – ranging from David Shrigley's deceptively naive illustrations to provocative photographic self-portraits by Matthias Herrmann – and operates a public reading room as well as a shop. Works by unknown and emerging artists share shelf space with those by veterans such as Yoko Ono and Edward Ruscha.

Nightlife

The Eagle

554 W 28th Street, between Tenth & Eleventh Avenues (1-646 473 1866, www.eaglenyc.com). Subway C, E to

23rd Street. **Open** 10pm-4am Tue-Sat; 5pm-4am Sun. No credit cards. **Map** p104 A3 ⓫

You don't have to be a kinky leather daddy to enjoy this manly outpost, but it definitely doesn't hurt. The gay fetish bar is home to an array of beer blasts, foot-worship fêtes and leather soirées, plus simple pool playing and cruising nights. In summer, the rooftop is a surprising oasis.

G Lounge

225 W 19th Street, between Seventh & Eighth Avenues (1-212 929 1085, www.glounge.com). Subway 1 to 18th Street. **Open** 4pm-4am daily. No credit cards. **Map** p104 C4 ⓬

The neighbourhood's original slick boy lounge – a rather moodily lit cave with a cool brick-and-glass arched entrance – wouldn't look out of place in an upscale boutique hotel. An excellent roster of DJs stays on top of the mood at this popular gay after-work cocktail spot.

Highline Ballroom

431 W 16th Street, between Ninth & Tenth Avenues (1-212 414 5994, www.highlineballroom.com). Subway A, C, E to 14th Street; L to Eighth Avenue. **Map** p104 B5 ⓭

This West Side club is LA-slick and bland, in a corporate sense. But it still has a lot to recommend it: the sound is top-of-the-heap and sightlines are pretty good. The bookings are also impressive, ranging from hip hop heatseekers such as Yelawolf and Wiz Khalifa, to singer-songwriter pop, world music and burlesque.

Upright Citizens Brigade Theatre

307 W 26th Street, between Eighth & Ninth Avenues (1-212 366 9176, www.ucbtheatre.com). Subway C, E to 23rd Street. No credit cards. **Map** p104 B3 ⓮

The Upright Citizens Brigade, which migrated from Chicago in the 1990s, has been the most visible catalyst in

New York's current alternative comedy boom. The improv troupes and sketch groups here are some of the best in the city. Stars of *Saturday Night Live* and writers for late-night talk shows gather on Sunday nights to wow crowds in the long-running *ASSSSCAT 3000.* Other premier teams include the Stepfathers (Fridays) and Death by Roo Roo (Saturdays). Arrive early so you can choose a good seat – the venue has challenging sightlines.

Event highlights *ASSSSCAT 3000* (7.30pm, 9.30pm Sun).

Arts & leisure

Atlantic Theater Company

336 W 20th Street, between Eighth & Ninth Avenues (1-212 691 5919, Ticket Central 1-212 279 4200, www.atlantictheater. org). Subway C, E to 23rd Street. **Map** p105 B4 ⓯

Created in 1985 as an offshoot of acting workshops led by playwright David Mamet and actor William H Macy, the dynamic Atlantic Theater Company has presented dozens of new plays, including Martin McDonagh's *The Lieutenant of Inishmore* and the rock musical *Spring Awakening.*

Chelsea Piers

Piers 59-62, W 17th to 23rd Streets, at Eleventh Avenue (1-212 336 6666, www.chelseapiers.com). Subway C, E to 23rd Street. **Open** times vary; phone or check website for details. **Map** p104 A4 ⓰

Chelsea Piers is still the most impressive all-in-one athletic facility in New York. Between the ice rink (Pier 61, 1-212 336 6100), the bowling alley (between Piers 59 & 60, 1-212 835 2695), the driving range (Pier 59, 1-212 336 6400) and scads of other choices, there's definitely something for everyone here. The Field House (between Piers 61 & 62, 1-212 336 6500) has a climbing wall, a gymnastics centre, batting cages and basketball courts. At the Sports Center Health Club (Pier 60, 1-212 336 6000), you'll find a gym complete with comprehensive weight deck and cardiovascular machines, plus classes covering everything from boxing to triathlon training in the 25yd pool.

Joyce Theater

175 Eighth Avenue, at 19th Street (1-212 691 9740, www.joyce.org). Subway A, C, E to 14th Street; 1 to 18th Street; L to Eighth Avenue. **Map** p104 B4 **17**
This intimate space houses one of the finest theatres – we're talking about sightlines – in town. Companies and choreographers that present work here, among them Ballet Hispanico, Pilobolus Dance Theater and Doug Varone, tend to be somewhat traditional. The Joyce hosts dance throughout much of the year – Pilobolus is a summer staple.

The Kitchen

512 W 19th Street, between Tenth & Eleventh Avenues (1-212 255 5793, www.thekitchen.org). Subway A, C, E to 14th Street; L to Eighth Avenue. **Map** p104 B4 **18**
The Kitchen offers some of the best experimental dance around – inventive, provocative and rigorous. Some of the artists who have presented work here are the finest in New York: Sarah Michelson, who also curates artists Jon Kinzel, Ann Liv Young and Jodi Melnick.

Sleep No More

McKittrick Hotel, 530 W 27th Street, between Tenth & Eleventh Avenues, Chelsea (Ovationtix 1-866 811 4111, www.sleepnomorenyc.com). Subway 1 to 28th Street; C, E to 23rd Street. **Map** p103 A3 **19**
A multitude of searing sights await at this bedazzling and uncanny installation by the English company Punchdrunk. Your sense of space is blurred as you wend through more than 90 discrete spaces, from a cloistral chapel to a ballroom floor. A Shakespearean can check off allusions to *Macbeth*; others can just revel in the haunted-house vibe.

Flatiron District & Union Square

Taking its name from the distinctive wedge-shaped **Flatiron Building**, this district extends from 14th to 29th Streets, between Sixth and Lexington Avenues. The former commercial district became more residential in the 1980s as buyers were drawn to its early 20th-century industrial architecture and 19th-century brownstones; clusters of restaurants and shops followed.

Sights & museums

Flatiron Building

175 Fifth Avenue, between 22nd & 23rd Streets. Subway N, R, 6 to 23rd Street. **Map** p105 D4 **20**
One of New York's most celebrated structures, the Flatiron Building was the world's first steel-frame skyscraper when it was completed in 1902. The 22-storey Beaux Arts edifice is clad in white limestone and terracotta, but it's the unique triangular shape as well as its singular position at the crossing of Fifth Avenue and Broadway that draws the stares of sightseers and natives alike.

Madison Square Park

23rd to 26th Streets, between Fifth & Madison Avenues (www.madison squarepark.org). Subway N, R, 6 to 23rd Street. **Map** p105 D3/D4 **21**
Madison Square Park, which first opened in 1847, is one of the most elegant spaces in New York, surrounded by some of the city's most fabled buildings. The world's tallest skyscraper from 1909 to 1913, the Metropolitan Life Tower at 1 Madison Avenue was designed to resemble the Campanile in Venice's Piazza San Marco, whose reconstruction (after a collapse in 1902) Met Life had funded. The Appellate Division Courthouse at 27 Madison Avenue is one of the finest Beaux Arts buildings in New York. The park itself hosts summer

Madison Square Park

concerts, literary readings and kids' events. The undoubted star of the initiative is Mad Sq Art, a year-round 'gallery without walls', featuring changing installations by big-name artists such as Antony Gormley and Jaume Plensa.

Museum of Sex

233 Fifth Avenue, at 27th Street (1-212 689 6337, www.museumofsex.com). Subway N, R, 6 to 28th Street. **Open** 10am-8pm Mon-Thur, Sun; 10am-9pm Fri, Sat. **Admission** $17.50; $15.25 reductions. **Map** p105 D3 ㉒

Situated in the former Tenderloin district, which bumped-and-grinded with dance halls and brothels in the 1800s, MoSex explores the subject within a cultural context. Highlights of the permanent collection range from the tastefully erotic to the outlandish: an 1890s antionanism device looks as uncomfortable as the BDSM gear donated by a local dominatrix, there is kinky art courtesy of Picasso and Keith Haring, and a life-size silicone Real Doll. Rotating exhibitions in the three-level space cover such topics as 'The Sex Lives of Animals'. The gift shop stocks books and arty sex toys, while the subterranean Oralfix bar dispenses aphrodisiac soft drinks and decadent cocktails.

Eating & drinking

230 Fifth

230 Fifth Avenue, between 26th & 27th Streets (1-212 725 4300, www.230-fifth.com). Subway N, R to 28th Street. **Open** 4pm-4am daily. **Bar**. **Map** p105 D3 ㉓

The 14,000sq ft roof garden dazzles with truly spectacular views, including a close-up of the Empire State Building, but the glitzy indoor lounge – with its ceiling-height windows, wraparound sofas and bold lighting – shouldn't be overlooked. While the sprawling outdoor space gets mobbed on sultry nights, it's less crowded in the cooler months when heaters, fleece robes and hot ciders make it a winter hotspot.

ABC Kitchen

ABC Carpet & Home, 35 E 18th Street, betwveen Broadway and Park Avenue South (1-212 475 5829, www.abckitchennyc.com). Subway L, N, Q, R, 4, 5, 6 to 14th Street-Union Square. **Open** noon-3pm, 5.30-10.30pm Mon-Wed; noon-3pm, 5.30-11pm Thur; noon-3pm, 5.30-11.30pm Fri; 11am-3.30pm, 5.30-11.30pm Sat; 11am-3.30pm, 5.30pm Sun. **$$ Eclectic**. **Map** p105 D4 ㉔

The haute green cooking at Jean-Georges Vongerichten's artfully decorated restaurant inside a landmark Flatiron furniture store is based on the most gorgeous ingredients from up and down the East Coast. Local, seasonal bounty finds its way into such dishes as a salad of cumin-and-citrus-laced roasted carrots with avocado and crunchy sunflower, pumpkin and sesame seeds, or kasha bowtie pasta with veal meatballs. A sundae of salted caramel ice-cream, candied peanuts and popcorn with chocolate sauce reworks the kids' treat to thrill a grownup palate. ABC delivers one message overall: food that's good for the planet needn't be any less opulent, flavourful or stunning to look at.

Breslin Bar & Dining Room

Ace Hotel, 16 W 29th Street, at Broadway (1-212 679 1939). Subway N, R to 28th Street. **Open** 7am-midnight daily. **$$$. Eclectic**. **Map** p105 D3 ㉕

The third project from restaurant savant Ken Friedman and Anglo chef April Bloomfield, the Breslin broke gluttonous new ground. Expect a wait at this no-reservations hotspot – you can quell your appetite at the bar with an order of scrumpets (fried strips of lamb belly). The overall ethos could best be described as late-period Henry VIII: groaning boards of housemade terrines feature thick slices of guinea hen, rabbit and pork. The pig's foot for two – half a leg, really – could feed the whole Tudor court.

Desserts include amped-up childhood treats like ice-cream sundaes.

The Cannibal

NEW *113 E 29th Street, between Park and Lexington Avenues (1-212 686 5480, www.thecannibalnyc.com). Subway 6 to 28th Street.* **Open** 11am-11.30pm Mon-Sat; 11am-10.30pm Sun. **$-$$.** **Steakhouse.** Map p105 D3 ㉖

Run by restaurateur Christian Pappanicholas and connected to his Belgian-American eatery, Resto, the Cannibal is an unusual retail-restaurant hybrid – a beer store and a butcher shop but also a laid-back place to eat and drink. The meat counter supplies whole beasts for Resto's large-format feasts, but the carnivore's paradise is otherwise autonomous, with its own chef, Michael Berardino (formerly of Dell'anima) and beer master, Ryan Colcannon. The food is best ordered in rounds, pairing beer and bites – wispy shavings of Kentucky ham, patés, sausages and tartares – as you work your way through some of the 400-plus selections on the drinks list.

Casa Mono

52 Irving Place, at 17th Street (1-212 253 2773, www.casamononyc.com). Subway L to Third Avenue; L, N, Q, R, 4, 5, 6 to 14th Street-Union Square. **Open** noon-midnight daily. **$-$$.** **Spanish.** Map p105 E4 ㉗

Offal-loving chef-partners Mario Batali and Andy Nusser broke new ground in NYC with their adventurous Spanish fare: oxtail-stuffed piquillo peppers, fried sweetbreads, foie gras with *cinco cebollas* (five types of onion), or the fried duck egg, a delicately flavoured breakfast-meets-dinner dish topping a mound of sautéed fingerling potatoes and salt-cured tuna loin. For a cheaper option, the attached Bar Jamón (125 E 17th Street; open 5pm-2am Mon-Fri; noon-2am Sat, Sun) offers tapas, treasured Ibérico hams and Spanish cheeses.

Eleven Madison Park

11 Madison Avenue, at 24th Street (1-212 889 0905, www.elevenmadisonpark.com). Subway N, R, 6 to 23rd Street. **Open** noon-2pm, 5.30-10.30pm Mon-Thur; noon-2pm, 5.30-10.30pm Fri; 5.30-10.30pm Sat. **$$$$.** **American.** Map p105 D4 ㉓

Originally a Danny Meyer restaurant, this vast art deco jewel is now owned by its award-winning chef Daniel Humm and general manager Will Guidara. Humm's lofty intentions are expressed in a four-course lunch or dinner and a multicourse tasting menu. A starter of *la ratte* potatoes featured Hawaiian prawns and delicate rings of calamares spiked with lemon, and an entrée of Muscovy duck was given a floral note with a lavender-honey glaze.

Flatiron Lounge

37 W 19th Street, between Fifth & Sixth Avenues (1-212 727 7741, www.flatironlounge.com). Subway F, M, N, R to 23rd Street. **Open** 4pm-2am Mon-Wed; 4pm-3am Thur; 4pm-4am Fri, Sat; 5pm-2am Sun. **Cocktail Bar.** Map p105 D4 ㉙

Red leather booths, mahogany tables and globe-shaped lamps amp up the vintage vibe at this art deco space. Julie Reiner's notable mixology skills have made the bar a destination for creative libations like the Sun Also Sets (pisco, silver tequila and blood orange shrub).

John Dory Oyster Bar

1196 Broadway, at 29th Street (1-212 792 9000, www.thejohndory.com). Subway N, R to 28th Street. **Open** noon-midnight daily. **$$.** **American.** Map p105 D3 ㉚

April Bloomfield and Ken Friedman's original Meatpacking District's John Dory was an ambitious, pricey endeavour, but its reincarnation in the Ace Hotel is an understated knockout. Tall stools face a raw bar stocked with East and West Coast oysters, all expertly handled and impeccably sourced. True to form, the rest of Bloomfield's tapas-style seafood dishes are intensely

NEW YORK BY AREA

Eataly

flavoured – meaty octopus with egg-
plant, garbanzo beans and harissa, for
example, or miniature mussels stuffed
with boisterous mortadella meatballs.

The NoMad

NEW *1170 Broadway, at 28th Street
(1-347 472 5660, www.thenomad
hotel.com). N, R to 28th Street.* **Open**
7am-10.30pm Mon-Thur; 7am-11pm Fri,
Sat; 7am-10pm Sun. **$$$**. **American**.
Map p105 D3 ③

The sophomore effort from chef
Daniel Humm and front-of-house part-
ner Will Guidara, who've been in
cahoots at Eleven Madison Park (see
p113) since 2006, the NoMad features
plush armchairs around well-spaced
tables and a stylish return to three-
course dining. The food, like the
space, exudes unbuttoned decadence:
a poached egg stars in one over-the-
top starter, its barely contained yolk
melting into a sweet, velvety soup of
brown butter and Parmesan, with
shaved white asparagus and toasted
quinoa for crunch. And while there are
plenty of rich-man roasted chickens
for two in New York, the amber-hued
bird here – with a foie gras, brioche
and black truffle stuffing under the
skin – is surely the new gold standard,
well worth its $78 price tag.

Rye House

*11 W 17th Street, between Fifth
& Sixth Avenues (1-212 255 7260,
www.ryehousenyc.com). Subway F,
M to 14th Street; L to Sixth Avenue.*
Open noon-2am Mon-Thur; 11am-2am
Sat, Sun. **Bar**. **Map** p105 D4 ③

As the name suggests, American spir-
its are the emphasis at this dark, sultry
bar. As well as bourbons and ryes,
there are gins, vodkas and rums, most
distilled in the States. Check out the
smoky bacon-infused bourbon, a pop-
ular take on a Kentucky favourite.
While the focus is clearly on drinking,
there's excellent upscale pub grub,
such as truffle grilled cheese or house-
smoked pork cheeks.

Shopping

ABC Carpet & Home

*888 Broadway, at 19th Street (1-212
473 3000, www.abchome.com). Subway
L, N, Q, R, 4, 5, 6 to 14th Street-Union
Square.* **Open** 10am-7pm Mon-Wed, Fri,
Sat; 10am-8pm Thur; 11am-6.30pm Sun.
Map p105 D4 ③

Most of ABC's 35,000-strong carpet
range is housed in the store across the
street at No.881 – except the rarest rugs,
which reside on the sixth floor of the
main store. Browse everything from
organic soap to hand-beaded lamp-
shades on the ground floor. Furniture,
on the upper floors, spans every style,
from European minimalism to antique
oriental and mid-century modern.

Eataly

*200 Fifth Avenue, between 23rd
& 24th Streets (1-212 229 2560,
www.eataly.com). Subway F, M, N, R
to 23rd Street.* **Open** 8am-11pm daily.
Map p105 D4 ③

This massive foodie destination, from
Mario Batali and Joe and Lidia
Bastianich, sprawls across 42,500
square feet. A spin-off of an operation
by the same name just outside of Turin,
the complex encompasses six restau-
rants and a beer garden. Adjacent retail
areas offer gourmet provisions, includ-
ing artisanal breads baked on the
premises, fresh mozzarella, salumi and
a vast array of olive oils.

Idlewild

*12 W 19th Street, between Fifth
& Sixth Avenues (1-212 414 8888,
www.idlewildbooks.com). Subway F
to 14th Street; L to Sixth Avenue.*
Open noon-7.30pm Mon-Thur; noon-
6pm Fri-Sun. **Map** p105 D4 ③

Opened by a former United Nations
press officer, Idlewild stocks travel
guides to more than 100 countries and
all 50 states, which are grouped with
related works of fiction and non-fiction.
It also has a large selection of works in
French, Spanish and Italian. Fun fact:

Idlewild was the original name for JFK Airport before it was renamed to honour the assassinated president.

JJ Hat Center

310 Fifth Avenue, at 32nd Street (1-212 239 4368, www.jjhatcenter.com). Subway B, D, F, M, N, Q, R to 34th Street-Herald Square. **Open** 9am-6pm Mon-Fri; 9.30am-5.30pm Sat. **Map** p105 D3 ⑱

Trad hats may be back in fashion, but this venerable shop, in business since 1911, is oblivious to passing trends. Dapper gents sporting the shop's wares will help you choose from more than 2,000 fedoras, pork pies, caps and other styles on display in the splendid, chandelier-illuminated, wood-panelled showroom. Prices start at around $30 for a wool-blend cap.

Showplace Antique & Design Center

40 W 25th Street, between Fifth & Sixth Avenues (1-212 633 6063, www.nyshowplace.com). Subway F, M to 23rd Street. **Open** 10am-6pm Mon-Fri; 8.30am-5.30pm Sat, Sun. **Map** p104 C3 ⑰

Set over four expansive floors, this indoor market houses more than 200 high-quality dealers selling everything from vintage designer wear to Greek and Roman antiquities. Among the highlights are Joe Sundlie's colourful, spot-on-trend vintage pieces from Lanvin and Alaïa, and Mood Indigo – arguably the best source in the city for collectible bar accessories and dinnerware. The array of Bakelite jewellery and table accessories and Fiestaware is dazzling.

Union Square Greenmarket

From 16th to 17th Streets, between Union Square East & Union Square West (1-212 788 7476, www.grownyc. org/unionsquaregreenmarket). Subway L, N, Q, R, 4, 5, 6 to 14th Street-Union Square. **Open** 8am-6pm Mon, Wed, Fri, Sat. **Map** p105 D4 ⑱

There are more than 50 open-air Greenmarkets throughout the city run by the non-profit organisation GrowNYC. At this, the largest and best known, small producers of cheese, herbs, fruits and vegetables hawk their goods directly to the public.

Nightlife

Metropolitan Room

34 W 22nd Street, between Fifth & Sixth Avenues (1-212 206 0440, www.metropolitanroom.com). Subway F, M, N, R to 23rd Street. **Map** p105 D4 ⑲

The Met Room has established itself as the must-go venue for high-level nightclub singing that won't bust your wallet. Regular performers range from rising musical-theatre stars to established cabaret acts (including Baby Jane Dexter), plus legends such as Tammy Grimes, Julie Wilson and Annie Ross.

Splash

50 W 17th Street, between Fifth & Sixth Avenues (1-212 691 0073, www.splash bar.com). Subway F, M to 14th Street; L to Sixth Avenue. **Open** 5pm-4am daily. No credit cards. **Map** p104 C4 ⑳

This NYC queer institution offers 10,000sq ft of dance and lounge space, staffed by super-muscular (and shirtless) bartenders. Nationally known DJs still rock the house, while local drag celebs give good face, and in-house VJs flash hypnotic snippets of classic musicals spliced with videos.

Gramercy Park & Murray Hill

A key to Gramercy Park, the gated square at the southern end of Lexington Avenue (between 20th & 21st Streets), is the preserve and privilege of residents of the surrounding homes (and members of a couple of venerable private clubs). Murray Hill spans 30th to 40th Streets, between Third and Fifth Avenues. Townhouses of the rich and powerful were once clustered around Madison and Park Avenues, but these days, only a few streets retain their former elegance and the area is mainly populated by upwardly mobiles fresh out of university.

Sights & museums

Morgan Library & Museum

225 Madison Avenue, at 36th Street (1-212 685 0008, www.themorgan.org). Subway 6 to 33rd Street. **Open** 10.30am-5pm Tue-Thur; 10.30am-9pm Fri; 10am-6pm Sat; 11am-6pm Sun. **Admission** $15; free-$10 reductions. **Map** p105 D2/p105 D5 🟠

This Madison Avenue institution began as the private library of financier J Pierpont Morgan. It houses first-rate works on paper, including drawings by Michelangelo, Rembrandt and Picasso; a copy of *Frankenstein* annotated by Mary Shelley; manuscripts by Steinbeck, Twain and Wilde; sheet music handwritten by Beethoven and Mozart; and an original edition of Dickens' *A Christmas Carol* that's displayed every Yuletide.

Event highlights Dürer to de Kooning: 100 Master Drawings from Munich (12 Oct 2012-6 Jan 2013); Fantasy and Invention: Rosso Fiorentino and 16th-Century Florentine Drawing (16 Nov 2012-3 Feb 2013).

Eating & drinking

71 Irving Place Coffee & Tea Bar

71 Irving Place, between 18th & 19th Streets (1-212 995 5252, www.irvingfarm.com). Subway L, N, Q, R, 4, 5, 6 to 14th Street-Union Square. **Open** 7am-10pm Mon-Fri; 8am-10pm Sat. **$**. **Café**. **Map** p105 D4 🟠

Irving Farm's beans are roasted in a 100-year-old carriage house in the Hudson Valley; fittingly, its Gramercy

Park café, in a stately brownstone, also has a quaint, rustic edge. Breakfast (granola, oatmeal, waffles, bagels), sandwiches and salads accompany the superior-quality java.

Artisanal

2 Park Avenue, at 32nd Street (1-212 725 8585, www.artisanalbistro.com). Subway 6 to 33rd Street. **Open** 11.45am-10pm Mon-Wed; 11.45am-11pm Thur, Fri; 10.30am-11pm Sat; 10.30am-9pm Sun. **$$**. **French**. **Map** p105 D3 🟠

As New York's bistros veer towards uniformity, Terrance Brennan's high-ceilinged deco gem makes its mark with an all-out homage to *fromage*. Skip the appetisers and open with fondue, which comes in three varieties. Familiar bistro fare awaits, with such dishes as steak frites, mussels, and chicken baked 'under a brick', but the curd gets the last word with the cheese and wine pairings. These selections of three cheeses – chosen by region, style or theme (for example, each one produced in a monastery) – are matched with three wines (or beers or even sakés) for a sumptuous and intriguing finale.

Maialino

Gramercy Park Hotel, 2 Lexington Avenue, at 21st Street (1-212 777 2410). Subway 6 to 23rd Street. **Open** 7.30am-10.30pm Mon-Thur; 7.30am-11pm Fri; 10am-11pm Sat; 10am-10.30pm Sun. **$$**. **Italian**. **Map** p105 D4 🟠

Danny Meyer's first full-fledged foray into Italian cuisine is a dedicated homage to the Roman neighbourhood trattoria. Salumi and bakery stations between the front bar and the wood-beamed dining room – hog jowls and sausages dangling near shelves stacked with crusty loaves of bread – mimic a market off the Appian Way. Chef Nick Anderer's menu offers exceptional facsimiles of dishes specific to Rome: carbonara, braised tripe and suckling pig, among others.

Nightlife

Gramercy Theatre

*127 E 23rd Street, between Park
& Lexington Avenues (1-212 614
6932, www.thegramercytheatre.com).
Subway R, 6 to 23rd Street.* **Map**
p105 D4 **45**

The Gramercy Theatre looks exactly
like what it actually is, a run-down
former movie theatre; yet it has a
decent sound system and good sightlines. Concert-goers can lounge in
raised seats on the top level or get
closer to the stage lower down. Past
bookings have included such Baby
Boom underdogs as Todd Rundgren
and Loudon Wainwright III, and the
occasional hip hop show (Kool Keith,
Pusha T), but tilt towards niche metal
and emo bands.

Irving Plaza

*17 Irving Place, at 15th Street
(1-212 777 6800, www.irvingplaza.
com). Subway L, N, Q, R, 4, 5, 6
to 14th Street-Union Square.*
Map p105 D5 **46**

Lying just east of Union Square, this
midsize rock venue has served as a
Democratic Party lecture hall (in the
19th century), a Yiddish theatre and a
burlesque house (Gypsy Rose Lee made
an appearance). Most importantly, it's a
great place to see big stars keeping a low
profile (Jeff Beck, Jane's Addiction and
Lenny Kravitz) and medium heavies on
their way up.

Rodeo Bar & Grill

*375 Third Avenue, at 27th Street
(1-212 683 6500, www.rodeobar.
com). Subway 6 to 28th Street.*
Map p105 E3 **47**

The unpretentious, if sometimes raucous crowd, roadhouse atmosphere and
absence of a cover charge help make the
Rodeo the city's best roots club, with a
steady stream of rockabilly, country and
related sounds. Kick back with a beer
from the bar – a funked-up trailer in the
middle of the room.

Seventh Avenue is the main drag
of the Garment District (roughly
from 34th to 40th Streets, between
Broadway & Eighth Avenue),
where designers feed America's
multibillion-dollar clothing industry.
The world's largest store, Macy's,
looms over Herald Square (at the
junction of Broadway and Sixth
Avenue). To the east, the spas,
restaurants and karaoke bars
of Koreatown line 32nd Street,
between Fifth and Sixth Avenues.

Eating & drinking

Keens Steakhouse

*72 W 36th Street, between Fifth
& Sixth Avenues (1-212 947 3646,
www.keens.com). Subway B, D, F, M,
N, Q, R to 34th Street-Herald Square.*
Open 11.45am-10.30pm Mon-Fri;
5-10.30pm Sat; 5-9pm Sun. **$$**.
Steakhouse. **Map** p104 C2 **48**

The ceiling and walls are hung with
pipes, some from such long-ago Keens
regulars as Babe Ruth, JP Morgan and
Teddy Roosevelt. Even in these non-
smoking days, you can catch a whiff of
the restaurant's 120-plus years of his-
tory. Bevelled-glass doors, two work-
ing fireplaces and a forest's worth of
dark wood suggest a time when
'Diamond Jim' Brady piled his table
with bushels of oysters, slabs of seared
beef and troughs of ale. The menu still
lists a three-inch-thick mutton chop
(imagine a saddle of lamb but with
more punch), and the porterhouse (for
two or three) holds its own against any
steak in the city.

Mandoo Bar

*2 W 32nd Street, between Fifth Avenue
& Broadway (1-212 279 3075). Subway
B, D, F, M, N, Q, R to 34th Street-
Herald Square.* **Open** 11.30am-10pm
daily. **$**. **Korean**. **Map** p105 D3 **49**

If the staff painstakingly filling and crimping dough squares in the front window don't give it away, we will – this wood-wrapped industrial-style spot elevates *mandoo* (Korean dumplings) above mere appetiser status. Six varieties of the tasty morsels are filled with such delights as subtly piquant kimchi, juicy pork, succulent shrimp and vegetables. Try them miniaturised, as in the 'baby mandoo', swimming in a soothing beef broth or atop springy, soupy ramen noodles.

New York Kom Tang Kalbi House

32 W 32nd Street, between Fifth Avenue & Broadway (1-212 947 8482). Subway B, D, F, M, N, Q, R to 34th Street-Herald Square. **Open** 24hrs Mon-Sat. **$$. Korean. Map** p105 D3 🔟

Tender *kalbi* (barbecued short ribs) are indeed the stars here; their signature smoky flavour comes from being cooked over *soot bul* (wood chips). The oldest Korean restaurant in the city also makes crisp, seafood-laden *haemool pajun* (pancakes); sweet, juicy *yuk hwe* (raw beef salad); and garlicky *bulgogi*. *Kom tang*, or 'bear soup', is a milky beef broth that's deep and soothing.

Shopping

B&H

420 Ninth Avenue, at 34th Street (1 212 444 5040, www.bhphotovideo. com). Subway A, C, E to 34th Street-Penn Station. **Open** 9am-7pm Mon-Thur; 9am-1pm Fri; 10am-6pm Sun. **Map** p104 B2 🔟

In this huge, busy store, goods are transported from the stock room via an overhead conveyor belt. B&H is the ultimate one-stop shop for all your photographic, video and audio needs. Note that, due to the largely Hasidic Jewish staff, the store is closed on Saturdays.

Macy's

151 W 34th Street, between Broadway & Seventh Avenue (1-212 695 4400, www.macys.com). *Subway B, D, F, M, N, Q, R to 34th Street-Herald Square; 1, 2, 3 to 34th Street-Penn Station.* **Open** 10am-9.30pm Mon-Sat; 11am-8.30pm Sun. **Map** p104 C2/p106 C5 🔟

It may not be as glamorous as New York's other famous department stores, but for sheer breadth of stock, the 34th Street behemoth that is Macy's is hard to beat. You won't find exalted labels here, though; mid-priced fashion and designers' diffusion lines for all ages are its bread and butter, along with all the big beauty names. There's also a branch of the Metropolitan Museum of Art gift store and a Ben & Jerry's outpost.

Nepenthes New York

307 W 38th Street, between Eighth & Ninth Avenues (1-212 643 9540, www.nepenthesny.com). *Subway A, C, E, 1, 2, 3 to 34th Street-Penn Station.* **Open** noon-7pm Mon-Sat; noon-5pm Sun. **Map** p104 B2 🔟

Well-dressed dudes with an eye on the Japanese style scene will already be familiar with this Tokyo fashion retailer. The narrow, high-ceilinged Garment District shop – its first US location – showcases expertly crafted urban-rustic menswear from house label Engineered Garments, such as plaid flannel shirts and workwear-inspired jackets. There is also a small selection of its women's line, FWK.

Arts & leisure

Juvenex

5th Floor, 25 W 32nd Street, between Fifth Avenue & Broadway (1-646 733 1330, www.juvenexspa.com). Subway B, D, F, M, N, Q, R to 34th Street-Herald Square. **Open** 24hrs daily. **Map** p105 D3 🔟

This bustling Koreatown relaxation hub may be slightly rough around the edges (frayed towels, dingy sandals), but we embrace it for its bathhouse-meets-Epcot feel (igloo saunas, tiled 'soaking ponds' and a slatted bridge), and 24hr availability (women only before 5pm). A basic Purification Program – including soak and sauna, face, body and hair cleansing and a salt scrub – is great value at $115.

Madison Square Garden

Seventh Avenue, between 31st & 33rd Streets (1-212 465 6741, www.thegarden.com). Subway A, C, E, 1, 2, 3 to 34th Street-Penn Station. **Map** p104 C3 ⑤⑤

Some of music's biggest acts – Jay-Z, Lady Gaga, Rush – come out to play at the world's most famous basketball arena, home to the Knicks and also hockey's Rangers. Whether you'll actually be able to get a look at them depends on your seat number or the quality of your binoculars. While it is undoubtedly a part of the fabric of New York, the arena is far too vast for a rich concert experience, ugly and a little bit musty, though the latter should soon be a thing of the past – a major renovation, wrapping up in 2014, is bringing new seats and upgraded lighting, sound and video systems among other improvements.

Theater District & Hell's Kitchen

Times Square is the gateway to the Theater District, the zone roughly between 41st Street and 53rd Street, from Sixth Avenue to Ninth Avenue. Thirty-eight of the opulent show houses here – those with more than 500 seats – are designated as being part of Broadway (plus the Vivian Beaumont Theater, uptown at Lincoln Center; p155). Just west of Times Square is Hell's Kitchen, which maintained a crime-ridden, tough veneer well into the 1970s. Today, it's emerging as the city's new queer mecca. Pricey Restaurant Row (46th Street, between Eighth & Ninth Avenues) caters to theatregoers, but Ninth Avenue

itself, with its cornucopia of cheap ethnic eateries, is a better bet.

Sights & museums

Circle Line Cruises

Pier 83, 42nd Street, at the Hudson River (1-212 563 3200, www.circleline 42.com). Subway A, C, E to 42nd Street-Port Authority. **Tickets** $36; $23-$31 reductions. **Map** p104 A1/p106 A4 ⑤⑥

Circle Line's famed three-hour guided circumnavigation of Manhattan Island is a fantastic way to get your bearings and see many of the city's sights as you pass under its iconic bridges. Themed tours include an evening 'Harbor Lights' sailing (Mar-late Nov) and an autumn foliage ride to Bear Mountain in the Hudson Valley. If you don't have time for the full round trip, there's a two-hour 'Liberty' tour that takes you around Downtown to the Brooklyn Bridge and back.

Intrepid Sea, Air & Space Museum

USS Intrepid, Pier 86, Twelfth Avenue & 46th Street (1-877 957 7447, www. intrepidmuseum.org). Subway A, C, E to 42nd Street-Port Authority, then M42 bus to Twelfth Avenue or 15min walk. **Open** *Apr-Oct* 10am-5pm Mon-Fri; 10am-6pm Sat, Sun. *Nov-Mar* 10am-5pm Tue-Sun. **Admission** $24-$30; free-$26 reductions. **Map** p104 A1/p106 A4 ⑤⑦

Commissioned in 1943, this 27,000-ton, 898ft aircraft carrier survived torpedoes and kamikaze attacks in World War II, served during Vietnam and the Cuban Missile Crisis, and recovered two space capsules for NASA. It was decommissioned in 1974, then resurrected as an educational institution. On its flight deck and portside aircraft elevator are top-notch examples of American military might, including the US Navy F-14 Tomcat (from *Top Gun*), an A-12 Blackbird spy plane and a fully restored Army AH-1G Cobra gunship helicopter. In summer 2011, the museum became home to the *Enterprise* (OV-101), the

Circle Line Cruises

first Space Shuttle Orbiter, which was recently retired (entry to the new Space Shuttle Pavilion costs extra).

Times Square

From 42nd to 47th Streets, between Broadway & Seventh Avenue. Subway N, Q, R, S, 1, 2, 3, 7 to 42nd Street-Times Square; N, Q, R to 49th Street. **Map** p104 C1/p106 C4 ⑤

Times Square's evolution from a traffic-choked fleshpot to a tourist-friendly theme park has accelerated in the past year. Not only has the 'crossroads of the world' gained an elevated viewing platform atop the new TKTS discount booth, but in 2009 Mayor Bloomberg designated stretches of Broadway, including the area from 47th to 42nd Streets, as pedestrian zones.

Originally called Longacre Square, Times Square was renamed after the *New York Times* moved here in the early 1900s. The first electrified billboard graced the district in 1904. The same year, the inaugural New Year's Eve party in Times Square doubled as the *Times'* housewarming party in its new HQ. Today, around a million people gather here to watch a mirrorball descend every 31 December. The paper left the building only a decade after it arrived. However, it retained ownership of its old headquarters until the 1960s, and erected the world's first scrolling electric news 'zipper' in 1928. The readout, now sponsored by Dow Jones, has trumpeted breaking stories from the stock-market crash of 1929 to the death of Osama bin Laden in 2011.

TKTS

Father Duffy Square, Broadway & 47th Street (www.tdf.org). Subway N, Q, R to 49th Street; N, Q, R, S, 1, 2, 3, 7 to 42nd Street-Times Square. **Open** *Evening tickets* 3-8pm Mon, Wed-Sat, Sun; 2-8pm Tue. *Same-day matinée tickets* 10am-2pm Wed, Sat; 11am-3pm Sun. **Map** p104 C1/p106 C4 ⑤

At the architecturally striking new TKTS base, you can get tickets on the day of the performance for as much as 50% off face value. Although there's often a queue when it opens for business, this has usually dispersed one to two hours later, so it's worth trying your luck an hour or two before the show. The Downtown and Brooklyn branches (see website for details) are much less busy and open earlier (so you can secure your tickets on the morning of the show); they also sell matinée tickets the day before a show. Never buy tickets from anyone who approaches you in the queue as they may have been obtained illegally.

Eating & drinking

Ardesia

510 W52nd Street, between Tenth & Eleventh Avenues (1-212 247 9191, www.ardesia-ny.com). Subway C, E to 50th Street. **Open** 5pm-midnight Mon-Wed; 5pm-2am Thur-Sat; 5-11pm Sun. **$. Wine bar. Map** p106 B3 ⑥

Le Bernardin vet Mandy Oser's iron-and-marble gem offers superior wines in an extremely relaxed setting. The 75-strong collection of international bottles is a smart balance of Old and New World options that pair beautifully with the eclectic small plates. Our grüner veltliner – a dry, oaky white from the Knoll winery in Wachau, Austria – had enough backbone to stand up to a duck *banh mi* layered with house-made pâté and duck prosciutto. A blended red from Spain's Cellar Can Blau, meanwhile, was a spicy, velvety match for coriander-rich homemade mortadella.

Café Edison

Hotel Edison, 228 W 47th Street, between Broadway & Eighth Avenues (1-212 354 0368). Subway N, Q, R to 49th Street; 1 to 50th Street. **Open** 6am-9.30pm Mon-Sat; 6am-7.30pm Sun. **$. No credit cards. American. Map** p106 C4 ⑥

This old-school no-frills eatery draws tourists, theatregoers, actors and just about everyone else in search of deli staples such as cheese blintzes and giant open-faced Reubens. The matzo ball soup is so restorative, you can almost feel it bolstering your immune system.

Don Antonio by Starita

NEW *309 W 50th Street, between Eighth & Ninth Avenues (1-646 719 1043). Subway C, E to 50th Street.* **Open** noon-11pm Mon-Thur; noon-midnight Fri, Sat; noon-10pm Sun. **$. Pizza. Map** p106 C3 ②

Pizza aficionados have been busy colonising this pedigreed newcomer, a collaboration between Kesté's (see p98) talented Roberto Caporuscio and his decorated Naples mentor, Antonio Starita. Start with tasty bites like the *frittatine* (a deep-fried spaghetti cake oozing *prosciutto cotto* and béchamel sauce). The main event should be the habit-forming Montanara Starita, which gets a quick dip in the deep fryer before hitting the oven to develop its puffy, golden crust. Topped with tomato sauce, basil and intensely smoky buffalo mozzarella, it's a worthy new addition to the pantheon of classic New York pies.

Kashkaval

856 Ninth Avenue, between 55th & 56th Streets (1-212 581 8282, www.kashkavalfoods.com). Subway C, E to 50th Street. **Open** 11am-midnight daily. **$. Wine bar. Map** p106 B3 ③

This charming cheese-shop-cum-wine-bar evokes fondue's peasant origins, with deep cast-iron pots and generous baskets of crusty bread – steer clear of the bland and rubbery kashkaval (a Balkan sheep's-milk cheese) and order the gooey and surprisingly mild Gorgonzola. Or choose from the selection of tangy Mediterranean spreads – vinegary artichoke dip, hot-pink beet skordalia – and the impressive roster of charcuterie. End the meal with the bittersweet dark-chocolate fondue, a guaranteed crowd-pleaser served with fruit and mini marshmallows.

Pony Bar

637 Tenth Avenue, at 45th Street (1-212 586 2707, www.thepony bar.com). Subway C, E to 50th Street. **Open** 3pm-4am Mon-Fri; noon-4am Sat, Sun. **Bar. Map** p106 B4 ④

Hell's Kitchen has long been a dead zone for civilised bars, but this sunny paean to American microbrews is an oasis. Choose from a constantly changing selection of two cask ales and 20 beers on tap; daily selections are artfully listed on signboards according to provenance and potency. The expert curation, combined with low prices (all beers cost $5), suggest that the drought may finally be easing.

Shopping

Amy's Bread

672 Ninth Avenue, between 46th & 47th Streets (1-212 977 2670, www.amys bread.com). Subway C, E to 50th Street; N, Q, R to 49th Street. **Open** 7.30am-11pm Mon-Fri; 8am-11pm Sat; 8am-8pm Sun. **Map** p104 B1/p106 B4 ⑤

Whether you want sweet (double chocolate pecan Chubbie cookies) or savoury (hefty French sourdough boules), Amy's never disappoints. Breakfast and snacks such as the grilled cheese sandwich (made with New York State cheddar) are served.

Colony Records

Brill Building, 1619 Broadway, at 49th Street (1-212 265 2050, www.colony music.com). Subway N, Q, R to 49th Street; 1 to 50th Street. **Open** 9am-1am Mon-Sat; 10am-midnight Sun. **Map** p106 C4 ⑥

Push the musical-note door handles to enter a portal to Times Square's past; Colony, a longtime resident of storied music-industry hub the Brill Building, was founded in 1948. In addition to sheet music (the selection covers everything from an AC/DC songbook to hot Broadway musicals such as *The Book of Mormon*), CDs and vinyl, there are glass cases full of era-spanning

Stage debuts

New spaces are reinvigorating Off Broadway

New York's Off Broadway world has seen a boom of late, with several key institutions – including the **Public Theater** (see p93) and **Atlantic Theater Company** (see p109) – undergoing major renovations to their venues. But the most significant changes have been at **Lincoln Center Theater** (see p156) and **Signature Theatre Company** (see p127).

Lincoln Center has opened the 112-seat Claire Tow Theater, a striking glass-framed rectangle perched atop the Vivian Beaumont. It will use the Tow as a platform for emerging talent, with ticket prices capped at $20.

More than any other troupe in town, Signature focuses on playwrights in depth, with whole seasons devoted to works by individual living writers. Founded in 1991, it started out in a 79-seat theatre, then moved to a 160-seat venue. But in 2012, it finally moved into a base equal to its lofty ambitions.

Designed by Frank Gehry, the new Pershing Square Signature Center has three major spaces: a 299-seat main stage; a 199-seat miniature opera house; and a malleable courtyard theatre. Over the next five years, the company is commissioning three new plays apiece from five writers on the cusp of major fame – while keeping the sponsorship initiative that caps ticket prices at $25 during all plays' initially scheduled runs. Who says great theatre doesn't come cheap?

NEW YORK BY AREA

ephemera. Get a whiff of the King with Elvis 'Teddy Bear' perfume from the '50s ($500) or pay tribute to the original superwaif in a pair of cream lace tights 'inspired by Twiggy' ($50).

Domus

413 W 44th Street, between Ninth & Tenth Avenues (1-212 581 8099, www.domusnewyork.com). Subway A, C, E to 42nd Street-Port Authority. **Open** noon-8pm Tue-Sat; noon-6pm Sun. **Map** p106 C4 ⑰

Scouring the globe for unusual design products is nothing new, but owners Luisa Cerutti and Nicki Lindheimer take the concept a step further; each year they visit a far-flung part of the world to forge links with and support co-operatives and individual craftspeople. The beautiful results, such as vivid baskets woven from telephone wire by South African Zulu tribespeople, reflect a fine attention to detail and a sense of place. It's a great place to find reasonably priced gifts, from handmade Afghan soaps to Italian throws.

Grast

Port Authority subway concourse, 625 Eighth Avenue, unit 17 between 41st & 42nd Sreets (1-212 244 4468). Subway A, C, E to 42nd Street-Port Authority. **Open** 10am-9pm Mon-Sat; 11am-8pm Sun. **Map** p106 C4 ⑱

A subway concourse is the last spot you'd expect to find a hip boutique, but that's exactly when Merwin Andrade decided to open this sleek sliver of a store. If you're passing through, be sure to check out Graft's giftable gear such as own-label silk-screened T-shirts and hoodies, Urbanears rainbow-bright headphones and collectible Japanese toys from Medicom.

Nightlife

54 Below

NEW *254 W 54th Street, between Seventh & Eighth Avenues (Ticketweb 1-866 468 7619, www.54below.com). B, D, E to*

Seventh Avenue; C, E, 1 to 50th Street; R to 57th Street. Map p106 C3 **69**
A team of top-drawer Broadway producers is behind this swank new supper club located in the bowels of the legendary Studio 54 space. The schedule is dominated by big Broadway talent – Patti LuPone and Ben Vereen had the first two major runs – but there is also room for edgier talents such as Justin Vivian Bond and Jackie Hoffman, as well as weekly showcases for emerging Broadway songwriters.

Birdland

315 W 44th Street, between Eighth & Ninth Avenues (1-212 581 3080, www.birdlandjazz.com). Subway A, C, E to 42nd Street-Port Authority. **Open** 5pm-1am daily. Map p104 B1/p106 C4 **70**
Its name is synonymous with jazz (Jim Hall, Greg Osby), but Birdland is also a prime cabaret destination (Christine Ebersole, various up-and-coming songwriters). Arturo O'Farrill's Afro Latin Jazz Orchestra owns Sundays, and David Ostwald's Louis Armstrong Centennial Band hits on Wednesdays; Mondays see cabaret's waggish Jim Caruso and his Cast Party.

Carolines on Broadway

1626 Broadway, between 49th & 50th Streets (1-212 757 4100, www.carolines.com). Subway N, Q, R to 49th Street; 1 to 50th Street. Map p106 C3 **71**
This New York City institution's long-term relationships with national comedy headliners, sitcom stars and cable-special pros ensure that its stage always features marquee names. Although a majority of the bookings skew towards mainstream appetites, the club also makes time for undisputedly darker fare such as Louis CK.

Don't Tell Mama

343 W 46th Street, between Eighth & Ninth Avenues (1-212 757 0788, www.donttellmamanyc.com). Subway A, C, E to 42nd Street-Port Authority. Map p104 B1/p106 C4 **72**

Showbiz pros and piano bar buffs adore this dank but homey Theater District stalwart, where acts range from the strictly amateur to potential stars of tomorrow. The line-up may include pop, jazz and musical-theatre singers, as well as female impersonators, comedians and musical revues.

Fairytail Lounge

NEW *500 W 48th Street, between Tenth & Eleventh Avenues (1-646 684 3897, www.twitter.com/fairytaillounge). Subway C, E to 50th Street.* **Open** 5pm-2am Mon, Tue; 5pm-3am Thur-Sun. Map p106 B4 **73**
This Hell's Kitchen gay watering hole packs a lot of glittery, pseudo-Victorian personality into a small space. Patrons can sip cocktails off the backs of sexy centaur mannequins, or park at the bar while bobbing their heads to tunes from various DJs during weekly theme nights.

Flaming Saddles

NEW *793 Ninth Avenue, at 53rd Street (1-212 713 0481, www.flaming saddles.com). Subway C, E to 50th Street.* **Open** 4pm-4am Mon-Fri; 2pm-4am Sat, Sun. No credit cards. Map p106 B3 **74**
City boys can party honky-tonk-style at this country and western gay bar. The place is outfitted to look like a Wild West bordello, complete with red velvet drapes, antler sconces and rococo wallpaper. Performances by bartenders dancing in cowboy boots add to the raucous vibe.

Industry

355 W 52nd Street, between Eighth & Ninth Avenues (1-646 476 2747, www.industry-bar.com). Subway C, E to 50th Street. **Open** 4pm-4am daily. No credit cards. Map p106 B3 **75**
This sultry, cosy gay nightspot is the latest venture from Bob Pontarelli and Stephen Heighton, the duo behind several successful venues including Elmo restaurant. There's a small stage for

regular drag shows and other performances, a pool table, and couches for lounging. DJs spin nightly to a sexy, fashionable crowd.

Pacha

618 W 46th Street, between Eleventh & Twelfth Avenues (1-212 209 7500, www.pachanyc.com). Subway C, E to 50th Street. **Open** 7pm-5am Fri; 7pm-9am Sat. **Map** p104 A1/p106 A4 **76**

The worldwide glam-club chain Pacha hit the US market in 2005 with this swanky joint helmed by superstar spinner Erick Morillo. The spot attracts heavyweights ranging from local hero Danny Tenaglia to to international crowd-pleasers such as Fedde Le Grande and Benny Benassi. As with most big clubs, it pays to check the line-up in advance if you're into underground beats.

Arts & leisure

Avenue Q

New World Stages, 340 W 50th Street, between Eighth & Ninth Avenues (Telecharge 1-212 239 6200, www.avenueq.com). Subway C, E, 1 to 50th Street. **Map** p106 C3 **77**

After many years, which have included a Broadway run followed by a return to its Off Broadway roots, the sassy and clever puppet musical doesn't show its age. The current cast is capable and likable, and Robert Lopez and Jeff Marx's deft *Sesame Street*-esque novelty tunes about porn and racism still earn their laughs. *Avenue Q* remains a sly and winning piece of metamusical tomfoolery.

The Book of Mormon

Eugene O'Neill Theatre, 230 W 49th Street, between Broadway & Eighth Avenue (Telecharge 1-212 239 6200, www.bookofmormon broadway.com). Subway C, E to 50th Street; N, Q, R, S, 1, 2, 3, 7 to 42nd Street-Times Square; N, R to 49th Street. **Map** p106 C4 **78**

If theatre is your religion, and the Broadway musical your particular sect, it's time to rejoice. This gleefully obscene and subversive satire is one of the funniest shows to grace the Great White Way since *The Producers* and *Urinetown*. Writers Trey Parker and Matt Stone of *South Park*, along with composer Robert Lopez (*Avenue Q*), find the perfect blend of sweet and nasty for this tale of mismatched Mormon proselytisers in Uganda.

Carnegie Hall

154 W 57th Street, at Seventh Avenue (1-212 247 7800, www.carnegiehall.org). Subway N, Q, R to 57th Street. **Map** p106 C3 **79**

Artistic director Clive Gillinson continues to put his stamp on Carnegie Hall. The stars still shine the most brightly in the Isaac Stern Auditorium – but it's the upstart Zankel Hall that has generated the most buzz, offering an eclectic mix of classical, contemporary, jazz, pop and world music.

Newsies

NEW *Nederlander Theatre, 208 W 41st Street, between Broadway & Eighth Avenue (Ticketmaster 1-866 870 2717, www.newsiesthemusical.com). Subway A, C, E to 42nd Street-Port Authority; N, Q, R, S, 1, 2, 3, 7 to 42nd Street-Times Square.* **Map** p106 C5 **80**

Not since *Wicked* has there been a big-tent, family-friendly Broadway musical that gets so much so right. Disney's barnstorming, four-alarm delight focuses on the newsboy strike of 1899, in which spunky (and high-kicking) newspaper hawkers stood up to media magnates. The Alan Menken tunes are pleasing, the book is sharp, and the dances are simply spectacular.

New York City Center

131 W 55th Street, between Sixth & Seventh Avenues (1-212 581 7907, www.nycitycenter.org). Subway B, D, E to Seventh Avenue; F, N, Q, R to 57th Street. **Map** p106 C3 **81**

Street art

A MoMA exhibition spotlights an artist's downtown vision.

Claes Oldenburg's name is synonymous with monumental sculptures of common household items or appliances, mostly rendered in a style that, while cartoonish, is still crisp and refined. But as a survey of his nascent career opening at the Museum of Modern Art (see p130) in spring 2013 makes clear, the Pop Art pioneer's aesthetic started out as something funkier, more expressionistic – and tied to a distinct locale.

Much of Oldenburg's early oeuvre was inspired by his downtown milieu of the late 1950s and early '60s, especially two pieces in the exhibition: *the Store* and *the Street*. In both, Oldenburg created installations out of a multitude of objects, portraying the East Village and Lower East Side as a landscape of consumption and its inevitable byproduct, garbage. In the case of *the Store*, he did so site-specifically, renting a storefront and filling its display cases with

food items such as cakes and ice-cream sundaes made of painted papier mâché. In *the Street*, he evoked the neighbourhood as a decaying slum, rendering figures and commercial signage as large cardboard silhouettes with charred edges. This, then, was the flip side to the American Dream embodied by the postwar suburban house.

Other offerings in the show – a collaboration with Vienna's Museum Moderner Kunst Siftung Ludwig Wien – include pieces from later in the 1960s: soft-sculptural, oversized fans, light switches, egg-beaters and toilets that made Oldenburg famous and served as stepping stones to his monumental works. They were more singular manifestations of his imagination than either *the Store* or *the Street*, but they maintained his exquisite balance of whimsy and acid wit, and his augural vision of a culture about to be undone by its own prosperity – a foretelling this show revisits with clarity and taste.

Museum of Modern Art p130

Before Lincoln Center changed the city's cultural geography, this was the home of American Ballet Theatre, the Joffrey Ballet and the New York City Ballet. City Center's lavish decor is golden – as are the companies that pass through here. Regular events include Alvin Ailey American Dance Theater in December and the popular Fall for Dance Festival, in autumn, which features mixed bills for just $10.

Pershing Square Signature Center

NEW *480 W 42nd Street, at Tenth Avenue (1-212 244 7529, www. signaturetheatre.org). Subway A, C, E to 42nd Street-Port Authority.* **Map** p106 B4 ❸❷
See box p124.

Playwrights Horizons

416 W 42nd Street, between Ninth & Tenth Avenues, Theater District (Ticket Central 1-212 279 4200, www.playwrightshorizons.org). Subway A, C, E to 42nd Street-Port Authority. **Map** p106 B4 ❸❸
More than 300 important contemporary plays have premièred here, among them dramas such as *Driving Miss Daisy* and *The Heidi Chronicles* and musicals such as Stephen Sondheim's *Assassins* and *Sunday in the Park with George*. Recent seasons have included works by Edward Albee and Craig Lucas, as well as Bruce Norris's Pulitzer Prize-winning *Clybourne Park*.

Spider-Man: Turn Off the Dark

Foxwoods Theatre, 213 W 42nd Street, between Seventh & Eighth Avenues, Theater District (Ticketmaster 1-877 250 2929, www.spidermanonbroadway.com). Subway A, C, E to 42nd Street-Port Authority; N, Q, R, S, 1, 2, 3, 7 to 42nd Street-Times Square. **Map** p104 C1, p106 C4 ❸❹
The woe-plagued, $75-million musical based on the Marvel superhero ends its

long, strange journey (grisly injuries, Julie Taymor fired, 183 previews) as a moderately enjoyable show that is still a hotchpotch of rock, circus and romantic comedy. You care about Peter Parker and Mary Jane Watson more, but the show is still dragged down by plot holes and a lumbering, bland score by Bono and the Edge.

Fifth Avenue & around

The stretch of Fifth Avenue between Rockefeller Center and Central Park South showcases retail palaces bearing names that were famous long before the concept of branding was developed. Bracketed by Saks Fifth Avenue (49th to 50th Streets) and Bergdorf Goodman (57th to 58th Streets), tenants include Gucci, Prada and Tiffany & Co (and the parade of big names continues east along 57th Street). A number of landmarks and first-rate museums are on, or in the vicinity of, the strip.

Sights & museums

Empire State Building

350 Fifth Avenue, between 33rd & 34th Streets (1-212 736 3100, www.esbnyc. com). Subway B, D, F, M, N, Q, R to 34th Street-Herald Square. **Open** 8am 2am daily (last elevator at 1.15am). **Admission** *86th floor* $23; free-$20 reductions. *102nd floor* $17 extra (see website for express ticket options). **Map** p105 D2 ❸❺
Financed by General Motors executive John J Raskob at the height of New York's skyscraper race, the Empire State sprang up in a mere 14 months, weeks ahead of schedule and $5 million under budget. Since its opening in 1931, it's been immortalised in countless photos and films, from the original *King Kong* to *Sleepless in Seattle*. Following the destruction of the World Trade Center in 2001, the 1,250ft tower resumed its title as New York's tallest

building but has since been overtaken by the new 1 World Trade Center. The nocturnal colour scheme of the tower lights – recently upgraded to flashy LEDs – often honours holidays, charities or special events.

The enclosed observatory on the 102nd floor is the city's highest look-out point, but the panoramic deck on the 86th floor, 1,050ft above the street, is roomier. From here, you can enjoy views of all five boroughs and five neighbouring states too (when the skies are clear).

International Center of Photography

1133 Sixth Avenue, at 43rd Street (1-212 857 0000, www.icp.org). Subway B, D, F, M, 7 to 42nd Street-Bryant Park; N, Q, R, S, 1, 2, 3 to 42nd Street-Times Square; 7 to Fifth Avenue. **Open** 10am-6pm Tue-Wed, Sat, Sun; 10am-8pm Thur, Fri. **Admission** $12; free-$8 reductions. Pay what you wish 5-8pm Fri. **Map** p107 D4 ⑯

Since 1974, the ICP has served as a pre-eminent library, school and museum devoted to the photographic image. Photojournalism remains a vital facet of the centre's programming, which also includes contemporary photos and video. Recent shows in the two-floor exhibition space have focused on the work of Elliott Erwitt, Richard Avedon and Weegee.

Event highlights Rise and Fall of Apartheid: Photography and the Bureaucracy of Everyday Life (14 Sept 2012-6 Jan 2013); Roman Vishniac (18 Jan-5 May 2013)

Museum of Modern Art

11 W 53rd Street, between Fifth & Sixth Avenues (1-212 708 9400, www.moma.org). Subway E, M to Fifth Avenue-53rd Street. **Open** 10.30am-5.30pm Mon, Wed, Thur, Sat, Sun; 10.30am-8pm Fri. **Admission** (incl admission to film programmes & MoMA PS1) $25; free-$18 reductions; free 4-8pm Fri. **Map** p107 D3 ⑰

After a two-year redesign by Japanese architect Yoshio Taniguchi, MoMA reopened in 2004 with almost double the space to display some of the most impressive artworks from the 19th-21st centuries. The museum's permanent collection is divided into seven curatorial departments: Architecture and Design, Drawings, Film, Media, Painting and Sculpture, Photography, and Prints and Illustrated Books. Among the highlights are Picasso's *Les Demoiselles d'Avignon*, Dali's *The Persistence of Memory* and Van Gogh's *The Starry Night* as well as masterpieces by Giacometti, Hopper, Matisse, Monet, O'Keefe, Pollock, Rothko, Warhol and others. Outside, the Philip Johnson-designed Abby Aldrich Rockefeller Sculpture Garden contains works by Calder, Rodin and Moore. There's also a destination restaurant: the Modern, which overlooks the garden.

Event highlights Tokyo 1955-1970 (18 Nov 2012-25 Feb 2013); Inventing Abstraction, 1912-1925 (23 Dec 2012-15 Apr 2013); Claes Oldenburg: The 60s (14 Apr-5 Aug 2013); Le Corbusier: Landscapes for the Machine Age (6 June-23 Sept 2013). See also box p127.

New York Public Library

455 Fifth Avenue, at 42nd Street (1-917 275 6975, www.nypl.org). Subway B, D, F, M to 42nd Street-Bryant Park; 7 to Fifth Avenue. **Open** 10am-6pm Mon, Thur-Sat; 10am-8pm Tue, Wed; 1-5pm Sun (except July, Aug). **Admission** free. **Map** p105 D1/p105 D5 ⑱

Guarded by the marble lions Patience and Fortitude, this austere Beaux Arts edifice, designed by Carrère and Hastings, was completed in 1911. The building was renamed in honour of philanthropist Stephen A Schwarzman in 2008, but Gothamites still know it as the New York Public Library, although the citywide library system consists of 91 locations. Free hour-long tours (11am, 2pm Mon-Sat; 2pm Sun, except July & Aug) take in the Rose Main Reading Room on the third floor, which at 297 feet long and 78 feet wide is almost the size of a football field. Specialist departments include the Map Division, containing some 431,000 maps and 16,000 atlases, and the Rare Books Division boasting Walt Whitman's personal copies of the first (1855) and third (1860) editions of *Leaves of Grass*.

Paley Center for Media

25 W 52nd Street, between Fifth & Sixth Avenues (1-212 621 6600, www.paley center.org). Subway B, D, F, M to 47th-50th Streets-Rockefeller Center; E, M to Fifth Avenue-53rd Street. **Open** noon-6pm Wed, Fri-Sun; noon-8pm Thur. **Admission** $10; $5-$8 reductions. No credit cards. **Map** p107 D3 ⑥⑨
A nirvana for TV addicts and pop-culture junkies, the Paley Center houses an immense archive of almost 150,000 radio and TV shows. Head to the fourth-floor library to search the system for your favourite episode of *Star Trek*, *Seinfeld*, or rarer fare, and watch it on your assigned console. Radio shows are also available.

Rockefeller Center

From 48th to 51st Streets, between Fifth & Sixth Avenues (tours & Top of the Rock 1-212 698 2000, NBC Studio Tours 1-212 664 3700, www.rockefeller center.com). Subway B, D, F, M to 47th-50th Streets-Rockefeller Center. **Open** Tours vary. *Observation deck* 8am-midnight daily (last elevator 11pm). **Admission** *Rockefeller Center tours* $15; (under-6s not admitted). *NBC Studio tours* $24; $21 reductions (under-6s not admitted). *Observation deck* $25; free-$23 reductions. **Map** p107 D3/D4 ⑨⓪
Constructed under the aegis of industrialist John D Rockefeller in the 1930s, this art deco city-within-a-city is inhabited by NBC, Simon & Schuster, McGraw-Hill and other media giants, as well as Radio City Music Hall, Christie's auction house, and an underground shopping arcade. Guided tours of the entire complex are available daily, and there's a separate NBC Studio tour too.

The buildings and grounds are embellished with works by several well-known artists; look out for Isamu Noguchi's stainless-steel relief, *News*, above the entrance to 50 Rockefeller Plaza, and José Maria Sert's mural *American Progress* in the lobby of 30 Rockefeller Plaza. The most breathtaking sights are those seen from the 70th-floor Top of the Rock observation deck. In winter, the Plaza's sunken courtyard transforms into an ice skating rink.

St Patrick's Cathedral

Fifth Avenue, between 50th & 51st Streets (1-212 753 2261, www.saint patrickscathedral.org). Subway B, D, F, M to 47th-50th Streets-Rockefeller Center; E, M to Fifth Avenue-53rd Street. **Open** 6.30am-8.45pm daily. **Admission** free. **Map** p107 D3 ⑨①
The largest Catholic church in the US, St Patrick's was built 1858-79. The Gothic-style façade features intricate white-marble spires, but just as impressive is the interior, including the Louis Tiffany-designed altar, solid bronze baldachin, and the rose window by stained-glass master Charles Connick.

Eating & drinking

Bar Room at the Modern

9 W 53rd Street, between Fifth & Sixth Avenues (1-212 333 1220, www.the modernnyc.com). Subway E, M to Fifth Avenue-53rd Street. **Open** 11.30am-10.30pm Mon-Thur; 11.30am-11pm Fri, Sat; 11.30am-9.30pm Sun. **$$**. **American creative**. **Map** p107 D3 ⑨②
Those who can't afford to drop a pay cheque at award-winning chef Gabriel Kreuther's formal MoMA dining room, the Modern, can still dine in the equally stunning and less pricey bar at the front. The Alsatian-inspired menu is constructed of around 30 small and medium-sized plates that can be mixed and shared. Desserts come courtesy of pastry chef Marc Aumont, and the wine list is extensive to say the least.

Marea

240 Central Park South, between Seventh Avenue & Broadway (1-212 582 5100, www.marea-nyc.com). Subway A, B, C, D, 1 to 59th Street-Columbus Circle. **Open** noon-2.30pm, 5.30-11pm Mon-Thur; noon-2.30pm, 5-11.30pm Fri; 5-11.30pm Sat; 11.30am-2.30pm, 5-10.30pm Sun. **$$$**. **Italian/Seafood**. **Map** p106 C2 93

Chef Michael White's shrine to the Italian coastline seems torn between its high and low ambitions. You might find lofty items such as an unorthodox starter of cool lobster with creamy burrata, while basic platters of raw oysters seem better suited to a fish shack. Seafood-focused pastas – fusilli with braised octopus and bone marrow, or tortelli filled with langoustine, dandelion and butternut squash, for example – are the highlight.

Shopping

Bergdorf Goodman

754 Fifth Avenue, between 57th & 58th Streets (1-212 753 7300, www.bergdorfgoodman.com). Subway E to Fifth Avenue-53rd Street; N, Q, R to Fifth Avenue-59th Street. **Open** 10am-8pm Mon-Fri; 10am-7pm Sat; noon-6pm Sun. **Map** p107 D3 94

Synonymous with understated luxury, Bergdorf's is known for its designer clothes (the fifth floor is dedicated to younger, trend-driven labels) and accessories – seek out Kentshire's wonderful vintage-jewellery cache on the ground floor. The men's store is across the street at 745 Fifth Avenue.

FAO Schwarz

767 Fifth Avenue, at 58th Street (1-212 644 9400, www.fao.com). Subway N, Q, R to Fifth Avenue-59th Street. **Open** 10am-7pm Mon-Thur; 10am-8pm Fri, Sat; 11am-6pm Sun. **Map** p107 D2 95

Although it's now owned by the ubiquitous Toys 'R' Us company, this three-storey emporium is still the ultimate NYC toy box. Most people head straight to the 22ft-long floor piano that Tom Hanks famously tinkled in *Big*. Children will marvel at the giant stuffed animals, the detailed and imaginative Lego figures and the revolving Barbie fashion catwalk.

Henri Bendel

712 Fifth Avenue, at 56th Street (1-212 247 1100, www.henribendel.com). Subway E to Fifth Avenue-53rd Street; N, R to Fifth Avenue-59th Street. **Open** 10am-8pm Mon-Sat; noon-7pm Sun. **Map** p107 D3 96

While Bendel's merchandise (a mix of jewellery, fashion accessories, cosmetics and fragrances) is comparable to that of other upscale stores, it somehow seems more desirable when viewed in its opulent premises, a conglomeration of three 19th-century townhouses – and those darling brown-and-white striped shopping bags don't hurt, either.

Nightlife

Radio City Music Hall

1260 Sixth Avenue, at 50th Street (1-212 247 4777, www.radiocity.com). Subway B, D, F, M to 47th-50th Streets-Rockefeller Center. **Map** p107 D3 97

Few rooms scream 'New York City!' louder than this gilded hall, which has recently drawn Leonard Cohen, Drake and TV on the Radio as headliners. The greatest challenge for any performer is not to be upstaged by the awe-inspiring art deco surroundings. On the other hand, those same surroundings lend historic heft to even the flimsiest showing.

Event highlights Christmas Spectacular (9 Nov-30 Dec 2012).

Arts & leisure

Caudalie Vinothérapie Spa

4th Floor, 1 W 58th Street, at Fifth Avenue (1-212 265 3182, www.caudalie-usa.com). Subway N, Q, R

Rockefeller Center p131

Terminal trivia

Five facts about 100-year-old transport hub Grand Central.

The ceiling is backwards
The opulent ceiling mural in the main concourse, by French painter Paul Helleu, depicts the October zodiac in the Mediterranean sky, complete with 2,500 stars (some now lit by LEDs). There's just one problem. According to Daniel Brucker, manager of GCT Tours, an amateur-astronomer commuter wrote to the owning Vanderbilt family to point out the constellations were backwards. Their response? It had been done on purpose to represent God's view of the sky.

Campbell called it home
In the 1920s, the financier John Campbell was granted an office-cum-pied-à-terre in the terminal. 'He had a bond rating firm,' explains Brucker, 'he was a large shareholder in New York Central Railroad stock, and a good friend of the Vanderbilts. Putting it all together, he got New York's largest ground floor apartment with marble walls, a working fireplace and a wine cellar.' After Campbell's death, the space was used by railroad police, and the wine cellar was turned into a jail cell. In the late '90s it was restored and converted into a bar.

It has a phantom track
In the 1930s, FDR's private train would arrive via a secret subterranean track. According to Brucker, the train car that carried his Pierce-Arrow limousine is still there. Brucker surmises the disabled president was driven off the train into an extra-large elevator

at the end of the platform, which brought him into the grand ballroom of the Waldorf-Astoria Hotel.

It was a lofty art hub
In early 1920s, a group of artists including John Singer Sargent established art galleries on the top floor. The vast space now houses the state-of-the-art control centre for Metro-North Railroad.

There's a Kennedy connection
Because CBS studios were on the third floor from 1939 to 1964, the midcentury's biggest news stories issued from Grand Central – it was here that Walter Cronkite announced the assassination of JFK in 1963. Five years later, when a developer proposed building an office tower above the terminal, Jacqueline Kennedy Onassis was one of Grand Central's strongest supporters. It is now a protected landmark.

to *Fifth Avenue-59th Street*. **Open** noon-6pm Mon; 11am-7pm Tue, Wed; 11am-8pm Thur, Fri; 10am-7pm Sat; 11am-6pm Sun. **Map** p107 D2 ❸

The first Vinothérapie outpost in the US, this original spa harnesses the antioxidant power of grapes and vine leaves. The 8,000sq ft facility in the Plaza offers such treatments as a Red Vine bath ($75) in one of its cherry-wood 'barrel' tubs.

Midtown East

Shopping, dining and entertainment options wane east of Fifth Avenue in the 40s and 50s. However, this area is home to a number of landmarks. What the area lacks in street-level attractions it makes up for with an array of world-class architecture.

Sights & museums

Chrysler Building

405 Lexington Avenue, between 42nd & 43rd Streets. Subway S, 4, 5, 6, 7 to 42nd Street-Grand Central. **Map** p105 E1/p107 E4 ❻

Completed in 1930 by architect William Van Alen, the gleaming Chrysler Building is a pinnacle of art deco architecture, paying homage to the automobile with vast radiator-cap eagles in lieu of traditional gargoyles and a brickwork relief sculpture of racing cars complete with chrome hubcaps. During the famed three-way race for New York's tallest building, a needle-sharp stainless-steel spire was added to the blueprint to make it taller than 40 Wall Street, under construction at the same time – but the Chrysler Building was soon outdone by the Empire State Building.

Grand Central Terminal

From 42nd to 44th Streets, between Lexington & Vanderbilt Avenues (audio tours 1-917 566 0008, www.grandcentralterminal.com). Subway S, 4, 5, 6, 7 to 42nd Street-Grand Central. **Map** p105 D1/p107 D4 ❿

Each day, the world's largest terminal sees more than 750,000 people shuffle through its Beaux Arts threshold. Designed by Warren & Wetmore and Reed & Stern, the gorgeous transport hub opened in 1913 with lashings of Botticino marble and staircases modelled after those of the Paris opera house. After midcentury decline, the terminal underwent extensive restoration between 1996 and 1998 and is now a destination in itself with shopping and dining options including the Campbell Apartment (1-212 953 0409), the Grand Central Oyster Bar & Restaurant (see p136) and, since late 2011, the city's newest Apple Store. On 1 February 2013, Grand Central kicks off its centenniel celebrations with performances and a multimedia exhibition about the terminal's history. Check the website for information about events and self-guided audio tours ($7; $5-$6 reductions). See box left.

United Nations Headquarters

Visitors' Entrance: First Avenue, at 46th Street (tours 1-212 963 8687, http://visit.un.org). Subway S, 4, 5, 6, 7 to 42nd Street Grand Central. **Tours** 9.45am-4.45pm Mon-Fri; 10am-4.15pm Sat, Sun (Mar-Dec; escorted audio tours only). **Admission** $16; $9-$11 reductions (under-5s not admitted). **Map** p105 F1/p107 F4 ❿

The UN is undergoing extensive renovations that have left the Secretariat building, designed by Le Corbusier, gleaming – though that building is off-limits to the public. The 45-minute public tours discuss the history and role of the UN, and currently visit the General Assembly Hall and the temporary Security Council Chamber (when not in session), which has been recreated to resemble the original in the construction zone; however, at some point in 2013, the General Assembly Hall will close for construction and the newly refurbished Security Council will reopen. Though many artworks and objects given by

NEW YORK BY AREA

member nations are not on public display during this period, one of the best-known, the stained-glass window by Marc Chagall memorialising Secretary-General Dag Hammarskjöld, is in the public lobby of the General Assembly.

Eating & drinking

Grand Central Oyster Bar & Restaurant

Grand Central Terminal, Lower Concourse, 42nd Street, at Park Avenue (1-212 490 6650, www.oysterbarny.com). Subway S, 4, 5, 6, 7 to 42nd Street-Grand Central. **Open** 11.30am-9.30pm Mon-Fri; noon-9.30pm Sat. **$$.**
Seafood. Map p107 D4 **102**

At the legendary 100-year-old Grand Central Oyster Bar, located in the epic and gorgeous hub that shares its name, the surly countermen at the mile-long bar (the best seats in the house) are part of the charm. Avoid the more complicated fish concoctions and play it safe with a reliably awe-inspiring platter of iced, just-shucked oysters – there can be a whopping 30 varieties to choose from at any given time.

Melt Shop

601 Lexington Avenue, at 53rd Street (1-212 759 6358, www.meltshop nyc.com). Subway E, M to Lexington Avenue-53rd Street; 6 to 51st Street. **Open** 7am-9pm Mon-Fri; 10.30am-9pm Sat, Sun. **$. Café. Map** p107 E3 **103**

This breakfast-to-dinner sandwich shop pays homage to the comfort food favourite: grilled cheese. Go for the classic American cheese on white pull-man bread, or try a sophisticated twist on the theme such as the Shroom (havarti and goat's cheese with roasted wild mushrooms and house-made parsley pesto on multigrain bread) or buttermilk-fried chicken with jalapeño Jack cheese and red cabbage coleslaw on sourdough. Accompany your sarnie with tomato soup or a shake in such inner-child-pleasing flavours as peanut butter and jelly and cookies and cream.

The Monkey Bar

60 E 54th Street, between Madison & Park Avenues (1-212 288 1010, www.monkeybarnewyork.com). Subway E, M to Lexington Avenue-53rd Street; 6 to 51st Street. **Open** noon-midnight Mon-Fri; 5.30-11pm Sat. **$$$.**
American. Map p107 D3 **104**

After the repeal of Prohibition in 1933, this one-time piano bar in the swank Hotel Elysée became a boozy club-house for glitzy artistic types, among them Tallulah Bankhead, Dorothy Parker and Tennessee Williams. Recently, publishing tycoon Graydon Carter assembled a dream team here, including chef Damon Wise, cocktail doyenne Julie Reiner and downtown restaurateur Ken Friedman, to bring new buzz to the historic space. Perched at the bar with a pitch-perfect Vieux Carré or ensconced in a red leather booth with a plate of caviar-crowned smoked fettuccine, you'll find yourself seduced by that rare alchemy of old New York luxury and new-school flair. The only question remaining is how long the star-power magic can last.

Sushi Yasuda

204 E 43rd Street, between Second & Third Avenues (212 972 1001, www.sushiyasuda.com). Subway S, 4, 5, 6, 7 to 42nd St-Grand Central. **Open** noon-2.15pm, 6-10.15pm Mon-Fri; 6-10.15pm Sat. **$$.**
Japanese Map p105 E1/ p107 E4 **105**

Seeing the sushi master practice in this bamboo-embellished space is the culinary equivalent of observing Buddhist monks at prayer. Counter seating, where you can witness – and chat up – the chefs, is the only way to go. Prime your palate with a miso soup and segue into the raw stuff: petals of buttery fluke; rich eel; dessert-sweet egg custard; nearly translucent discs of sliced scallop over neat cubes of milky sushi rice. Still craving a California roll? Move along.

Central Park

Uptown

In the 19th century, the area above 59th Street was a bucolic getaway for locals living at the southern tip of the island. Today, much of this locale maintains an air of serenity, thanks largely to Central Park and the presence of a number of New York's premier cultural institutions.

Central Park

In 1858, the newly formed Central Park Commission chose landscape designer Frederick Law Olmsted and architect Calvert Vaux to turn a vast tract of rocky swampland into a rambling oasis of lush greenery. When their vision of an urban 'greensward' was realised in 1873, Central Park became the first man-made public park in the US.

As well as a wide variety of landscapes, from open meadows to woodland, the park offers numerous family-friendly attractions and activities, from the **Central Park**

Zoo (830 Fifth Avenue, between 63rd & 66th Streets, 1-212 439 6500, www.centralparkzoo.org, Apr-Sept 10am-5.30pm daily, Nov-Mar 10am-4.30pm daily; $12, free $9 reductions) to marionette shows in the quaint **Swedish Cottage** (west side, at 81st Street). Stop by the visitor centre in the 1870 Gothic Revival **Dairy** (midpark at 65th Street, 1-212 794 6564, www.centralparknyc.org) for information on activities and events. In winter, ice-skaters lace up at the picturesque **Trump Wollman Rink** (midpark at 62nd Street, 1-212 439 6000, www.wollman skatingrink.com). A short stroll to about 64th Street brings you to the **Friedsam Memorial Carousel** (closed weekdays in winter), a bargain at $2.50 a ride.

Come summer, kites, Frisbees and soccer balls seem to fly every which way across **Sheep Meadow**, the designated quiet zone that begins at

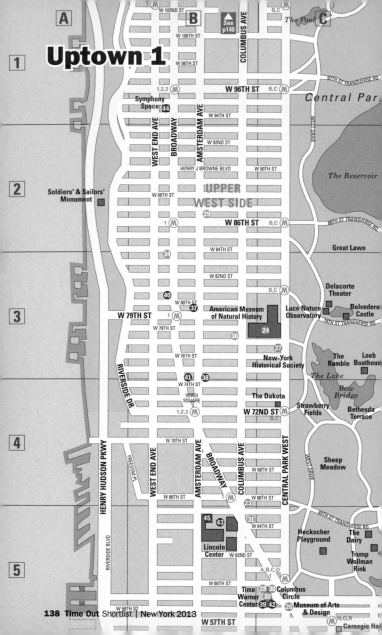

Uptown 1

A **B** **C**

1

W 102ND ST

W 100TH ST

See p140

B,C

The Pool

COLUMBUS AVE

W 98TH ST

97TH ST TRANSVERSE RD

1,2,3 Ⓜ W 96TH ST B,C Ⓜ

Central Par

Symphony
Space 44

W 94TH ST

WEST END AVE

BROADWAY

AMSTERDAM AVE

W 92ND ST

W 90TH ST

HENRY J BROWNE BLVD

The Reservoir

2

Soldiers' &
Sailors'
Monument

W 88TH ST

W 86TH ST

UPPER
WEST SIDE

29

1 Ⓜ W 86TH ST B,C Ⓜ

86TH ST TRANSVERSE RD

Great Lawn

34

W 84TH ST

W 82ND ST

B,C Ⓜ

Delacorte
Theater

40

W 80TH ST

37

Belvedere
Castle

3

W 79TH ST

1 Ⓜ

W 78TH ST

American Museum
of Natural History

24

Luce Nature
Observatory

78TH ST TRANSVERSE RD

RIVERSIDE DR

36

The
Ramble

Loeb
Boathous

New-York
Historical Society

27

41 38

The Lake

W 74TH ST

VERDI
SQUARE

Bow
Bridge

The Dakota

Strawberry
Fields

Bethesda
Terrace

1,2,3 Ⓜ W 72ND ST Ⓜ

B,C

4

W 70TH ST

W 68TH ST

Sheep
Meadow

HENRY HUDSON PKWY

WEST END AVE

FREEDOM PL

AMSTERDAM AVE

BROADWAY

COLUMBUS AVE

CENTRAL PARK WEST

WEST DRIVE

W 66TH ST

1 Ⓜ

W 66TH ST

23

65TH ST TRANSVERSE RD

45 43

31

W 64TH ST

Heckscher
Playground

The
Dairy

Lincoln
Center

W 62ND ST

Trump
Wollman
Rink

5

A,B,C,D Ⓜ

RIVERSIDE BLVD

W 60TH ST

99

98

W 58TH ST

Time
Warner
Center

28 30
Columbus
35 Circle
39 42

26

Museum of Arts
& Design

Ⓜ N,Q,R

138 Time Out Shortlist | New York 2013

W 57TH ST

Carnegie Hal

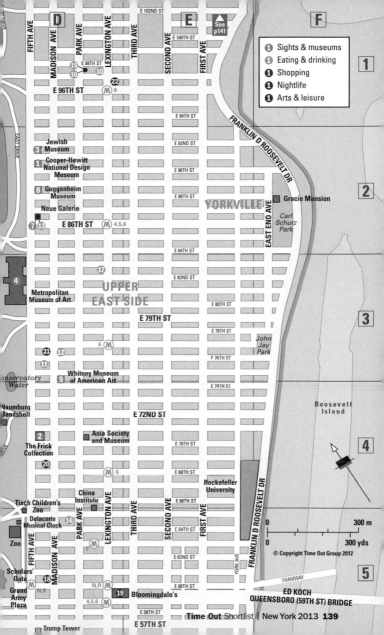

D **E** **F**

FIFTH AVE
MADISON AVE
PARK AVE
LEXINGTON AVE
THIRD AVE
SECOND AVE
FIRST AVE

E 102ND ST

See
p141

E 100TH ST

1

1 🔴 Sights & museums
1 🔴 Eating & drinking
1 🔴 Shopping
1 🔴 Nightlife
1 🔴 Arts & leisure

15 E 98TH ST
16   10

22
Ⓜ 6   E 96TH ST

E 94TH ST

FRANKLIN D ROOSEVELT DR

E 92ND ST

3 Jewish
Museum

1 Cooper-Hewitt
National Design
Museum

E 90TH ST

E 88TH ST

8 Guggenheim
Museum

2

Neue Galerie

🔴 Gracie Mansion

YORKVILLE

EAST END AVE

Carl
Schutz
Park

7 **13** E 86TH ST Ⓜ 4,5,6

E 84TH ST

E 82ND ST

17

UPPER
EAST SIDE

Metropolitan
Museum of Art

4

E 80TH ST

E 79TH ST

E 78TH ST

EAST DRIVE

21   **12**
11

6 Ⓜ

John
Jay
Park

F 76TH ST

3

Whitney Museum
9 of American Art

E 74TH St

Conservatory
Water

E 72ND ST

Roosevelt
Island

Naumburg
Bandshell

Asia Society
and Museum

E 70TH ST

2
The Frick
Collection

20

E 68TH ST

Ⓜ 6

4

Rockefeller
University

China
Institute

PARK AVE
LEXINGTON AVE
THIRD AVE
SECOND AVE
FIRST AVE

E 66TH ST

FRANKLIN D ROOSEVELT DR

Tisch Children's
Zoo

14

Delacorte
Musical Clock

Ⓜ 6

E 64TH ST

E 62ND ST

Zoo

FIFTH AVE
MADISON AVE

F Ⓜ

YORK AVE

0   300 m
0   300 yds

© Copyright Time Out Group 2012

Scholars'
Gate

18

E 60TH ST

TRAMWAY

Ⓜ
N,R
Grand
Army
Plaza

N,R

19 Bloomingdale's

Ⓜ 4,5,6

ED KOCH
QUEENSBORO (59TH ST) BRIDGE

5

E 58TH ST

Trump Tower

E 57TH ST

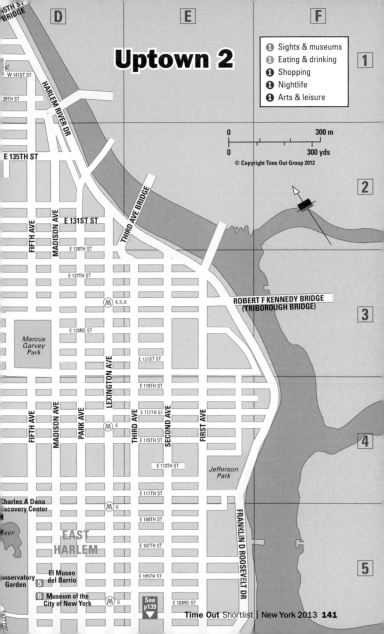

Uptown 2

D   **E**   **F**

1 Sights & museums
2 Eating & drinking
3 Shopping
4 Nightlife
5 Arts & leisure

0   300 m
0   300 yds
© Copyright Time Out Group 2012

5TH ST
BRIDGE
W 141ST ST
39TH ST
HARLEM RIVER DR
E 135TH ST
E 131ST ST
MADISON AVE
FIFTH AVE
E 129TH ST
THIRD AVE BRIDGE
E 127TH ST
M 4,5,6
E 123RD ST
Marcus
Garvey
Park
E 121ST ST
LEXINGTON AVE
E 119TH ST
ROBERT F KENNEDY BRIDGE
(TRIBOROUGH BRIDGE)
E 117TH ST
PARK AVE
MADISON AVE
FIFTH AVE
THIRD AVE
SECOND AVE
FIRST AVE
M 6
E 115TH ST
E 113TH ST
Jefferson
Park
E 111TH ST
Charles A Dana
Discovery Center
M 6
E 109TH ST
Meer
EAST
HARLEM
E 107TH ST
FRANKLIN D ROOSEVELT DR
Conservatory
Garden
5 El Museo
del Barrio
E 105TH ST
6 Museum of the
City of New York
M 6
See
p139
E 103RD ST

66th Street. Sheep did indeed graze here until 1934, but they've since been replaced by sunbathers. East of Sheep Meadow, between 66th and 72nd Streets, is the **Mall**, an elm-lined promenade that attracts street performers and in-line skaters. And just east of the Mall's Naumburg Bandshell is Rumsey Playfield – site of the mainstage for the citywide **SummerStage** (see p41) series, an eclectic roster of free and benefit concerts.

One of the most popular meeting places in the park is north of the Mall: the grand **Bethesda Fountain & Terrace**, near the midpoint of the 72nd Street Transverse Road. *Angel of the Waters*, the sculpture in the centre of the fountain, was created by Emma Stebbins, the first woman to be granted a major public art commission in New York. Be sure to admire the Minton-tiled ceiling of the ornate passageway that connects the plaza around the fountain to the Mall.

To the west of the fountain, near the W 72nd Street entrance, sits **Strawberry Fields**, a section of the park that memorialises John Lennon, who lived in the nearby Dakota Building. It features a mosaic of the word 'imagine' and more than 160 species of flowers and plants from all over the world. Just north of the Bethesda Fountain is the **Loeb Boathouse** (midpark, at 75th Street). From here, you can take a rowboat or gondola out on the lake, which is crossed by the elegant Bow Bridge. The Loeb houses the **Central Park Boathouse Restaurant** (Central Park Lake, park entrance on Fifth Avenue, at 72nd Street, 1-212 517 2233, www.thecentral parkboathouse.com, closed dinner Nov-Mar), which commands a great view of the lake, and has a popular outdoor bar.

Further north is **Belvedere Castle**, a restored Victorian structure that sits atop the park's second-highest peak. Besides offering excellent views, it also houses the **Henry Luce Nature Observatory**. The nearby Delacorte Theater hosts **Shakespeare in the Park** (see p41). And further north still sits the **Great Lawn** (midpark, between 79th & 85th Streets), a sprawling stretch of grass that serves as sports fields, a rallying point for political protests, and a concert spot – the Metropolitan Opera and the New York Philharmonic perform here during the summer. East of the Great Lawn, behind the **Metropolitan Museum of Art** (see right), is the **Obelisk**, a 69-foot hieroglyphics-covered granite monument dating from around 1500 BC, which was given to the US by the Khedive of Egypt in 1881.

In the mid 1990s, the **Jacqueline Kennedy Onassis Reservoir** (midpark, between 85th & 96th Streets) was renamed in honour of the late first lady, who used to jog around it. The path affords great views of the surrounding skyscrapers, especially at the northern end, looking south.

In the northern section, the exquisite **Conservatory Garden** (entrance on Fifth Avenue, at 105th Street) comprises formal gardens inspired by English, French and Italian styles.

Upper East Side

Although Manhattan's super-rich now live all over town, the air of old money is most pronounced on the Upper East Side. Along Fifth, Madison and Park Avenues, from 61st to 81st Streets, you'll see the great old mansions, many of which are now foreign consulates.

Philanthropic gestures made by the moneyed classes over the past 130-odd years have helped create an impressive cluster of art collections, museums and cultural institutions. Indeed, Fifth Avenue from 82nd to 110th Streets is known as Museum Mile because it's lined with half a dozen celebrated institutions.

Sights & museums

Cooper-Hewitt, National Design Museum

2 E 91st Street, at Fifth Avenue (1-212 849 8400, www.cooperhewitt. org). Subway 4, 5, 6 to 86th Street. Closed until 2014 (see website for updates and off-site exhibitions). **Map** p139 D2 **1**
Founded in 1897 by the Hewitt sisters, granddaughters of industrialist Peter Cooper, the only museum in the US solely dedicated to design (both historic and modern) has been part of the Smithsonian since the 1960s. In 1976, it took up residence in the former home of steel magnate Andrew Carnegie. The museum is currently closed during a major renovation and expansion project, which will more than double its exhibition space. Meanwhile, the Cooper-Hewitt is staging exhibitions off-site; see website for information.

Frick Collection

1 E 70th Street, between Fifth & Madison Avenues (1-212 288 0700, www.frick.org). Subway 6 to 68th Street-Hunter College. **Open** 10am-6pm Tue-Sat; 11am-5pm Sun. **Admission** $18; $10-$15 reductions; under-10s not admitted. Pay what you wish 11am-1pm Sun. **Map** p139 D4 **2**
Industrialist, robber baron and collector Henry Clay Frick commissioned this opulent mansion with a view to leaving his legacy to the public. Designed by Thomas Hastings of Carrère & Hastings and built in 1914, the building was inspired by 18th-century British and French architecture.

In an effort to preserve the feel of a private residence, labelling is minimal, but you can opt for a free audio guide or pay $2 for a booklet. Works spanning the 14th to the 19th centuries include masterpieces by Rembrandt, Vermeer, Whistler, Monet and Bellini and exquisite period furniture and objects. A new gallery in the enclosed garden portico is devoted to decorative arts and sculpture. The interior fountain court is a serene spot in which to rest your feet.
Event highlights Mantegna to Matisse: Master Drawings from the Courtauld Gallery (2 Oct 2012-27 Jan 2013); Vermeer, Rembrandt, and Hals: Masterpieces from the Mauritshuis (22 Oct 2013-21 Jan 2014).

Jewish Museum

1109 Fifth Avenue, at 92nd Street (1-212 423 3200, www.thejewishmuseum. org). Subway 4, 5, 6 to 86th Street; 6 to 96th Street. **Open** 11am-5.45pm Mon, Tue, Sat, Sun; 11am-8pm Thur; 11am-4pm (5.45pm Mar-Nov) Fri. Closed on Jewish holidays. **Admission** $12; free-$10 reductions; free Sat. **Map** p139 D2 **3**
The Jewish Museum is housed in a magnificent 1908 French Gothic-style mansion – the former home of the financier, collector and Jewish leader Felix Warburg. A far-reaching collection of more than 28,000 works of art, artefacts and media installations are arranged thematically in a two-floor permanent exhibition, 'Culture and Continuity: The Jewish Journey', which traces the evolution of Judaism from antiquity to the present day. The excellent temporary shows appeal to a broad audience.

Metropolitan Museum of Art

1000 Fifth Avenue, at 82nd Street (1-212 535 7710, www.metmuseum.org). Subway 4, 5, 6 to 86th Street. **Open** 9.30am-5.30pm Tue-Thur, Sun; 9.30am-9pm Fri, Sat. **Admission** suggested donation (incl same-day admission to the Cloisters) $25; free-$17 reductions. **Map** p139 D3 **4**

Occupying 13 acres of Central Park, the Metropolitan Museum of Art, which opened in 1880, is impressive in terms both of quality and scale. The neo-classical façade (added in 1895 by McKim, Mead & White) can appear daunting, but the museum is easy to negotiate, particularly if you come early on a weekday to avoid the crowds.

In the first floor's north wing sit the collection of Egyptian art and the glass-walled atrium housing the Temple of Dendur, moved en masse from its original Nile-side setting and now overlooking a reflective pool. Antiquity is also well represented in the southern wing by the halls housing Greek and Roman art. Turning west brings you to the Arts of Africa, Oceania and the Americas collection; it was donated by Nelson Rockefeller as a memorial to his son Michael, who disappeared while visiting New Guinea in 1961.

A wider-ranging bequest, the two-storey Robert Lehman Wing, is at the western end of the floor. This eclectic collection is housed in a re-creation of the Lehman family townhouse and features works by Botticelli, Bellini, Ingres and Rembrandt, among others.

On the north-west corner is the American Wing, which was recently revamped in stages. Its grand, conservatory-style Engelhard Court reopened in 2009 – the light-filled sculpture court is flanked by the façade of Wall Street's Branch Bank of the United States (saved when the building was torn down in 1915) and a stunning loggia designed by Louis Comfort Tiffany for his Long Island estate.

Upstairs, the central western section is dominated by the European Paintings galleries, which hold an amazing reserve of old masters; the Dutch section boasts five Vermeers, the largest collection of the artist in the world. To the south, the 19th-century European galleries contain some of the Met's most popular works – in particular the two-room Monet holdings and a colony of Van Goghs that includes his oft-reproduced *Irises*.

Walk eastward and you'll reach the new Galleries of the Art of the Arab Lands, Turkey, Iran, Central Asia and Later South Asia. In the northern wing of the floor, you'll find the sprawling collection of Asian art; be sure to check out the ceiling of the Jain Meeting Hall in the South-east Asian gallery. If you're still on your feet, give them a deserved rest in the Astor Court, a tranquil re-creation of a Ming Dynasty garden, or head up to the Iris & B Gerald Cantor Roof Garden (open May-late Oct). For the Cloisters, which houses the Met's medieval art collection, see p158.

Event highlights Regarding Warhol: Sixty Artists, Fifty Years (18 Sept-31 Dec 2012); Matisse: In Search of True Painting (11 Dec 2012-17 Mar 2013); Impressionism, Fashion and Modernity (26 Feb-27 May 2013); The Civil War and American Art (28 May-2 Sept 2013

El Museo del Barrio

1230 Fifth Avenue, at 104th Street (1-212 831 7272, www.elmuseo.org). Subway 6 to 103rd Street. **Open** 11am-6pm Tue-Sat; 1-5pm-Sun. **Admission** suggested $9; free-$5 reductions. **Map** p141 D5 ❺

Founded in 1969 by the artist (and former MoMA curator) Rafael Montañez Ortiz, El Museo del Barrio takes its name from its East Harlem locale. Dedicated to the art and culture of Puerto Ricans and Latin Americans all over the US, El Museo reopened in 2009 following a $35-million renovation. The redesigned spaces within the museum's 1921 Beaux Arts building provide a polished, contemporary showcase for the diversity and vibrancy of Hispanic art. The new galleries allow more space for rotating installations from the museum's 6,500-piece holdings – from pre-Columbian artefacts to contemporary installations – as well as around three temporary shows a year.

Event highlights Caribbean: Crossroads of the World (until 6 Jan 2013), in collaboration with the Queens Museum of Art and the Studio Museum in Harlem.

Museum of the City of New York

1220 Fifth Avenue, between 103rd & 104th Streets (1-212 534 1672, www.mcny.org). Subway 6 to 103rd Street. **Open** 10am-6pm daily. **Admission** suggested donation $10; free-$6 reductions. **Map** p141 D5 ❻

A great introduction to New York, this institution contains a wealth of city history. *Timescapes*, a 22-minute multimedia presentation that illuminates the history of NYC, is shown free with admission every half hour. A spacious new gallery opened in late 2008 to allow more space for five to seven temporary exhibitions each year, which spotlight the city from different angles.

The museum's holdings include prints, drawings and photos of NYC, decorative arts and furnishings and an extensive collection of toys. The undoubted jewel is the amazing Stettheimer Dollhouse: it was created in the '20s by Carrie Stettheimer, whose artist friends reinterpreted their masterpieces in miniature to hang on the walls. Look closely and you'll even spy a tiny version of Marcel Duchamp's famous *Nude Descending a Staircase*.

Event highlights From Farm to City: Staten Island 1661-2012 (13 Sept 2012-21 Jan 2013).

Neue Galerie

1048 Fifth Avenue, at 86th Street (1-212 628 6200, www.neuegalerie.org). Subway 4, 5, 6 to 86th Street. **Open** 11am-6pm Mon, Thur-Sun; 11am-8pm 1st Fri of mth. **Admission** $20; $10 reductions. Under-16s must be accompanied by an adult; under-12s not admitted. **Map** p139 D2 ❼

This elegant gallery is devoted to late 19th- and early 20th-century German

Museum secrets

Behind-the-scenes stories at three NYC institutions.

American Museum of Natural History: An American chipmunk in Congo
'All the dioramas are real places from a specific expedition... But in the okapi diorama, one of the artists drew his signature creature in the background: somewhere, if you really search, in our Congo rain forest, there's a little [North American] eastern chipmunk.' – *Stephen C Quinn, senior project manager and artist*

Museum of Modern Art: The purchase of Meret Oppenheim's Object (fur-covered cup, saucer and spoon)
'Director Alfred Barr wanted to buy it in 1936, but the trustees disagreed. Barr was so convinced that it belonged in the collection that he bought it with his own money for $50... It's one of the great stars of our Surrealism collection; to think that our director had to sneak it in!' – *Ann Temkin, chief curator, Painting and Sculpture*

The Metropolitan Museum of Art: A seaman's handiwork
'There are all kinds of carved names on the Temple of Dendur, but the only inscription to be positively attached to a specific person belongs to Armar Lowry Corry, a lieutenant in the British Royal Navy.' – *Bret Watson, founder and president Watson Adventures (www.watsonadventures.com)*

and Austrian fine and decorative arts. The creation of the late art dealer Serge Sabarsky and cosmetics mogul Ronald S Lauder, it has the largest concentration of works by Gustav Klimt and Egon Schiele outside Vienna.

Solomon R Guggenheim Museum

1071 Fifth Avenue, at 89th Street (1-212 423 3500, www.guggenheim.org). Subway 4, 5, 6 to 86th Street. **Open** 10am-5.45pm Mon-Wed, Fri, Sun; 10am-7.45pm Sat. **Admission** $22; free-$18 reductions; pay what you wish 5.45-7.15pm Fri. **Map** p139 D2 ❽

The Guggenheim is as famous for its landmark building – designed by Frank Lloyd Wright – as it is for its impressive collection and daring temporary shows. The museum opened in 1959, and the addition of a ten-storey tower in 1992 provided space for a sculpture gallery (with park views), an auditorium and a café. The institution owns Peggy Guggenheim's trove of Cubist, Surrealist and Abstract Expressionist works, along with the Panza di Biumo Collection of American Minimalist and Conceptual art from the 1960s and '70s. As well as works by Manet, Picasso, Chagall and Bourgeois, it includes the largest collection of Kandinskys in the US.

Event highlights Picasso Black and White (5 Oct 2012-23 Jan 2013); Gutai: Splendid Playground (Feb-May 2013)

Whitney Museum of American Art

945 Madison Avenue, at 75th Street (1-212 570 3600, www.whitney.org). Subway 6 to 77th Street. **Open** 11am-6pm Wed, Thur, Sat, Sun; 1-9pm Fri. **Admission** $18; free-$12 reductions; pay what you wish 6-9pm Fri. **Map** p139 D3 ❾

When sculptor and art patron Gertrude Vanderbilt Whitney opened the museum in 1931, she dedicated it to living American artists. Today, the Whitney holds more than 19,000 pieces

by around 2,700 artists, including Willem de Kooning, Edward Hopper, Jasper Johns, Georgia O'Keeffe and Claes Oldenburg. Like the Guggenheim, the Whitney is set apart by its unique architecture, but the museum will only occupy the Marcel Breuer-designed granite cube with its all-seeing upper-storey 'eye' for a few more years.

In spring 2011, architect Renzo Piano broke ground on the museum's new nine-storey home at the foot of the High Line (see p97) in the Meatpacking District. Once it opens in 2015, there will be space for a comprehensive display of the collection for the first time. In the run-up to the move, the Whitney is rummaging through its holdings to stage a series of exhibitions based on its permanent collection, each covering roughly two decades of American art; the next istallment is 'Sinister Pop', giving a dark spin on its cache of Pop Art. The Whitney's reputation rests primarily on its temporary shows – particularly the Whitney Biennial, the exhibition that everyone loves to hate. Launched in 1932 and held in even-numbered years, it's the most prestigious and controversial assessment of contemporary art in the US.

Event highlights Richard Artschwager! (25 Oct 2012-3 Feb 2013); Sinister Pop (15 Nov 2012-Mar 2013); Jay Defeo: A Retrospective (28 Feb-2 June 2013).

Eating & drinking

ABV

NEW *1504 Lexington Avenue, at 97th Street (1-212 722 8959, www.abvny.com). Subway 6 to 96th Street.* **Open** 5-11pm Mon-Thur; 5pm-1am Fri; 5pm-midnight Sat; 5-11pm Sun. **Wine bar**. **Map** p139 D1 ❿
See box right.

Bar Pleiades

The Surrey, 20 E 76th Street, between Fifth & Madison Avenues (1-212 772 2600, www.danielnyc.com). Subway 6

Uptown cheer

A hip food-and-drink enclave takes root.

While you'll agonise over which of the Upper East Side's many top museums to cram into your itinerary, the area is less well endowed with hip bars. Recently, however, an informal web of pioneering young upstarts have brought Downtown swagger to the top of the Upper East Side. With spots focused on beer, wine and spirits, you can literally choose your poison.

Adam Clark and Michael Cesari's pint-size **Earl's Beer and Cheese** (see p148) instantly makes you want to be a regular. Expertly chosen drafts ($5-$7) change nearly every day, and the lineup cycles through mostly local pours, including the citrus-tinged Bronx Pale Ale and Southern Tier's Krampus, a high-alcohol take on a traditional German *helles* lager. Yet, amid all the top-notch brews, the kitchen steals the show. Momofuku Ssäm Bar alum Corey Cova's menu deploys local curds in a variety of kitchen-sink creations such as the NY State Cheddar – a grilled cheese featuring braised pork belly, fried egg and house-made kimchi – or an Eggo waffle topped with coffee-cured bacon, reduced maple syrup, aged cheddar and grilled foie gras.

Next door, Clark's new cocktail bar **Guthrie Inn** (see p148) is Earl's fancier, pricier sibling, with a plush back room for more mellow boozing. Bustling wine bar **ABV** (see left), co-owned by Cesari, also offers classic drinks and creative American grub courtesy of Cova, but it's at least four times the size of the other

Earl's Beer and Cheese

two venues, with plenty of room for drinkers and diners alike. Post work, young professionals fill long communal tables for tartare pizza and cocktails like the lemony Piedmont Fizz.

While you're here, check out Cesari's music-themed retail store, **Vinyl Wine** (see p149). With the intention of selling records in addition to bottles, he joined forces with Michael Faircloth, a viticulture and cellar assistant at Napa Wine Company and former jazz-studies major. The pair soon found that liquor-store laws barred the sale of non-wine accessories, meaning that they couldn't sell any vinyl – instead, their stock of small-production, organic and biodynamic bottles now shares shelf space with more than 10,000 decorative records.

to 77th Street. **Open** noon-midnight daily. **Bar**. Map p139 D3 ⑪

Designed as a nod to Coco Chanel, Daniel Boulud's bar – across the hotel lobby from Café Boulud – is framed in black lacquered panels that recall an elegant make-up compact. The luxe setting and moneyed crowd might seem a little stiff, but the drinks are so exquisitely executed, you won't mind sharing your banquette with a suit. Light eats are provided by Café Boulud next door (about $15 a plate).

Bemelmans Bar

The Carlyle, 35 E 76th Street, at Madison Avenue (1-212 744 1600, www.thecarlyle.com). Subway 6 to 77th Street. **Open** noon-1am daily. **Bar**. Map p139 D3 ⑫

The Plaza may have Eloise, but the Carlyle has its own children's book connection – the wonderful 1947 murals of Central Park by *Madeline* creator Ludwig Bemelmans in this, the quintessential classy New York bar. A jazz trio adds to the atmosphere every night (a cover charge of $15-$30 applies from 9.30pm Tue-Sat and 9pm Mon, Sun, when they take up residence).

Café Sabarsky

Neue Galerie, 1048 Fifth Avenue, at 86th Street (1-212 288 0665, www.neuegalerie.org). Subway 4, 5, 6 to 86th Street. **Open** 9am-6pm Mon, Wed; 9am-9pm, Thur-Sun. $$ **Café**. Map p139 D2 ⑬

Purveyor of indulgent pastries and whipped-cream-topped *einspänner* coffee for Neue Galerie patrons by day, this sophisticated, high-ceilinged room becomes an upscale restaurant four nights a week. Appetisers are most adventurous – the creaminess of the *spätzle* is a perfect base for sweetcorn, tarragon and wild mushrooms – while main course specials, such as the *wiener schnitzel* tartly garnished with lingonberries, are capable yet ultimately feel like the calm before the *Sturm und Drang* of dessert. Try the *klimttorte*,

which masterfully alternates layers of hazelnut cake with chocolate.

Daniel

60 E 65th Street, between Madison & Park Avenues (1-212 288 0033, www.danielnyc.com). Subway F to Lexington Avenue-63rd Street; 6 to 68th Street-Hunter College. **Open** 5.30-11pm Mon-Sat. $$$$. **French**. Map p139 D5 ⑭

The cuisine at Daniel Boulud's elegant fine-dining flagship, designed by Adam Tihany, is rooted in French technique with *au courant* flourishes like fusion elements and an emphasis on local produce. Although the menu changes seasonally, it always includes a few signature dishes – Boulud's black truffle and scallops in puff pastry remains a classic, and the duo of beef is a sumptuous pairing of Black Angus short ribs and seared Wagyu tenderloin. His other restaurant, Café Boulud, is at 20 76th Street, between Fifth & Madison Avenues (1-212 772 2600).

NEW Earl's Beer & Cheese

1259 Park Avenue, between 97th & 98th Streets (1-212 289 1581, www.earlsny.com). Subway 6 to 96th Street. **Open** 4pm-midnight Mon-Wed; 11am-midnight Thur, Sun; 11am-2am Fri, Sat. **Bar**. Map p139 D1 ⑮
See box p147.

NEW Guthrie Inn

1259 Park Avenue, between 97th & 98th Streets (1-212 423 9900). Subway 6 to 96th Street. **Open** 5pm-2am Tue-Sat; 5pm-midnight Mon, Sun. **Cocktail bar**. Map p139 D1 ⑯
See box 147.

Lexington Candy Shop

1226 Lexington Avenue, at 83rd Street (1-212 288 0057, www.lexingtoncandy shop.net). Subway 4, 5, 6 to 86th Street. **Open** 7am-7pm Mon-Sat; 8am-6pm Sun. $. **American**. Map p139 D3 ⑰

You won't see much candy for sale at Lexington Candy Shop. Instead, you'll

find a wonderfully preserved retro diner
(it was founded in 1925), its long counter
lined with chatty locals on their lunch
hours, tucking into burgers and chocolate malts. If you come for breakfast,
order the doorstop slabs of french toast.

Shopping

Madison Avenue, between 57th
and 86th Streets, is packed with
international designer names:
Gucci, Prada, Chloé, Donna Karan,
Tom Ford, Lanvin, multiple Ralph
Lauren outposts and many more.

Barneys New York

*660 Madison Avenue, at 61st Street
(1-212 826 8900, www.barneys.com).
Subway N, R to Fifth Avenue-59th
Street; 4, 5, 6 to 59th Street.* **Open**
10am-8pm Mon-Fri; 10am-7pm Sat;
11am-6pm Sun. **Map** p139 D5 ⓲
Barneys has a reputation for spotlight-
ing more independent designer labels
than other upmarket department
stores, and has its own quirky-classic
line. Its hip Co-op boutiques (see website for locations) carry contemporary
threads and the latest hot denim lines.
Every February and August, the
Chelsea Co-op hosts the Barneys
Warehouse Sale, when prices are
slashed by 50-80%.

Bloomingdale's

*1000 Third Avenue, at 59th Street (1-
212 705 2000, www.bloomingdales.com).
Subway N, Q, R to Lexington Avenue-
59th Street; 4, 5, 6 to 59th Street.* **Open**
10am-8.30pm Mon-Sat; 11am-7pm Sun.
Map p139 D5/E5 ⓳
Ranking among the city's top tourist
attractions, Bloomie's is a gigantic,
glitzy department store stocked with
everything from bags to beauty products, home furnishings to designer
duds. The beauty hall, complete with
an outpost of globe-spanning apothecary Space NK and a Bumble &
Bumble dry-styling bar, recently got
a glam makeover. The compact Soho

outpost concentrates on contemporary
labels, denim and cosmetics.

NEW Fivestory

*18 E 69th Street, between Fifth &
Madison Avenues (1-212 288 1338,
www.fivestoryny.com). Subway 6 to
68th Street-Hunter College.* **Open**
10am-6pm Mon-Fri; noon-6pm Sat.
Map p139 D4 ⓴
At just 26 (with a little help from her
fashion-industry insider dad), Claire
Distenfeld has opened this glamorous,
grown-up boutique, which sprawls
over two floors of – yes – a five-storey
townhouse. The space is stocked with
clothing, shoes and accessories for
men, women and children, plus select
home items. The emphasis is on less-
ubiquitous American and European
labels, including New York-based Lyn
Devon and Thakoon, and Peter Pilotto,
created by two alums of Antwerp's
Royal Academy of Fine Arts.

Lisa Perry

*988 Madison Avenue, at 77th Street
(1-212 334 1956, www.lisaperry
style.com). Subway 6 to 77th Street.*
Open 10am-6pm Mon-Sat; noon-5pm
Sun. **Map** p139 D3 ㉑
Upon graduation from FIT in 1981,
designer Lisa Perry launched her line
of retro women's threads inspired by
her massive personal collection of '60s
and '70s pieces. Ultrabright pieces,
such as her signature colour-blocked
minidresses, pop against the stark
white walls of her Madison Avenue
flagship. You'll also find the
designer's cheerful accessories, such
as candy-colored duffel bags, and her
mod home collection, which includes
place mats and throw pillows.

NEW Vinyl Wine

*1491 Lexington Avenue, between
96th & 97th Streets (1-646 370 4100,
www.vinylwineshop.com). Subway 6 to
96th Street.* **Open** 1-9pm Mon-Wed,
Sun; 1-10pmThur-Sat. **Map** p139 D1 ㉒
See box p147.

Reinventing history

A venerable institution embraces the 21st century.

Founded in 1804 by merchant John Pintard and a group of prominent New Yorkers that included Mayor Dewitt Clinton, the **New-York Historical Society** (see p152) is the city's oldest museum. Originally based at City Hall, the institution was set up to preserve colonial and federal documents for posterity. It had subsequent stints in several locations before settling into its stately current home in 1908. In November 2011, the museum reopened after a three-year, $65-million renovation that literally opened up the interior spaces to make the collection more accessible to a 21st-century audience.

Previously a warren of smaller rooms, the Robert H and Clarice Smith New York Gallery of American History provides an overview of the collection and a broad sweep of New York's place in American history – Revolutionary-era maps are juxtaposed with a piece of the ceiling mural from Keith Haring's Pop Shop (the artist's Soho store, which closed after his death in 1990). Touch-screen monitors illuminate artworks, documents and other objects from the early Federal period, while large-scale HD screens display a continuous slide show of highlights of the museum's holdings, such as original watercolours from Audubon's *Birds of America* and some of its 132 Tiffany lamps. A dozen circular exhibition cases in the floor, resembling manholes, contain items dug up by a group of amateur archaeologists founded by the Society in 1918, including Lenape Indian arrowheads and a pair of baby shoes that survived the 1904 fire on the *General Slocum* pleasure boat. At the back of the gallery, the updated auditorium screens an 18-minute film tracing the city's development, while downstairs the DiMenna Children's History Museum engages the next generation.

The upper floors house changing shows and a visible-storage display that spans everything from spectacles, canes and toys to Washington's Valley Forge camp bed and a 1770 coach. The Society's name is itself a historical preservation – placing a hyphen between 'New' and 'York' was common in the early 19th century. In fact, according to the Society, *The New York Times* maintained the convention until 1896.

Upper West Side

The gateway to the Upper West Side is Columbus Circle, where Broadway meets 59th Street, Eighth Avenue, Central Park South and Central Park West – a rare roundabout in a city that is largely made up of right angles. The cosmopolitan neighbourhood's seat of culture is **Lincoln Center**, a complex of concert halls and auditoriums that's home to the New York Philharmonic, the New York City Ballet, the Metropolitan Opera and various other notable arts organisations.

Further uptown, Morningside Heights, between 110th and 125th Streets, from Morningside Park to the Hudson, is dominated by Columbia University. The sinuous Riverside Park, designed by Central Park's Frederick Law Olmsted, starts at 72nd Street and ends at 158th Street, between Riverside Drive and the Hudson River; in the 1990s, work began to develop the abandoned Penn Central Railyard between 59th and 72nd Streets into Riverside Park South, now a peaceful city retreat with a pier and undulating waterside paths.

Sights & museums

American Folk Art Museum

2 Lincoln Square, Columbus Avenue, at 66th Street (1-212 595 9533, www.folkartmuseum.org). Subway 1 to 66th Street-Lincoln Center. **Open** noon-7.30pm Tue-Sat; noon-6pm Sun. **Admission** free. **Map** p138 B5 ㉓
In 2011, the financially troubled American Folk Art Museum sold its building on W 53rd Street to the neighbouring Museum of Modern Art and decamped to its smaller, original premises where it will continue to celebrate the work of self-taught artists and traditional crafts such as pottery, quilting, woodwork and jewellery design.

American Museum of Natural History/Rose Center for Earth & Space

Central Park West, at 79th Street (1-212 769 5100, www.amnh.org). Subway B, C to 81st Street-Museum of Natural History. **Open** 10am-5.45pm daily. **Admission** suggested donation $19; free-$14.50 reductions. **Map** p138 C3 ㉔
The American Museum of Natural History's fourth-floor dino halls are home to the largest and arguably most fabulous collection of dinosaur fossils in the world. Roughly 80% of the bones on display were dug out of the ground by Indiana Jones types, but during the museum's mid 1990s renovation, several specimens were remodelled to incorporate discoveries made during the intervening years. The tyrannosaurus rex, for instance, was once believed to have walked upright, *Godzilla*-style; it now stalks prey with its head lowered and tail raised parallel to the ground.

The rest of the museum is equally dramatic. The Hall of Human Origins houses a fine display of our old cousins, the Neanderthals. The Hall of Biodiversity examines world ecosystems and environmental preservation, and a life-size model of a blue whale hangs from the cavernous ceiling of the Hall of Ocean Life. In the Hall of Meteorites, the focal point is Ahnighito, the largest iron meteor on display anywhere in the world, weighing in at 34 tons.

The spectacular $210 million Rose Center for Earth & Space – dazzling at night – is a giant silvery globe where you can discover the universe via 3-D shows in the Hayden Planetarium and light shows in the Big Bang Theater. An IMAX theatre screens larger-than-life nature programmes, and the roster of temporary exhibitions is thought-provoking for all ages.
Event highlights Creatures of Light: Nature's Bioluminescence (until 6 Jan 2013).

NEW YORK BY AREA

Cathedral Church of St John the Divine

1047 Amsterdam Avenue, at 112th Street (1-212 316 7540, www. stjohndivine.org). Subway B, C, 1 to 110th Street-Cathedral Parkway. **Open** 7am-6pm Mon-Sat; 7am-7pm Sun. **Admission** suggested donation $10; $5 reductions. **Map** p140 B4 ㉕

Construction of this massive house of worship, affectionately nicknamed 'St John the Unfinished', began in 1892 in Romanesque style, was put on hold for a Gothic Revival redesign in 1911, then ground to a halt in 1941, when the US entered World War II. It resumed in earnest in 1979, but a fire in 2001 that destroyed the church's gift shop and damaged two 17th-century Italian tapestries further delayed completion. It's still missing a tower and a north transept, among other things, but the nave has been restored and the entire interior reopened and rededicated. No further work is planned… for now.

In addition to Sunday services, the cathedral hosts concerts and tours. It bills itself as a place for all people – and it certainly means it. Annual events include both winter and summer solstice celebrations, and even a Blessing of the Bicycles every spring.

Museum of Arts & Design

2 Columbus Circle, at Broadway (1-212 299 7777, www.madmuseum.org). Subway A, B, C, D, 1 to 59th Street-Columbus Circle. **Open** 11am-6pm Tue, Wed, Sat, Sun; 11am-9pm Thur, Fri. **Admission** $15; free-$12 reductions; pay what you wish 6-9pm Thur, Fri. **Map** p138 C5 ㉖

This institution brings together contemporary objects created in a wide range of media – including clay, glass, wood, metal and cloth – with a strong focus on materials and process. And in 2008 the museum crafted itself a new home. Originally designed in 1964 by Radio City Music Hall architect Edward Durell Stone to house the Gallery of Modern Art, 2 Columbus Circle was a windowless monolith that had sat empty since 1998. The redesigned ten-storey building now has four floors of exhibition galleries, including the Tiffany & Co Foundation Jewelry Gallery. Curators are able to display more of the 2,000-piece permanent collection, including porcelain ware by Cindy Sherman, stained glass by Judith Schaechter, basalt ceramics by James Turrell and Robert Arneson's mural *Alice House Wall*.

In addition to checking out temporary shows, you can also watch resident artists create works in studios on the sixth floor, while the ninth-floor bistro has views over the park.

Event highlights Doris Duke's Shangri La (7 Sept 2012-6 Jan 2013); Daniel Brush: Blue Steel Gold Light (16 Oct-17 Feb 2013).

New-York Historical Society

170 Central Park West, between 76th & 77th Streets (1-212 873 3400, www. nyhistory.org). Subway B, C to 81st Street-Museum of Natural History. **Open** 10am-6pm Tue-Thur, Sat; 10am-8pm Fri; 11am-5pm Sun. **Admission** $15; free-$12 reductions. Pay what you wish 6-8pm Fri. **Map** p138 C3 ㉗ See box p150.

Event highlights WW1 & NYC (5 Oct 2012-27 May 2013); Audubon's Aviary: Part I of the Complete Flock (8 Mar-19 May 2013).

Eating & drinking

A Voce Columbus

3rd Floor, 10 Columbus Circle, at Broadway (1-212 823 2523, www. avocerestaurant.com). Subway A, B, C, D, 1 to 59th Street-Columbus Circle. **Open** 11.30am-2.30pm, 5-10pm Mon-Wed; 11.30am-2.30pm, 5-10.30pm Thur-Sat; 11am-3pm, 5-10pm Sun. **$$-$$$. Italian. Map** p138 C5 ㉓

Want views over Columbus Circle and the park without paying Per Se (see p154) prices? A Voce's sleek uptown out-post also has a solid menu and impeccable service. Brick-flattened chicken, infused with roasted garlic, lemon and dried Calabrian chillies and served with Tuscan kale, white beans and potatoes, is a comfort-food triumph. The owner's art collection, including a massive Frank Stella mixed-media piece that hangs near the host stand, is a feast for the eyes.

Barney Greengrass

541 Amsterdam Avenue, between 86th & 87th Streets (1-212 724 4707, www. barneygreengrass.com). Subway B, C, 1 to 86th Street. **Open** 8.30am-4pm Tue-Fri; 8.30am-5pm Sat, Sun. **$-$$**. No credit cards. **American**. Map p138 B2 ㉙

Despite decor that Jewish mothers might call 'schmutzy', this legendary deli is a madhouse at breakfast and brunch. Egg platters come with the usual choice of smoked fish (such as sturgeon or Nova Scotia salmon). Prices are on the high side, but portions are large, and that goes for the sandwiches too. Or try the less costly items like matzo-ball soup or cold pink borscht.

Bouchon Bakery

3rd Floor, Time Warner Center, 10 Columbus Circle, at Broadway (1-212 823 9366, www.bouchonbakery.com). Subway A, B, C, D, 1 to 59th Street-Columbus Circle. **Open** 11.30am-7pm daily. **$**. **Café**. Map p138 C5 ㉚

Chef Thomas Keller's café, in the same mall as his lauded fine-dining room Per Se (see p154), lacks ambience, and the soups, tartines and salads are a bit basic, though prices are more palatable. Sandwiches such as a dry-cured ham and emmenthaler baguette are around a tenner. Focus on the bakery: French classics and Keller's takes on American ones – Oreo cookies and Nutter Butters – are the real highlights.

Boulud Sud

NEW *20 W 64th Street, between Broadway & Central Park West (1-212 595 1313, www.danielnyc.com).*

Subway 1 to 66th Street-Lincoln Center. **Open** noon-2.30pm, 5-11pm Mon-Sat; noon-3pm, 5-10pm Sun. **$$$**. **Mediterranean**. Map p138 B5 ㉛

At his most international restaurant yet, superchef Daniel Boulud highlights the new French cuisine of melting-pot cities like Marseille and Nice. With his executive chef, Aaron Chambers (Café Boulud), he casts a wide net – looking to Israel and Egypt, Turkey and Greece. Budget-minded diners can build a full tapas meal from shareable snacks like octopus à la plancha, with marcona almonds and arugula. Heartier dishes combine Gallic finesse with polyglot flavours: sweet-spicy chicken tagine and a fragrant bowl of harira lamb soup borrow from the Moroccan pantry. Tunisian-born Ghaya Oliveira's audacious desserts – such as grapefruit givré stuffed with sorbet, sesame mousse and rose-scented nuggets of Turkish delight – take the exotic mix to even loftier heights.

Ding Dong Lounge

929 Columbus Avenue, between 105th & 106th Street (Duke Ellington Boulevard) (1-212 663 2600, www. dingdonglounge.com). Subway B, C to 103rd Street. **Open** 4pm-4am daily. **Bar**. Map p140 B5 ㉜

Goth chandeliers and kick-ass music mark this dark dive as punk – with broadened horizons. The tap pulls, dispensing Stella Artois, Guinness and Bass, are sawn-off guitar necks, and the walls are covered with vintage concert posters (from Dylan to the Damned). The affable local clientele and mood-lit conversation nooks make it surprisingly accessible (even without a working knowledge of Dee Dee Ramone).

Hungarian Pastry Shop

1030 Amsterdam Avenue, between 110th & 111th Street (1-212 866 4230). Subway 1 to 110th Street-Cathedral Parkway. **Open** 7.30am-11.30pm Mon-Fri; 8.30am-11.30pm Sat; 8.30am-10.30pm Sun. **$**. **Café**. Map p140 B4 ㉝

So many theses have been dreamed up, procrastinated over or tossed aside in the Hungarian Pastry Shop since it opened more than five decades ago that the Columbia University neighbourhood institution merits its own dissertation. The java is strong enough to make up for the erratic array of pastries, and the Euro feel is enhanced by the view of St John the Divine cathedral from outdoor tables.

Ouest

2315 Broadway, between 83rd & 84th Streets (1-212 580 8700, www.ouest ny.com). Subway 1 to 86th Street. **Open** 5-9.30pm Mon, Tue; 5-10pm Wed, Thur; 5-11pm Fri, Sat; 11am-2pm (except June-Aug), 5-9pm Sun. **$$$.** **American.** Map p138 B3 ㉞

A prototypical well-heeled local clientele calls chef Tom Valenti's Uptown fixture its local canteen. And why not? The friendly servers ferry pitch-perfect cocktails and rich, Italian-inflected cuisine from the open kitchen to immensely comfortable round red booths. Valenti adds some unexpected flourishes to the soothing formula: salmon gravadlax is served with a chickpea pancake topped with caviar and potent mustard oil, while the house-smoked sturgeon presides over frisée, lardons and a poached egg.

Per Se

4th Floor, Time Warner Center, 10 Columbus Circle, at Broadway (1-212 823 9335, www.perseny.com). Subway A, B, C, D, 1 to 59th Street-Columbus Circle. **Open** 5.30-10pm Mon-Thur; 11.30am-1.30pm, 5.30-10pm Fri-Sun. **$$$$.** **French.** Map p138 C5 ㉟

Expectations are high at Per Se – and that goes both ways. You're expected to wear the right clothes (jackets are required for men), pay a non-negotiable service charge, and pretend you aren't eating in a mall. The restaurant, in turn, is expected to deliver one hell of a tasting menu for $295. And it does. Dish after dish is flawless, beginning

with Thomas Keller's signature 'Oysters and Pearls' (a sabayon of pearl tapioca with oysters and caviar). Other hits include a buttery poached lobster and house-made sorbets; an all-vegetable version is also available. If you can afford it, it's worth every penny, but avoid the recently introduced à la carte option in the lounge, which offers miserly portions at high prices, making it less of a deal than the celebrated tasting menu in the formal dining room.

Shake Shack

366 Columbus Avenue, at 77th Street (1-646 747 8770, www.shakeshack nyc.com). Subway B, C to 81st Street-Museum of Natural History; 1 to 79th Street. **Open** 10.45am-11pm daily. **$.** **American.** Map p138 B3 ㊱

The spacious offspring of Danny Meyer's popular Madison Square Park concession stand is now one of several locations across the city. Shake Shack gets several local critics' votes for New York's best burger. Sirloin and brisket are ground daily for the prime patties, while franks are served Chicago-style on poppy seed buns with a 'salad' of toppings. Frozen-custard shakes hit the spot, but there's beer and wine if you want something stronger.

Shopping

Allan & Suzi

416 Amsterdam Avenue, at 80th Street (1-212 724 7445, www.allanandsuzi.net). Subway 1 to 79th Street. **Open** 12.30-7pm daily. Map p138 B3 ㊲

Models and celebs drop off worn-once Gaultiers, Muglers, Pradas and Manolos here. The platform shoe collection is flashback-inducing and incomparable, as is the selection of vintage jewellery.

Levain Bakery

167 W 74th Street, between Columbus & Amsterdam Avenues (1-212 874 6080, www.levainbakery.com). Subway 1 to 79th Street. **Open** 8am-7pm Mon-Sat; 9am-7pm Sun. Map p138 B3 ㊳

Levain's cookies are a full 6oz, and the massive mounds stay gooey in the middle. The lush, brownie-like double-chocolate variety, made with extra-dark French cocoa and semi-sweet chocolate chips, is truly decadent.

Shops at Columbus Circle

Time Warner Center, 10 Columbus Circle, at 59th Street (1-212 823 6300, www.shopsatcolumbuscircle.com). Subway A, B, C, D, 1 to 59th Street-Columbus Circle. **Open** 10am-9pm Mon-Sat; 11am-7pm Sun (hrs vary for some shops, bars and restaurants). **Map** p138 C5 ❸❾

Classier than your average mall, the retail contingent of the 2.8 million-sq-ft Time Warner Center features upscale stores such as Coach, Cole Haan and LK Bennett for accessories and shoes, London shirtmaker Thomas Pink, Bose home entertainment, the fancy kitchenware purveyor Williams-Sonoma, as well as shopping centre staples J Crew, Aveda, and organic grocer Whole Foods. Some of the city's top restaurants (including Thomas Keller's gourmet destination Per Se, p154, and his café Bouchon Bakery, p153) have made it a dining destination that transcends the stigma of eating at the mall.

Zabar's

2245 Broadway, at 80th Street (1-212 787 2000, www.zabars.com). Subway 1 to 79th Street. **Open** 8am-7.30pm Mon-Fri; 8am-8pm Sat; 9am-6pm Sun. **Map** p138 B3 ❹⓪

Zabar's is more than just a market – it's a New York City landmark. It began in 1934 as a tiny storefront specialising in Jewish 'appetising' delicacies and has gradually expanded to take over half a block of prime Upper West Side real estate. What never ceases to surprise, however, is its reasonable prices, even for high-end foods. Besides the famous smoked fish and rafts of delicacies, Zabar's has fabulous bread, cheese, olives and coffee and an entire floor dedicated to homewares.

Nightlife

Beacon Theatre

2124 Broadway, between 74th & 75th Streets (1-212 465 6500, www.beacontheatrenyc.com). Subway 1, 2, 3 to 72nd Street. **Map** p138 B3 ❹❶

This spacious former vaudeville theatre, resplendent after a recent renovation, hosts a variety of popular acts, from 'Weird Al' Yankovic to Crosby, Stills & Nash. While the vastness can be daunting to performers and audience alike, the gilded interior and Uptown location make you feel as though you're having a real night out on the town.

Jazz at Lincoln Center

Frederick P Rose Hall, Broadway, at 60th Street (1-212 258 9800, www.jalc.org). Subway A, B, C, D, 1 to 59th Street-Columbus Circle. **Map** p138 C5 ❹❷

The jazz arm of Lincoln Center is several blocks away from the main campus, high atop the Time Warner Center. It features three separate rooms: the Rose Theater is a traditional mid-size space, but the crown jewels are the Allen Room and the smaller Dizzy's Club Coca-Cola, which feel like a Hollywood cinematographer's vision of a Manhattan jazz club. Some of the best players in the business regularly grace the spot, among them Wynton Marsalis, Jazz at Lincoln Center's famed artistic director.

Arts & leisure

Lincoln Center

Columbus Avenue, between 62nd & 65th Streets (1-212 546 2656, www.lincoln center.org). Subway 1 to 66th Street-Lincoln Center. **Map** p138 B5 ❹❸

Built in the early 1960s, this massive complex is the nexus of Manhattan's performing arts scene, and a recent revamp of its campus included a redesign of the public spaces, refurbishment of the various halls, a new film centre and a visitor centre: the

NEW YORK BY AREA

Time Out Shortlist | New York 2013 155

David Rubenstein Atrium (between W 62nd & W 63rd Streets, Broadway & Columbus Avenue) sells same-day discounted tickets to Lincoln Center performances and stages free genre-spanning concerts on Thursday nights (see website for details). It's also the starting point for guided tours of the complex (1-212 875 5350, $15, $8-$12 reductions), which, in addition to the hallowed concert halls, contains several notable artworks, including Henry Moore's *Reclining Figure* in the plaza near Lincoln Center Theater, and two massive music-themed paintings by Marc Chagall in the lobby of the Metropolitan Opera House.

Event highlights see pp36-44 Calendar.

Alice Tully Hall *1-212 875 5050.*

An 18-month renovation turned the cosy home of the Chamber Music Society of Lincoln Center (www.chambermusicsociety.org) into a world-class, 1,096-seat theatre. The new contemporary foyer with an elegant (if rather pricey) café is immediately striking, but, more importantly, the revamp brought some dramatic acoustical improvements.

Avery Fisher Hall *1-212 875 5030.*

This handsome, comfortable 2,700-seat hall is the headquarters of the New York Philharmonic (1-212 875 5656, www.nyphil.org), the country's oldest symphony orchestra (founded in 1842) – and one of its finest. Depending on who you ask, the sound ranges from good to atrocious. Inexpensive, early evening 'rush hour' concerts and open rehearsals are presented on a regular basis. The ongoing Great Performers series features top international soloists and ensembles.

David H Koch Theater
1-212 870 5570.

The neoclassical New York City Ballet headlines at this opulent theatre, which Philip Johnson designed to resemble a jewellery box. The company offers its popular *Nutcracker* at the very end of November, carrying just into the new year, followed by a winter repertory season. The spring season begins in April. Ballets by George Balanchine are performed by a wonderful crop of young dancers; there are also plenty by Jerome Robbins, Peter Martins (the company's ballet master in chief) and former resident choreographer Christopher Wheeldon.

Lincoln Center Theater *Telecharge 1-212 239 6200, www.lct.org.*

The majestic and prestigious Lincoln Center Theater complex has a pair of amphitheatre-style drama venues. The Broadway house, the 1,138-seat Vivian Beaumont Theater is home to star-studded and elegant major productions. (When the Beaumont is tied up in long runs, such as the current puppet smash *War Horse*, LCT presents its larger works at available Times Square theatres.) Downstairs from the Beaumont is the 338-seat Mitzi E Newhouse Theater, an Off Broadway space devoted to new work by the upper layer of American playwrights. In an effort to shake off its reputation for stodginess, Lincoln Center launched LCT3, which presents the work of emerging playwrights in the new Claire Tow Theater, at the top of the Beaumont. See box p124.

Metropolitan Opera House *1-212 362 6000, www.metoperafamily.org.*

The grandest of the Lincoln Center buildings, the Met is a spectacular place to see and hear opera. It hosts the Metropolitan Opera from September to May, with major visiting companies appearing in summer. Opera's biggest stars appear here regularly, and artistic director James Levine has turned the orchestra into a true symphonic force. Audiences are knowledgeable and fiercely devoted, with subscriptions remaining in families for generations.

The Met had already started becoming more inclusive before current impresario Peter Gelb took the reins in 2006. Now, the company is placing a priority on creating novel theatrical experiences with visionary directors

(Robert Lepage, Bartlett Sher, Michael Grandage, David McVicar) and assembling a new company of physically graceful, telegenic stars (Anna Netrebko, Danielle de Niese, Jonas Kaufmann, Erwin Schrott). Its high-definition movie-theatre broadcasts continue to reign supreme outside the opera house.

Although most tickets are expensive, 200 prime seats for all performances from Monday to Thursday are sold for $20 apiece two hours before curtain up.

Film Society of Lincoln Center *1-212 875 5600, www.filmlinc.com.*
Founded in 1969 to promote contemporary film, the FSLC now also hosts the prestigious New York Film Festival, among other annual fests. Programmes are usually thematic, with an international perspective. The new $40-million Elinor Bunin Munroe Film Center houses two plush cinemas with built-in cameras for post-screening Q&As. Between these state-of-the-art screens and the operational Walter Reade Theater across the street, a small multiplex has been born. The Bunin also houses a café and bookstore.

Symphony Space

2537 Broadway, at 95th Street (1-212 864 5400, www.symphonyspace.org). Subway 1, 2, 3 to 96th Street.
Map p138 B1 ㉔
Despite the name, programming at Symphony Space is anything but orchestra-centric: recent seasons have featured sax quartets, Indian classical music, a capella ensembles and HD opera simulcasts from Europe. Annual Wall to Wall marathons (usually in spring) serve up a full day of music free of charge, all focused on a particular composer. Members of the New York Philharmonic are regular guests here in more intimate chamber concerts. The multidisciplinary performing arts centre also stages works by contemporary choreographers and traditional dancers from around the globe.

War Horse

Vivian Beaumont Theater at Lincoln Center, 150 W 65th Street, at Broadway (Telecharge 1-212 239 6200, www. warhorseonbroadway.com). Subway 1 to 66th Street-Lincoln Center.
Map p138 B5 ㊺
Based on Michael Morpurgo's young-adult novel, this stark and thrilling drama tells a coming-of-age tale of compassion and survival. Devon country lad Albert bonds with a horse named Joey (a stunning life-size puppet crafted by the Handspring Puppet Company) before both are thrown into the hellish crucible of World War I. Directors Marianne Elliott and Tom Morris blend painterly design elements and a sterling ensemble to build a triumphant epic of human and animal spirit.

Harlem & beyond

Extending north from the top of Central Park at 110th Street as far as 155th Street, Harlem is the cultural capital of black America – the legacy of the Harlem Renaissance. By the 1920s, it had become the country's most populous African-American community, attracting some of black America's greatest artists: writers such as Langston Hughes and musicians like Duke Ellington and Louis Armstrong. West Harlem, between Fifth and St Nicholas Avenues, is the Harlem of popular imagination, and 125th Street is its lifeline. The area around the landmarked Mount Morris Historic District (from 119th to 124th Streets, between Malcolm X Boulevard/Lenox Avenue & Mount Morris Park West) continues to gentrify, and new boutiques, restaurants and cafés dot the double-wide Malcolm X Boulevard. Further uptown, Strivers' Row, from 138th to 139th Streets, between Adam Clayton Powell Jr Boulevard (Seventh

Avenue) and Frederick Douglass Boulevard (Eighth Avenue), was developed in 1891. East of Fifth Avenue is East Harlem, better known to its primarily Puerto Rican residents as El Barrio. (For El Museo del Barrio, see p144.)

From 155th Street to Dyckman (200th) Street is Washington Heights, which contains a handful of attractions and, at the tip of Manhattan, picturesque riverside Fort Tryon Park.

Sights & museums

The Cloisters

Fort Tryon Park, Fort Washington Avenue, at Margaret Corbin Plaza (1-212 923 3700, www.metmuseum.org). Subway A to 190th Street, then M4 bus or 10min walk. **Open** *Mar-Oct* 9.30am-5.15pm Tue-Sun. *Nov-Feb* 9.30am-4.45pm Tue-Sun. **Admission** suggested donation (incl same-day admission to Metropolitan Museum of Art) $25; free-$17 reductions.
Set in a lovely park overlooking the Hudson River, the Cloisters houses the Met's medieval art and architecture collections. A path winds through the peaceful grounds to a castle that seems to date from the Middle Ages; in fact it was built in the 1930s using pieces from five medieval French cloisters. Highlights include the 12th-century Fuentidueña Chapel, the Unicorn Tapestries and Rober Campin's *Annunciation* triptych.

Studio Museum in Harlem

144 W 125th Street, between Malcolm X Boulevard (Lenox Avenue) & Adam Clayton Powell Jr Boulevard (Seventh Avenue) (1-212 864 4500, www.studio museum.org). Subway 2, 3 to 125th Street. **Open** noon-9pm Thur-Fri; 10am-6pm Sat; noon-6pm Sun. **Admission** suggested donation $7; free-$3 reductions; free Sun. No credit cards. **Map** p140 C3 ④⑥
The first black fine arts museum in the country when it opened in 1968, the Studio Museum is an important player in the art scene of the African diaspora. Under the leadership of director and chief curator Thelma Golden, this vibrant institution, housed in a stripped down, three-level space, presents shows in a variety of media by black artists from around the world.

Eating & drinking

Amy Ruth's

113 W 116th Street, between Malcolm X Boulevard (Lenox Avenue) & Adam Clayton Powell Jr Boulevard (Seventh Avenue) (1-212 280 8779, www.amy ruthsharlem.com). Subway 2, 3 to 116th Street. **Open** 11.30am-11pm Mon; 8.30am-11pm Tue-Thur; 8.30am-5.30am Fri; 7.30am-5.30am Sat; 7.30am-11pm Sun. **$**.
American regional. **Map** p140 C4 ④⑦
This popular no-reservations spot is the place for soul food. Delicately fried okra is delivered without a hint of slime, and the mac and cheese is gooey inside and crunchy-brown on top. Dishes taste their names from notable African-Americans – vote for the President Barack Obama (fried, smothered, baked or barbecued chicken).

Ginny's Supper Club

NEW *310 Malcolm X Boulevard (Lenox Avenue), between 125th & 126th Streets (1-212 792 9001, www.redroosterharlem. com). Subway 2, 3 to 125th Street.* **Open** 6pm-midnight daily. **Bar**. **Map** p140 C3 ④⑧
Red Rooster's sprawling new basement lounge is modelled after the Harlem speakeasies of the '20s. With its own menu, cocktails from star mixologist Eben Klemm and a steady lineup of live music, the venue seems to have caught fire overnight.

Red Rooster

310 Malcolm X Boulevard (Lenox Avenue), between 125th & 126th Streets (1-212 792 9001, www.redrooster harlem.com). Subway 2, 3 to 125th Street. **Open** 11.30am-3pm, 5.30-10.30 Mon-Wed; 11.30am-3pm, 5.30-11.30

Ginny's Supper Club

Thur, Fri; 10am-3pm, 5.30-11.30pm Sat; 10am-3pm, 5-10pm Sun. **$$. Eclectic**. **Map** p140 C3 ❹
With its hobnobbing bar scrum, potent cocktails and lively jazz, this buzzy eaterie serves as a worthy clubhouse for the new Harlem. Superstar chef Marcus Samuelsson is at his most populist here, drawing on a 'We Are the World' mix of Southern-fried, East African, Scandinavian and French flavours to feed the lively crowd. Harlem politicos mix at the teardrop bar with Downtown fashionistas, everyone happily swilling fine cocktails and gorging on rib-sticking food: chicken-liver-enriched dirty rice topped with plump barbecued shrimp, homey desserts, and crispy fried chicken with hot sauce, mace gravy and a smoky spice shake. It all adds up to a place that has earned its status as a local hub.

Shrine
2271 Adam Clayton Powell Jr Boulevard (Seventh Avenue), between 133rd & 134th Streets (1-212 690 7807, www.shrinenyc.com). Subway B, C, 2, 3 to 135th Street. **Open** 4pm-4am daily. **Bar**. **Map** p140 C2 ❺
Playfully adapting a sign left over from previous tenants (the Black United Foundation), the Shrine deems itself a 'Black United Fun Plaza'. The interior is tricked out with African art and vintage album covers (the actual vinyl adorns the ceiling). Harlemites and downtowners pack the Shrine for nightly concerts, which might feature indie rock, jazz, reggae, or DJ sets. The cocktail menu aspires to similar diversity: drinks range from a smooth mango mojito to signature tipples like a snappy Afro Trip (lime and ginger enhanced by Jamaican or Brazilian rum), and a sweet vodka-and-Bailey's-driven Muslim Jew.

Shopping

Hue-Man Bookstore & Café
2319 Frederick Douglass Boulevard (Eighth Avenue), between 124th & 125th Streets (1-212 665 7400, www.hueman

bookstore.com). Subway A, B, C, D to 125th Street. **Open** 10am-8pm Mon-Sat; 11am-7pm Sun. **Map** p140 C3 ❺
Focusing on African-American non-fiction and fiction, this Harlem indie also stocks bestsellers and general interest books. It hosts readings, as well as in-store appearances by authors such as Chris Abani and Marlon James. At press time, the owner announced plans to relocate – check the website.

Nightlife

Apollo Theater
253 W 125th Street, between Adam Clayton Powell Jr Boulevard (Seventh Avenue) & Frederick Douglass Boulevard (Eighth Avenue) (1-212 531 5300, www.apollotheater.org). Subway A, B, C, D, 1 to 125th Street. **Map** p140 C3 ❺
Visitors may think they know this venerable theatre from TV's Showtime at the Apollo. But as the saying goes, the small screen adds about ten pounds: the city's home of R&B and soul music is actually quite cosy. One of the Apollo's first Amateur Nights was won in 1934 by a 17-year-old Ella Fitzgerald (she took home $25), and the legendary Bessie Smith wowed the crowds with a New Year's Eve concert in 1935. Two years later, Count Basie and his Orchestra had his Apollo debut, featuring a young (and very stage-frightened) Billie Holiday. The Apollo continues to mix veteran talents such as Dianne Reeves with younger artists such as John Legend.

Lenox Lounge
288 Malcolm X Boulevard (Lenox Avenue), between 124th & 125th Streets (1-212 427 0253, www.lenoxlounge. com). Subway 2, 3 to 125th Street. **Open** noon-4am daily. **Map** p140 C3 ❺
This classy art deco lounge, where Billie Holiday, John Coltrane, and numerous other Harlem luminaries have performed, is a true Harlem landmark and has featured in numerous films evoking Harlem's past, including *Malcolm X* and the remake of *Shaft*.

Williamsburg p163

Outer Boroughs

The Bronx

Sights & museums

Bronx Zoo/Wildlife Conservation Society

Bronx River Parkway, at Fordham Road (1-718 367 1010, www.bronxzoo.org). Subway 2, 5 to E Tremont/W Farms Square, then walk 2 blocks to the zoo's Asia entrance; or Metro-North (Harlem Line local) from Grand Central Terminal to Fordham, then take the Bx9 bus to 183rd Street and Southern Boulevard. **Open** *Apr-Oct* 10am-5pm Mon-Fri; 10am-5.30pm Sat, Sun. *Nov-Mar* 10am-4.30pm daily. **Admission** $16; $12-$14 reductions; pay what you wish Wed. Some rides & exhibitions cost extra.

The Bronx Zoo shuns cages in favour of indoor and outdoor environments that mimic natural habitats. There are more than 60,000 creatures and more than 600 species here (including invertebrates and fish). Monkeys, leopards and tapirs live inside the lush, steamy Jungle World, a re-creation of an Asian rainforest inside a 37,000sq ft building, while lions, giraffes, zebras and other animals roam the African Plains. The super-popular Congo Gorilla Forest has turned 6.5 acres into a dramatic Central African rainforest habitat. A glass-enclosed tunnel winds through the forest, allowing visitors to get close to the dozens of primate families in residence, including majestic western lowland gorillas. Tiger Mountain has Siberian tigers, while the Himalayan Highlands features snow leopards and red pandas. Madagascar! is an exhibit focused on the species-rich island off the coast of East Africa.

New York Botanical Garden

Bronx River Parkway, at Fordham Road (1-718 817 8700, www.nybg.org). Subway B, D, 4 to Bedford Park Boulevard, then Bx26 bus to the garden's Mosholu Gate; or Metro-North (Harlem Line local) from Grand Central Terminal to Botanical

Garden. **Open** 10am-6pm Tue-Sun.
Admission $20; free-$18 reductions.
Grounds only $10; free-$5 reductions;
grounds free Wed, 10-11am Sat.

The serene 250 acres of the New York
Botanical Garden comprise 50 gardens
and plant collections, including the
Rockefeller Rose Garden, the Everett
Children's Adventure Garden and the
last 50 original acres of a forest that once
covered all of New York City. In spring,
clusters of lilac, cherry, magnolia and
crab apple trees burst into bloom; in
autumn you'll see vivid foliage in the
oak and maple groves. The Enid A
Haupt Conservatory – the nation's
largest greenhouse, built in 1902 – contains the World of Plants, a series of
environmental galleries that take you on
an eco-tour through tropical rainforests,
deserts and a palm tree oasis.

Brooklyn

Sights & museums

Brooklyn Botanic Garden

*1000 Washington Avenue, at Eastern
Parkway, Prospect Heights (1-718 623
7200, www.bbg.org). Subway B, Q,
Franklin Avenue S to Prospect Park;
2, 3 to Eastern Parkway-Brooklyn
Museum.* **Open** *early Mar-Oct* 8am-6pm
Tue-Fri; 10am-6pm Sat, Sun. *Nov-early
Mar* 8am-4.30pm Tue-Fri; 10am-4.30pm
Sat, Sun. **Admission** $10; free-$5
reductions; free Tue, 10am-noon Sat.

This 52-acre haven of luscious greenery
was founded in 1910. In spring, when
Sakura Matsuri, the annual Cherry
Blossom Festival, takes place, prize buds
and Japanese culture are in full bloom.
The restored Eastern Parkway entrance
and the Osborne Garden – an Italian-
style formal garden – are also well worth
a peek. A cool new visitor centre has a
roof covered in 45,000 plants.

Brooklyn Bridge

*Subway A, C to High Street; J, Z to
Chambers Street; 4, 5, 6 to Brooklyn
Bridge-City Hall.*

Even if your trip to New York doesn't
include a romp in the boroughs, it's
worth walking to the centre of the
Brooklyn Bridge along its wide, wood-
planked promenade. Designed by civil
engineer John Augustus Roebling, the
bridge was constructed in response to
the harsh winter of 1867 when the East
River froze over, severing the connection between Manhattan and what was
then the nation's third most populous
city. When it opened in 1883, the
5,989ft-long structure was the world's
longest bridge, and the first in the
world to use steel suspension cables.
From it, there are striking vistas of the
Statue of Liberty, the skyline of Lower
Manhattan and New York Harbor.

Brooklyn Bridge Park

*Riverside, from the Manhattan Bridge,
Dumbo, to Atlantic Avenue, Brooklyn
Heights (www.brooklynbridgepark.org).
Subway A, C to High Street; F to
York Street.*

The views of Manhattan from this
still-evolving riverside strip are spectacular. Brooklyn Bridge Park has
been undergoing a rolling redesign
that includes lawns, freshwater gardens, a water fowl-attracting salt
marsh and the Granite Prospect, a set
of stairs fashioned from salvaged
granite facing downtown's skyline.
There's also an open-air wine bar and
cult food carts. The restored merry-
go-round known as Jane's Carousel
(www.janescarousel.org) made its
long-awaited debut in a Jean Nouvel-
designed pavilion in autumn 2011.

Brooklyn Museum

*200 Eastern Parkway, at Washington
Avenue, Prospect Heights (1-718 638
5000, www.brooklynmuseum.org).
Subway 2, 3 to Eastern Parkway-
Brooklyn Museum.* **Open** 11am-6pm
Wed, Fri-Sun; 11am-10pm Thur; 11am-
11pm 1st Sat of mth (except Sept).
Admission suggested donation $12;
free-$8 reductions; free 5-11pm 1st Sat
of mth (except Sept).

Three bridges, not too far

Gantry Plaza State Park

Now that Manhattanites think nothing of crossing the river for a night out in Brooklyn or Queens, these boroughs no longer seem so far out. Walk over a bridge to one of these essential destinations – or take the subway if you must.

Brooklyn Bridge > Dumbo

Its waterside warehouses were colonised by artists seeking cheap live/work spaces, but Dumbo (Down Under the Manhattan Bridge Overpass) is now bursting with million-dollar apartments. After taking in the skyline panorama in **Brooklyn Bridge Park** (see left), head east on Water or Front Streets to discover the forgotten neighbourhood of Vinegar Hill. Among the row houses is cosy seasonal eaterie **Vinegar Hill House** (72 Hudson Avenue, between Front & Water Streets, 1-718 522 1018, www.vinegarhill house.com). After dinner, catch a cabaret show or concert at **Galapagos Art Space** (16 Main Street, at Water Street, 1-718 222 8500,www.galapagosartspace.com).

Ed Koch Queensboro Bridge > Long Island City

In this evolving Queens 'hood, a short walk takes you from desolate industrial streetscapes to the urban riviera created by gleaming high-rises fronting waterside **Gantry Plaza State Park**. Once you've perused contemporary art at **MoMA PS1** (see p165), grab a bite at the museum's hot new eaterie **M Well's Dinette**, then get an eyeful of **5Pointz Aerosol Art Center**, (www.5ptz.com), an old warehouse across the street covered in vivid graffiti murals. Afterwords, sip classic cocktails at Sasha Petroske's vintage saloon, **Dutch Kills** (27-24 Jackson Avenue, at Dutch Kills, 1-718 383 2724, www.dutchkillsbar.com).

Williamsburg Bridge > Williamsburg

The semi-industrial Brooklyn hub attracts coolhunters from all over the city. Snag a table at **Isa** (348 Wythe Avenue, at South 2nd Street, 1-347 689 3594, www.isa.gg), the latest venture from tastemaker Taavo Somer, or combine dinner and a movie at theatre-cum-restaurant **Nitehawk Cinema** (136 Metropolitan Avenue, between Berry Street & Wythe Avenue, 1-718 384 3980, www.nitehawkcinema.com). The 'Burg is also the place to catch a gig – check who's playing at **Music Hall of Williamsburg** (66 North 6th Street, between Kent & Wythe Avenues, 1-718 486 5400, www.musichallofwilliamsburg.com).

Among the many assets of Brooklyn's premier institution is the third-floor Egyptian galleries. Highlights include the Mummy Chamber, an installation of 170 objects related to the post-mortem practice, including human and animal mummies. Also on this level, works by Cézanne, Monet and Degas, part of an impressive European art collection, are displayed in the museum's skylighted Beaux-Arts Court. The Elizabeth A Sackler Center for Feminist Art on the fourth floor is dominated by Judy Chicago's monumental mixed-media installation, *The Dinner Party*; its centrepiece is a massive, triangular 'table' with 39 place settings, each representing important women down the ages. The fifth floor is mainly devoted to American works, including Albert Bierstadt's immense *A Storm in the Rocky Mountains, Mt Rosalie*, and the Visible Storage-Study Center, where paintings, furniture and other objects are intriguingly juxtaposed. **Event highlights** John Singer Sargent Watercolors (5 Apr-28 July 2013).

Green-Wood Cemetery

Fifth Avenue, at 25th Street, Sunset Park (1-718 768 7300, www.green-wood.com). Subway M, R to 25th Street. **Open** varies by season; usually 8am-5pm daily. **Admission** free.
Filled with Victorian mausoleums, cherubs and gargoyles, Green-Wood is the resting place of some half-million New Yorkers, among them Jean-Michel Basquiat, Leonard Bernstein, Boss Tweed and Horace Greeley. Battle Hill, the highest point in Brooklyn offering prime Manhattan skyline views, is on cemetery grounds.

New York Aquarium

610 Surf Avenue, at West 8th Street (1-718 265 3474, www.nyaquarium.com). Subway D, N, Q to Coney Island-Stillwell Avenue; F, Q to W 8th Street-NY Aquarium. **Open** *Sept, Oct, Apr, May* 10am-5pm Mon-Fri; 10am-5.30pm Sat, Sun. *Nov-Mar* 10am-4.30pm daily.

June-Aug 10am-6pm Mon-Fri; 10am-7pm Sat, Sun. **Admission** $15; free-$12 reductions.
Like much of Coney Island, this aquarium has seen better times, but it's sprucing itself up with new exhibits including Glovers Reef, a 150,000-gallon tank simulating the famed tropical ecosystem of Belize, and Alien Stingers, an impressive indoor jellyfish display. Among the aquarium's most beloved inhabitants are its walruses and sea lions.

New York Transit Museum

Corner of Boerum Place & Schermerhorn Street, Brooklyn Heights (1-718 694 1600, www.mta.info/mta/museum). Subway A, C, G to Hoyt-Schermerhorn; 2, 3, 4, 5 to Borough Hall. **Open** 10am-4pm Tue-Fri; 11am-5pm Sat, Sun. **Admission** $7; free-$5 reductions.
Located in a historic 1936 IND subway station, this is the largest museum in the United States devoted to urban public transport history. Exhibits explore the social and practical impact of public transport on the development of greater New York; among the highlights is an engrossing walkthrough display charting the construction of the city's century-old subway system. A line-up of turnstyles shows their evolution from the 1894 'ticket chopper' to the current Automatic Fare Card model. But the best part is down another level to a real platform where you can board an exceptional collection of vintage subway and El ('Elevated') cars.

Queens

Sights & museums

MoMA PS1

22-25 Jackson Avenue, at 46th Avenue, Long Island City (1-718 784 2084, www.momaps1.org). Subway E, M to Court Square -23rd Street; G to 21st Street-Jackson Avenue; 7 to 45th Road-Court House Square. **Open** noon-6pm Mon, Thur-Sun. **Admission** suggested donation $10; $5 reductions.

Housed in a distinctive Romanesque Revival former public school, MoMA PS1 mounts cutting-edge shows and hosts an acclaimed international studio programme. The contemporary art centre became an affiliate of MoMA in 1999, and the two institutions sometimes stage collaborative exhibitions. The museum's DJed summer Warm Up parties are an unmissable fixture of the city's dance-music scene, and as this guide went to press, M Wells Dinette, an offshoot of the shuttered cult Queens eaterie M Wells Diner, was poised to open.

Exhibition highlights Now Dig This! Art and Black Los Angeles 1960-1980 (Oct 2012-Feb 2013).

Museum of the Moving Image

35th Avenue, at 36th Street, Astoria (1-718 777 6888, www.movingimage.us). Subway M, R to Steinway Street; N, Q to 36th Avenue. **Open** *Galleries* 10.30am-5pm Tue-Thur; 10.30am-8pm Fri; 10.30am-7pm Sat, Sun. **Admission** $12; free-$9 reductions; free 4-8pm Fri. No pushchairs/strollers.

In January 2011, the Museum of the Moving Image reopened after a major renovation that doubled its size and made it one of the foremost museums in the world dedicated to TV, film and video. The collection and state-of-the-art screening facilities are housed in the Astoria Studios complex, which was once the New York production head-quarters of Paramount Pictures. Architect Thomas Leeser's sleek new design integrates moving pictures into the space itself. As visitors pass through the mirrored, screen-like entrance into the lobby, they'll encounter a panoramic video installation of constantly changing work. The upgraded core exhibition, 'Behind the Screen', on the second and third floors, contains artefacts from more than 1,000 productions (including the super creepy stunt doll used in *The Exorcist*, with full head-rotating capabilities, and the famous diner booth from *Seinfeld*) and interactive displays.

Noguchi Museum

9-01 33rd Road, between Vernon Boulevard & 10th Street, Long Island City (1-718 204 7088, www.noguchi.org). Subway N, Q to Broadway, then Q104 bus to 11th Street; 7 to Vernon Boulevard-Jackson Avenue, then Q103 bus to 10th Street. **Open** 10am-5pm Wed-Fri; 11am-6pm Sat, Sun. **Admission** $10; free-$5 reductions; pay what you wish 1st Fri of mth. No pushchairs/strollers.

Created by Japanese-American sculptor Isamu Noguchi (1904-88), this museum is a monument to the artist's harmonious sensibility. The building was designed, inside and out, by Noguchi as a meditative oasis carved from its gritty, industrial setting – it occupies a former photo-engraving plant that was across the street from his studio. Galleries and a garden are populated by Noguchi's sculptures, as well as painted and collaged studies, architectural models, and stage and furniture designs.

Queens Museum of Art

New York City Building, park entrance on 49th Avenue, at 111th Street, Flushing Meadows-Corona Park (1-718 592 9700, www.queensmuseum.org). Subway 7 to 111th Street, then walk south on 111th Street, turning left on to 49th Avenue; continue into the park and over Grand Central Parkway Bridge. **Open** noon-6pm Wed-Sun. **Admission** suggested donation $5; $2.50 reductions.

Housed in a building constructed for the 1939 World's Fair (and which hosted the United Nations for four years after its founding in 1946), the Queens Museum of Art holds one of the city's most curious sights: the Panorama of the City of New York, a 9,335sq ft scale model of all five boroughs, featuring 895,000 buildings. An expansion project to double the museum's size will provide more space for changing exhibitions when completed by the end of 2013.

Essentials

Dream Downtown p179

Hotels

Accommodation is more expensive in New York City than in the rest of the country and, while the average room rate dipped sharply in the wake of the financial crisis to under $200 a night, reports suggest it has been creeping up steadily since then. New construction has continued, albeit more slowly, throughout the recent economic slump, and, according to the city's official tourist authority hotel occupancy figures are strong. The city now has more than 90,000 hotel rooms, representing a 24 per cent increase over the past five years. But whether this will create a surplus that will benefit bargain-hunting travellers is anyone's guess.

Hotel hotspots

Growth areas include the Financial District, which is getting a new lease of life as the World Trade Center site redevelopment nears completion. Upscale chain **W Hotels** (www.starwoodhotels.com/whotels) opened a flashy new property directly opposite the WTC, and the stylish Hyatt offshoot **Andaz Wall Street** (see right) is anything but corporate. Recently, Hilton's **Conrad Hotel** debuted in Battery Park City (see p171). As condos rise in Hell's Kitchen, hotel development isn't far behind. The British team behind capsule hotel brand **Yotel** (see p181) introduced a super-size variation on the concept here in 2011, and the city's first gay resort, the **Out NYC** (see p181), recently arrived in the hot 'gaybourhood'. The long-awaited **NoMad Hotel** (see p180) opened in spring 2012 on the northern fringes of the Flatiron District, joining undisputed hipster hub the **Ace** (see p179) and signalling a revival in this run-down patch.

There is now more boutique choice in desirable areas like Soho, Nolita and Chelsea, with the arrival of the **James** (see p173), **The Nolitan** (see p174) and **Hôtel Americano** (see p179). It's also worth looking across the river for competitively priced accommodation (see box p178).

Prices & information

Rates can vary wildly according to room type and season, and those quoted here reflect that disparity. Unless indicated, prices are for a double room, from the cheapest in low season to the most expensive in high season. Of course, they're not guaranteed, but they offer a good indication of the hotel's average rack rates – what you would pay if you walked in off the street and asked for a room. Special deals are often available, especially if you book on the hotel's website. When budgeting, don't forget to factor in the hefty 14.75 per cent tax – which includes city, state and hotel-room occupancy tax – plus an extra $3.50 per night for most rooms.

Downtown

Financial District

Andaz Wall Street

75 Wall Street, at Water Street (1-212 590 1234, www.wallstreetandaz.com). Subway 2, 3, 4, 5 to Wall Street. **$$$**.
The New York outpost of this Hyatt subsidiary occupies the first 13 floors of a former Barclays Bank building. Inside, the vibe is anything but corporate: upon entering the spacious bamboo-panelled lobby-lounge, you're greeted by a free-range 'host', who acts as a combination check-in clerk and concierge. Chic, loft-style rooms are equally casual and user-friendly. The restaurant (Wall & Water), bar and spa are welcome attributes in an area with little action at weekends.

ESSENTIALS

Conrad New York

NEW *102 North End Avenue, at Vesey Street (1-212 945 0100, www.conrad newyork.com). Subway A, C to Chambers Street; 1, 2, 3 to Chambers Street; E to World Trade Center; R to Cortlandt Street; 2, 3 to Park Place.* $$$.
This sophisticated Hilton offshoot fronts Battery Park City's riverside Nelson A Rockefeller Park. West-facing rooms have views of the Hudson, but there's also plenty to see within the art-rich property. Sol LeWitt's vivid 100ft by 80ft painting *Loopy Doopy (Blue and Purple)* graces the dramatic 15-storey, glass-ceilinged, marble-floored lobby, and coolly understated guestrooms are adorned with pieces by the likes of Elizabeth Peyton and Mary Heilmann. Nespresso machines and marble bathrooms with Aromatherapy Associates are indulgent touches. Above the rooftop bar (open May-Oct), with views of the Statue of Liberty, is a vegetable patch providing fresh produce for the North End Grill (see p65) next door.

Tribeca & Soho

60 Thompson

60 Thompson Street, between Broome & Spring Streets (1-212 431 0400, 1-877 431 0400, www.60thompson.com). Subway C, E to Spring Street. $$$$.
An expansive, somewhat masculine second-floor lobby sets the tone for the rooms here, from the modest doubles to the spectacular duplex. A60, the exclusive guests-only rooftop bar with magnificent city views and Moroccan-inspired decor, is equally photogenic. The modern rooms are dotted with indulgent details such as pure down duvets and pillows, and Kiehl's products. The hotel's acclaimed restaurant, Kittichai, serves creative Thai cuisine.

Cosmopolitan

95 West Broadway, at Chambers Street (1-212 566 1900, 1-888 895 9400, www.cosmohotel.com). Subway A, C, 1, 2, 3 to Chambers Street. $$.

Despite the name, you won't find the legendary pink cocktail at this well-maintained hotel in two adjacent 1850s buildings, let alone a bar in which to drink it, though there is a café. Open continuously since the mid 19th century, the hotel remains a tourist favourite for its address, clean rooms and reasonable rates. A wide range of configurations is available, including a suite for families and – the best bargain – three cosy, bi-level, loft-style rooms.

Crosby Street Hotel

79 Crosby Street, between Prince & Spring Streets (1-212 226 6400, www.crosbystreethotel.com). Subway N, R to Prince Street; 6 to Spring Street. $$$$.
In 2009, Britain's hospitality power couple, Tim and Kit Kemp, brought their super-successful Firmdale formula across the Atlantic with the warehouse-style Crosby Street Hotel. Design director Kit's signature style – a fresh, contemporary take on classic English decor characterised by an oft-audacious mix of patterns, bold colours and judiciously chosen antiques – is instantly recognisable. There's a carefully selected, and predominantly British, art collection. Other Firmdale imports include a guests-only drawing room as well as a public restaurant and bar, a slick, 100-seat screening room and a verdant garden.

Greenwich Hotel

377 Greenwich Street, between Franklin & North Moore Streets (1-212 941 8900, www.thegreenwichhotel.com). Subway 1 to Franklin Street. $$$$.
'Deluxe guesthouse' might be a more fitting description of Robert De Niro's property, which has the vibe of a large villa located somewhere between Marrakech and Milan. Rooms are spare and comfortable, appointed with down-filled leather settees, kilims and oriental rugs, and small libraries of art books. Exquisite Moroccan tile or carrara marble envelops the bathrooms, while the main spaces feature wood-plank floors.

Many rooms overlook the charming courtyard. The centrepiece of the sub-terranean Eastern-inspired Shibui Spa is the low-lit pool, set within the frame of a 250-year-old Kyoto farmhouse.

James New York

27 Grand Street, at Thompson Street (1-212 465 2000, 1-888 526 3778, www.jameshotels.com). Subway A, C, E to Canal Street. **$$$**.

Hotel art displays are usually limited to eye-catching lobby installations or forgettable in-room prints. Not so at the James, which maintains a substantial showcase of local talent. The corridor of each guest floor is dedicated to the work of an individual artist, selected by a house curator and complete with museum-style notes. Although compact, bedrooms make the most of the available space with high ceilings and wall-spanning windows. Natural materials warm up the clean contemporary lines and bathroom products are courtesy of Intelligent Nutrients. While the attractions of Soho and Tribeca beckon, the hotel also offers tempting facilities: a three-level 'urban garden', which houses an outdoor bar and eatery, plus a rooftop bar, Jimmy, that opens on to the (admittedly tiny) pool.

Mercer

147 Mercer Street, at Prince Street (1-212 966 6060, 1-888 918 6060, www.mercerhotel.com). Subway N, R to Prince Street. **$$$$**.

Opened in 2001 by trendsetting hotelier André Balazs, the Mercer still has ample attractions that appeal to a celeb-heavy clientele. The lobby, with oversized white couches and chairs, and shelves lined with colourful books, acts as a bar, library and lounge – which is exclusive to hotel guests. Loft-like rooms are large by New York standards and feature furniture by Christian Liaigre. The restaurant, Mercer Kitchen, serves Jean-Georges Vongerichten's stylish version of casual American cuisine.

Chinatown, Little Italy & Nolita

Bowery House

[NEW] *220 Bowery, between Prince & Spring Streets (1-212 837 2373, www.theboweryhouse.com). Subway J, Z to Bowery.* **$**.

Two young real-estate developers transformed a 1927 Bowery flophouse into this stylish take on a hostel. History buffs will get a kick out of the original wainscotted corridors leading to cubicles (singles are a cosy 35sq ft and not all have windows) with lattice-work ceilings to allow air circulation. It might not be the best bet for light sleepers, but the place is hopping with pretty young things attracted to the hip aesthetic and the location (across the street from the New Museum and close to Soho and the Lower East Side). Quarters are decorated with vintage prints and historical photographs, and towels and robes are courtesy of Ralph Lauren. The (gender-segregated) communal bathrooms have rain shower-heads and products from local spa Red Flower, while the guest lounge is outfitted with chesterfield sofas, a huge LCD TV and an assortment of international style mags.

Sohotel

341 Broome Street, between Bowery & Elizabeth Street (1-212 226 1482, www.thesohotel.com). Subway J, Z to Bowery; 6 to Spring Street. **$$**.

Thanks to new exterior coloured-light effects, this formerly modest hotel at the nexus of Chinatown, Little Italy and Nolita piques the curiosity of passers-by. A recent overhaul, including a coat of chartreuse paint, flatscreen TVs and exposed-brick walls, has given the small rooms a quirky punch. Touches such as ceiling fans, hardwood floors, skylights and vaulted ceilings place the Sohotel a rung above similarly priced establishments. The many Regency Plus rooms ($199-$350), which can accommodate four to five guests, are the best bargain.

ESSENTIALS

Nolitan

NEW *30 Kenmare Street, at Elizabeth Street (1-212 925 2555, www.nolitanhotel.com). Subway J, Z to Bowery; 6 to Spring Street.* **$$$.**

The 55 airy rooms of this boutique hotel feature floor-to-ceiling windows, custom-made walnut beds, wooden floors and toiletries from Prince Street spa Red Flower. The emphasis on keeping it local is reflected in numerous guest perks: the luxuriously laid-back property lends out bikes and lays on free local calls and discounts at neighbourhood boutiques. The lobby's ceiling-height bookshelf is stocked with tomes from nearby Phaidon Books. Admire views of Nolita and beyond from the 2,400sq ft roof deck, complete with fire pit, or your private perch – more than half the guest quarters have balconies. Standard checkout is 2pm.

Lower East Side

Hotel on Rivington

107 Rivington Street, between Essex & Ludlow Streets (1-212 475 2600, www.hotelonrivington.com). Subway F to Delancey Street; J, Z to Delancey-Essex Streets. **$$$.**

When the Hotel on Rivington opened in 2005, its ultra-modern glass-covered façade was a novelty on the largely low-rise Lower East Side. Now, with condos popping up everywhere, the building seems less out of place, but it remains one of the few luxury hotels in the neighbourhood. Rooms are super-sleek, with black and white decorative touches, including velvet-covered lounge chairs, and floor-to-ceiling windows. A stylish crowd congregates in the hotel's two new restaurants, Coop Food & Drink, which serves sushi alongside modern American fare, and Viktor & Spoils, a contemporary taqueria and tequila bar.

Off Soho Suites Hotel

11 Rivington Street, between Bowery & Chrystie Street (1-212 979 9815, 1-800 633 7646, www.offsoho.com). Subway B,

D to Grand Street; F to Lower East Side-Second Avenue; J, Z to Bowery. **$$.**

These no-frills suites have become a lot more popular since the Lower East Side emerged as a nightlife hotspot. The rates are decent value for the now-thriving location, and the spartan but spacious rooms can accommodate either two or four guests.

East Village

Bowery Hotel

335 Bowery, at 3rd Street (1-212 505 9100, www.theboweryhotel.com). Subway B, D, F, M to Broadway-Lafayette Street; 6 to Bleecker Street. **$$$$.**

This fanciful boutique hotel from prominent duo Eric Goode and Sean MacPherson is the capstone in the gentrification of the Bowery. Shunning minimalism, they have created plush rooms that pair old-world touches (oriental rugs, wood-beamed ceilings, marble washstands) with modern amenities (flatscreen TVs, Wi-Fi).

East Village Bed & Coffee

110 Avenue C, between 7th & 8th Streets (1-917 816 0071, www.bedandcoffee.com). Subway F to Lower East Side-Second Avenue; L to First Avenue. **$.**

This East Village B&B (minus the breakfast) embodies quirky Downtown culture. Each of the guest rooms has a unique theme: for example, the 'Black and White Room' or the 'Treehouse' (with an ivory and olive colour scheme, animal-print linens and a whitewashed brick wall). Owner Anne Edris encourages guests to mingle in the communal areas, and when the weather's nice, sip your complimentary morning java in the private garden.

Hotel 17

225 E 17th Street, between Second & Third Avenues (1-212 475 2845, www.hotel17ny.com). Subway L to Third Avenue; L, N, Q, R, 4, 5, 6 to 14th Street-Union Square. **$.**

NYC's new nabe?

Two hip hotels are redefining a nondescript patch.

For years, a nameless, run-down corner just north of the Flatiron District has been characterised by cheap perfume and luggage stores. But the long-anticipated opening of the **NoMad Hotel** (see p180) in spring 2012 – a block south of hipster hub the **Ace Hotel** (see p179) – heralds what may emerge as a bona fide 'hood: North of Madison Square Park.

Both properties, which share a developer, are self-contained microcosms encompassing destination dining spots and cult retail. While the Ace's eateries were devised by smoking-hot duo April Bloomfield and Ken Friedman, the NoMad has its own food-and-beverage dream team, Daniel Humm and Will Guidara, of Michelin-three-starred Eleven Madison Park. Just as the Ace bagged a branch of NYC-fashion-insider favorite Opening Ceremony as its in-house boutique, NoMad scored the first stateside outpost of Parisian concept store Maison Kitsuné. But while the Ace has a raucous bohemian vibe fostered by its eclectic vintage-industrial decor and music-industry links, the refined NoMad evokes a traditional grand hotel crossed with a chic Parisian apartment.

Struck by the Haussmannesque facade of the 1903 limestone building (a former corporate HQ), owner Andrew Zobler enlisted Jacques Garcia, known for designing celebrated rue Saint-Honoré A-list crash pad Hôtel Costes, to create the opulent interiors. Original features in the public spaces, such as elaborate

NoMad Hotel

ceiling moldings and mosaic-tile floors, have been meticulously restored. After seeing a photograph in a design book of Garcia's old Paris flat, Zobler encouraged him to bring the same lived-in bohemian style to the hotel's guest quarters. Vintage Heriz rugs soften the weathered maple floor, salvaged from a 1905 factory, and in keeping with the residential aesthetic, the wall concealing the loo and shower cubicle is dressed up as a damask 'screen'. Many rooms feature old-fashioned claw-foot bathtubs, and the exclusive argan-oil products were supplied by provençal perfumer Côté Bastide. Each room has its own travel-themed art collection, amassed from French antique shops.

With two coolhunter magnets on this shabby stretch of Broadway, perhaps the NoMad nabe designation will finally stick.

Shabby chic is the best way to describe this hotel a few blocks from Union Square. Rooms are a study in contrast: antique dressers are paired with paisley bedspreads and vintage wallpaper. In most cases, bathrooms are shared, but they're kept immaculately clean. Over the years, the building has been featured in numerous films – including Woody Allen's *Manhattan Murder Mystery* – and has put up Madonna and, more recently, transgender Downtown diva Amanda Lepore.

Greenwich Village

Washington Square Hotel

103 Waverly Place, between MacDougal Street & Sixth Avenue (1-212 777 9515, 1-800 222 0418, www.washington squarehotel.com). Subway A, B, C, D, E, F, M to W 4th Street. **$$**.
A haven for writers and artists for decades, the Washington Square Hotel is suited to those seeking a quiet refuge in this historic neighbourhood. After a hotel-wide redecoration, rooms are done up with spare art deco furnishings and an odd but pleasant colour scheme of mauve and olive. The North Square restaurant and lounge – an unsung secret with an eclectic menu – is popular with locals and NYU profs. Rates include continental breakfast. Get a south-facing room for a glimpse of the park.

West Village & Meatpacking District

Gansevoort Meatpacking NYC

18 Ninth Avenue, at 13th Street (1-212 206 6700, 1-877 426 7386, www.hotel gansevoort.com). Subway A, C, E to 14th Street; L to Eighth Avenue. **$$$**.
The Gansevoort has made a name for itself as a coolhunters' hub. The lobby features four 18ft light boxes that change colour throughout the evening, while simple but elegant rooms offer a more muted colour scheme. Their real draw is floor-to-ceiling windows with incredible views, although, unfortunately, the glass is not quite thick enough to keep out noise from the street. But the mini-balconies, plush feather beds and Cutler toiletries counterbalance this minor gripe. A visit to the roof is a must: the garden has a heated pool (with underwater music) that is enclosed in winter, a bar (Plunge) and, of course, a 360-degree panorama.

Jane

113 Jane Street, at West Street (1-212 924 6700, www.thejanenyc.com). Subway A, C, E to 14th Street; L to Eighth Avenue. **$-$$**.
Opened in 1907 as the American Seaman's Friend Society Sailors Home, the 14-storey landmark was a residential hotel when hoteliers Eric Goode and Sean MacPherson took it over. The wood-panelled, 50sq ft rooms were inspired by vintage train sleeper compartments – there's a single bed with built-in storage and brass hooks for hanging up your clothes, but also iPod docks and wall-mounted flatscreen TVs. If entering the hotel feels like stepping on to a film set, there's good reason. Inspiration came from various celluloid sources, including *Barton Fink*'s Hotel Earle for the lobby.

Standard

848 Washington Street, at 13th Street (1-212 645 4646, www.standard hotels.com). Subway A, C, E to 14th Street; L to Eighth Avenue. **$$$**.
André Balazs's lauded West Coast minichain arrived in New York in 2009. Straddling the High Line, the retro 18-storey structure has been configured to give each room an exhilarating view, either of the river or a Midtown cityscape. Quarters are compact (from 230sq ft) but the combination of floor-to-ceiling windows, curving tambour wood panelling and 'peekaboo' bathrooms (with Japanese-style tubs or huge showerheads) give a sense of space.

Borough bargains

You'll get more bang for your buck in Brooklyn or Queens.

Z NYC Hotel

Although the growing attractions of Brooklyn and Queens have been luring visitors for several years, until more recently the outer boroughs haven't been seen as a base for tourists. Yet as ever-rising rents push young creative types out of Manhattan, visitors in search of New York's bohemian spirit may find it – not to mention better deals – off-island.

In Brooklyn, Williamsburg and Bushwick have adventurous music and art scenes, and some of the city's best restaurants and bars, while the overlapping neighbourhoods of Boerum Hill, Cobble Hill and Carroll Gardens (BoCoCa) are great for dining and shopping. In Queens, Long Island City is an evolving art destination with a rising number of hip watering holes. Supply is keeping up with demand: since 2008, more than 40 per cent of new hotel development has been outside Manhattan.

Now that apartments in Brooklyn's prime neighbourhoods are fetching millions of dollars,

it was inevitable that boutique hotels would follow. Williamsburg now has two: **King & Grove Williamsburg** (160 N 12th Street, between Bedford Avenue & Berry Street, 1-718 218 7500, www.kingandgrove.com), which launched as Hotel Williamsburg in fall 2011, has a 40-foot outdoor pool serviced by a cocktail bar, while the **Wythe Hotel** (80 Wythe Avenue, at N 11th Street, 1-718 460 8000, www.wythehotel.com), which opened in a former textile factory in spring 2012, houses an onsite eaterie from the team behind popular local spots Marlow & Sons and Diner. Boerum Hill's **Nu Hotel** (85 Smith Street, between Atlantic Avenue & State Street, 1-718 852 8585, www.nuhotelbrooklyn.com) is near Smith Street's many restaurants and the shops of Atlantic Avenue, and those who want to experience loft living in Bushwick's cutting-edge art enclave should check into the **New York Loft Hostel** (249 Varet Street, at Borgart Street, 1-718 366 1351, www.nylofthostel.com).

Visitors to Long Island City in Queens are discovering that rooms here offer something Manhattan properties can never have: a million-dollar view of the skyline from the other side of the East River. Although its industrial surroundings are somewhat desolate, the 11-storey **Z NYC Hotel** (11-01 43rd Avenue, at 11th Street, 1-212 319 7000, www.zhotelny.com) was designed so that each of the 100 rooms face the river.

ESSENTIALS

Eating and drinking options include a chop house, beer garden and an exclusive top-floor bar with a massive jacuzzi.

Midtown

Chelsea

Dream Downtown

NEW *355 W 16th Street, between Eighth & Ninth Avenues (1-212 229 2559, www.dreamdowntown.com). Subway A, C, E to 14th Street; L to Eighth Avenue.* **$$$**.

Be sure to pack your totem: staying at the latest property from hotel wunderkind Vikram Chatwal may make you wonder if you're in a dream within a Dream. The expansive, tree-shaded lobby, furnished with curvy, metallic-lizard banquettes, and presided over by a DJ nightly, provides an overhead view of swimmers doing laps in the glass-bottomed pool on the terrace above. Housed in the former annex of the New York Maritime Union (now the adjacent Maritime Hotel, see right), the surreal building is riddled with round windows. In the upper-floor rooms, these frame elements of the Manhattan skyline, such as the Empire State Building, in intriguing ways. Quarters combine classic elements (white chesterfield chairs or sofas, Tivoli radios, Turkish rugs) with futuristic touches like shiny steel bathtubs in some rooms.

Hôtel Americano

NEW *518 W 27th Street, between Tenth & Eleventh Avenues (1-212 216 0000, www.hotel-americano.com). Subway C, E to 23rd Street.* **$$$**.

You won't find any Talavera tiles in Grupo Habita's first property outside Mexico. Mexican architect Enrique Norten's sleek, mesh-encased structure stands alongside the High Line. Decor evokes classic mid-century American style, interpreted by a European (Colette designer Arnaud Montigny). The minimalist rooms have Japanese-style platform beds, iPads and, in one of several subtle nods to US culture, super-soft denim bathrobes. After a day of gallery-hopping, get an elevated view of the neighbourhood from the rooftop bar and grill, where a petite pool does double duty as a hot tub in winter.

Inn on 23rd

131 W 23rd Street, between Sixth & Seventh Avenues (1-212 463 0330, www.innon23rd.com). Subway F, M, 1 to 23rd Street. **$$**.

This renovated 19th-century townhouse offers the charm of a traditional bed and breakfast with enhanced amenities (a lift, pillow-top mattresses, private bathrooms, white-noise machines). Owners Annette and Barry Fisherman have styled each bedroom with a unique theme, such as Maritime, Bamboo and 1940s. One of the Inn's best attributes is the 'library', a cosy jumble of tables and chairs that's open 24/7 to guests for coffee and tea.

Maritime Hotel

363 W 16th Street, between Eighth & Ninth Avenues (1-212 242 4300, www. themaritimehotel.com). Subway A, C, E to 14th Street; L to Eighth Avenue. **$$$**.

Once the headquarters of the New York Maritime Union, this nautically themed hotel is outfitted with self-consciously hip details befitting a Wes Anderson film. Standard rooms are modelled on cruise cabins, lined with teak panelling and sporting a single porthole window. The hotel's busy Italian restaurant, La Bottega, also supplies room service, and the adjoining bar hosts a crowd of models and mortals, who throng the umbrella-lined patio in warmer weather. In the basement, Matsuri offers sushi, Japanese tapas and saké.

Flatiron District & Union Square

Ace Hotel

20 W 29th Street, at Broadway (1-212 679 2222, www.acehotel.com). Subway N, R to 28th Street. **$$-$$$**.

ESSENTIALS

Bourgeois hipsters tired of crashing on couches will appreciate the New York outpost of the cool chainlet founded in Seattle by a pair of DJs. The music influence is clear: many rooms in the 1904 building have playful amenities such as functioning turntables, stacks of vinyl and gleaming Gibson guitars. And while you'll pay for the sprawling loft spaces, there are options for those on a lower budget. The respectable 'medium' rooms have vintage furniture and original art; even cheaper are the snug bunk-bed set-ups. See also box p175.

NoMad Hotel

NEW *1170 Broadway, at 28th Street (212-796-1500, www.thenomadhotel.com). Subway N, R to 28th Street.* **$$$**.
See box p175.

Gershwin Hotel

7 E 27th Street, between Fifth & Madison Avenues (1-212 545 8000, www.gershwinhotel.com). Subway N, R, 6 to 28th Street. **$**.
Works by Lichtenstein line the hallways, and an original Warhol soup can painting hangs in the lobby of this Pop Art-themed budget hotel. Rooms are less than luxurious – especially the hostel-style dorms – but the rates are extremely reasonable for its location.

Gramercy Park & Murray Hill

Carlton Arms Hotel

160 E 25th Street, at Third Avenue (1-212 679 0680, www.carltonarms.com). Subway 6 to 23rd Street. **$**.
The Carlton Arms Art Project started in the late 1970s, when a small group of creative types brought fresh paint and new ideas to a run-down shelter. Today, the site is a bohemian backpackers' paradise and a live-in gallery, festooned with outré artwork. Themed quarters include the Money Room and a tribute to a traditional English cottage. Roughly half of the quarters have shared bathrooms. Reserve well in advance.

Gramercy Park Hotel

2 Lexington Avenue, at 21st Street (1-212 920 3300, 1-866 784 1300, www.gramercyparkhotel.com). Subway 6 to 23rd Street. **$$$$**.
Ian Schrager revamped this 1924 gem in 2006, but the reworked lobby retains the boho spirit with stuccoed walls, red banquettes, an enormous Venetian chandelier and art from Cy Twombly and Andy Warhol, among others. The eclectic elegance continues in the spacious rooms, which include tapestry-covered chairs and a Pre-Raphaelite colour scheme. Guests can lounge on the roof deck or sip cocktails at the Julian Schnabel-designed Rose and Jade bars. Danny Meyer's trattoria, Maialino, adds to the attractions, but the best amenity is a free key to Gramercy Park – one of the most exclusive outdoor spaces in the city.

Morgans

237 Madison Avenue, between 37th & 38th Streets (1-212 686 0300, 1-800 697 1791, www.morganshotelgroup. com). Subway S, 4, 5, 6, 7 to 42nd Street-Grand Central. **$$$**.
New York's original boutique hotel, Morgans opened in 1984. Some 25 years later, the hotel's original designer, Andrée Putnam, returned to officiate over a revamp that has softened its stark monochrome appearance. The boxy 1930s-inspired lobby now features a hypnotic coloured-light ceiling installation and unfussy bedrooms are cast in a calming palette of silver, grey, cream and white, and hung with original Robert Mapplethorpe prints.

Theater District & Hell's Kitchen

414 Hotel

414 W 46th Street, between Ninth & Tenth Avenues (1-212 399 0006, www. 414hotel.com). Subway A, C, E to 42nd Street-Port Authority. **$$**.
This is one hotel that truly deserves to be described as 'boutique'. Nearly everything about it is exquisite yet unshowy,

from its power-blasted brick exterior to the modern colour scheme in the rooms that pairs grey and brown furnishings with pale walls and white bedding. Bathrooms are immaculate. 414 is twice as big as it looks, as it consists of two townhouses separated by a leafy courtyard, which in warmer months is a lovely place to sip a glass of wine or eat your complimentary breakfast.

Chatwal New York

130 W 44th Street, between Sixth Avenue & Broadway (1-212 764 6200, www.the chatwalny.com). Subway N, Q, R, S, 1, 2, 3 to 42nd Street-Time Square. $$$$.
Hotelier Sant Chatwal entrusted the design of this 1905 Stanford White building (formerly the clubhouse for the Lamb's Club, America's first professional theatre organisation) to Thierry Despont, who worked on the centennial restoration of the Statue of Liberty. The lobby is adorned with murals recalling the hotel's New York roots and theatrical pedigree – members have included Charlie Chaplin and Fred Astaire. The elegant rooms feature vintage Broadway posters as well as hand-tufted Shifman mattresses, 400-thread count Frette linens and custom Asprey toiletries; select quarters have spacious terraces.

The Out NYC

NEW *512 W 42nd Street, between Tenth & Eleventh Avenues (212-947-2999, www.theoutnyc.com). Subway A, C, E to 42nd Street-Port Authority. $-$$.*
Homo hot spot Hell's Kitchen is the location of New York's first specifically gay (but 'straight-friendly') luxury hotel. Built in the husk of a 1960s motel, the sprawling all-in-one playground also houses XL, a club operated by nightlife bigwigs John Blair and FV Events' Tony Fornabaio and Brandon Voss; a restaurant, Kitchin, with a late-night menu; plus a gym. The hotel is designed around three courtyards, including the faux-ivy-lined sundeck, which leads to a glass-ceilinged area with two hot tubs. Despite a few style statements, the monochrome room decor is on the spare side. The 'sleep shares', with four curtained cubby-bunks reminiscent of sleeper compartments – upgraded with double beds and TVs – are a budget option for those who are travelling with a crowd or want to make new friends.

Yotel New York

NEW *570 Tenth Avenue, at 42nd Street (1-646 449 7700, www.yotel.com). Subway A, C, E to 42nd Street-Port Authority. $$.*
The British team behind this futuristic hotel is known for luxury airport-based capsule accommodations that give long-haul travellers just enough space to get horizontal between flights. Yotel New York has ditched the 75sq ft cubbies in favour of 'premium cabins' more than twice the size. Adaptable furnishings (such as motorised beds that fold up futon-style) maximise space, and the bathroom has streamlined luxuries such as a heated towel rail and monsoon shower. If you want to unload excess baggage, the 20ft tall robot (or Yobot, in the hotel's playful lingo) will stash it for you in a lobby locker. In contrast with the compact quarters, the sprawling public spaces include a wraparound terrace so large it's serviced by two bars.

Fifth Avenue & around

Plaza

768 Fifth Avenue, at Central Park South (1-212 759 3000, 1-888 850 0909, www.theplaza.com). Subway N, Q, R to Fifth Avenue-59th Street. $$$$.
This 1907 French Renaissance-style landmark building reopened in spring 2008 following a $400 million renovation. Although 152 rooms were converted into private condo units, guests can still check into one of 282 quarters complete with Louis XV-inspired furnishings and white-glove butler service. The opulent vibe extends to the bathrooms, which feature 24-carat gold-plated sink fittings and chandeliers.

Midtown East

Hotel Elysée

60 E 54th Street, between Madison & Park Avenues (1-212 753 1066, www.elysee hotel.com). Subway E, M to Lexington Avenue-53rd Street; 6 to 51st Street. **$$$**.
Since 1926, this discreet but opulent hotel has attracted luminaries. You may bump into one going from your antique-appointed room to the complimentary wine and cheese served every weekday evening in the second-floor lounge, or in the exclusive Monkey Bar (see p136), *Vanity Fair* editor Graydon Carter's restaurant that shares the building – a few tables are set aside for guests.

Pod Hotel

230 E 51st Street, at Third Avenue (1-212 355 0300, 1-800 742 5945, www.thepodhotel.com). Subway E, M to Lexington Avenue-53rd Street; 6 to 51st Street. **$**.
As its name suggests, the rooms in this minimalist bolthole are small-scale yet stylish. The 100sq ft single-bed 'pods' have nominal decor and under-bed dressers. There are also bunk-bed setups. At these levels, baths are shared; choose a roomier double or queen 'pod' if you want private facilities. The Pod Café, with both indoor and outdoor seating, serves inexpensive snacks from popular local purveyors including pastries from Balthazar Bakery and cheese and charcuterie from Murray's Cheese.

Uptown

Upper East Side

Surrey

20 E 76th Street, between Fifth & Madison Avenues (1-212 288 3700, 1-800 978 7739, www.thesurreyhotel. com). Subway 6 to 77th Street. **$$$$**.
The Surrey, in a solid pre-war Beaux Arts building given a $60 million overhaul, pitches at both traditionalists and the trend-driven. The coolly elegant limestone and marble lobby showcases

contemporary art, and rooms are dressed in a refined palette of cream, grey and beige, with luxurious white marble bathrooms. But the centrepiece is undoubtedly the incredibly comfortable DUX by Duxiana bed, swathed in luxurious Sferra linens. The hotel is flanked by top chef Daniel Boulud's Café Boulud and his chic cocktail destination, Bar Pleiades; there's also a five-room Darphin spa.

Upper West Side

On the Ave Hotel

2178 Broadway, at 77th Street (1-212 362 1100, 1-800 509 7598, www.onthe ave-nyc.com). Subway 1 to 79th Street. **$$**.
Given the affluent area, it's hardly surprising that On the Ave's rooms are stylish (industrial-style bathroom sinks, ergonomic Herman Miller chairs). On the upper floors, panoramic deluxe rooms and penthouse suites have fantastic private-balcony views of Central Park or the Hudson, but all guests have access to terraces on the 14th and 16th floors. The hotel houses the larger offshoot of Zak Pelaccio's Malaysian-inspired Meatpacking District eaterie, Fatty Crab.

Harlem

Harlem Flophouse

242 W 123rd Street, between Adam Clayton Powell Jr Boulevard (Seventh Avenue) & Frederick Douglass Boulevard (Eighth Avenue) (1-212 662 0678, www.harlemflophouse.com). Subway A, B, C, D to 125th Street. **$**.
The dark-wood interior, moody lighting and lilting jazz make musician Rene Calvo's Harlem inn feel more like a 1930s speakeasy than a 21st-century B&B. The airy suites, named for Harlem Renaissance figures such as Chester Himes and Cozy Cole, have restored tin ceilings, a quirky mix of junk-store furnishings and period knick-knacks, and working sinks in antique cabinets. There are just two suites per floor; each pair shares a bathroom.

Getting Around

Arriving and leaving

By air

John F Kennedy International Airport

1-718 244 4444, www.panynj.gov/ airports/jfk.html.

The subway (see below) is the cheapest option. The AirTrain ($5) links to the A train at Howard Beach or the E, J and Z trains at Sutphin Boulevard-Archer Avenue (www.airtrainjfk.com).

New York Airport Service (1-212 875 8200, www.nyairport service.com) buses run frequently to Manhattan ($15, round trip, available only, $25), with stops near Grand Central Terminal (Park Avenue, between 41st & 42nd Streets), near Penn Station (33rd Street, at Seventh Avenue), inside the Port Authority Bus Terminal (*see p184*) and outside a number of Midtown hotels (for an extra charge).

A **yellow cab** to Manhattan will charge a flat $52.50 fare, plus toll (usually $5) and tip (15 per cent is the norm). The fare to JFK from Manhattan is not a set rate, but is usually roughly the same (see p185 for taxi rates).

La Guardia Airport

1-718 533 3400, www.panynj.gov/ airports/laguardia.html.

Seasoned New Yorkers take the **M60 bus** ($2.25), which runs to 106th Street at Broadway. The ride takes 40-60mins and runs from 5am to 1am daily. The route crosses Manhattan at 125th Street in Harlem. Get off at Lexington Avenue for the 4, 5 and 6 trains; at Malcolm X Boulevard (Lenox Avenue) for the 2 and 3; or at St Nicholas Avenue for the A, B, C and D trains. You can also disembark on Broadway at 116th or 110th Street for the 1 train.

Less time-consuming options include **New York Airport Service** private buses (see left), which run frequently between Manhattan and La Guardia (one way $12, round trip $21). **Taxis** and **car services** charge about $30, plus toll and tip.

Newark Liberty International Airport

1-973 961 6000, www.panynj.gov/ airports/newark-liberty.html.

The best bet is the $12.50, half-hour trip via **New Jersey Transit** to or from Penn Station. The airport's monorail, **AirTrain Newark** (www.airtrainnewark.com), is linked to the NJ Transit and Amtrak train systems.

Bus services operated by **Coach USA** (1-877 894 9155, www. coachusa.com) run to Manhattan, stopping outside Grand Central Terminal (41st Street, between Park & Lexington Avenues), and inside the Port Authority Bus Terminal ($16, round trip $28); buses leave every 15-30mins. A **car** or **taxi** will run at $60-$75, plus toll and tip.

By bus

Most out-of-town buses come and go from the Port Authority Bus Terminal (*see p184*). **Greyhound** (1-800 231 2222, www.greyhound. com) offers long-distance travel to destinations across North America. Its **BoltBus** (1-877 265 8287, www. boltbus.com), serves several East Coast cities. **New Jersey Transit** (1-973 275 5555, www.njtransit.com) runs a service to nearly everywhere in the Garden State and parts of New York State. Finally, **Peter Pan** (1-800 343 9999, www.peterpanbus.com) runs extensive services to cities across the North-east; its tickets are also valid on Greyhound buses.

Port Authority Bus Terminal

625 Eighth Avenue, between 40th & 42nd Streets, Garment District (1-212 564 8484, www.panynj.gov/bus-terminals/port-authority-bus-terminal.html). Subway A, C, E to 42nd Street-Port Authority.
The hub for many commuter and long-distance services.

By rail

Grand Central Terminal

42nd to 44th Streets, between Vanderbilt & Lexington Avenues, Midtown East. Subway S, 4, 5, 6, 7 to 42nd Street-Grand Central.
Home to Metro-North, which runs trains to more than 120 stations in New York State and Connecticut.

Penn Station

31st to 33rd Streets, between Seventh & Eighth Avenues, Garment District. Subway A, C, E, 1, 2, 3 to 34th Street-Penn Station.
Amtrak, Long Island Rail Road and New Jersey Transit trains depart from this terminal.

Public transport

Metropolitan Transportation Authority (MTA)

1-718 330 1234 (or 511 within New York State), www.mta.info.
The MTA runs the subway and bus lines, as well as services to points outside Manhattan. News of service interruptions and MTA maps are on its website. Be warned: backpacks, handbags and large containers may be subject to random searches.

Fares & tickets

Although you can pay in cash or coins on the buses, you'll need to buy a MetroCard to enter the subway system. You can buy them from booths or vending machines in the stations; from the Official NYC Information Center; from the New York Transit Museum in Brooklyn or Grand Central Terminal; and from many hotels.

The standard fare across the subway and bus network on a MetroCard is $2.25, though a single-ride ticket purchased at a vending machine costs $2.50. Free transfers between the subway and buses are available only with a MetroCard (for bus-to-bus transfers on cash fares, see right). Up to four people can use a pay-per-ride MetroCard, sold in denominations from $4.50 to $80. If you put $10 or more on the card, you'll receive a seven per cent bonus. However, if you're planning to use the subway or buses often, an unlimited-ride MetroCard is great value. These cards are offered in two denominations, available at station vending machines but not at booths: a seven-day pass ($29) and a 30-day pass ($104). Note that you can't share a card with travel companions.

Subway

Far cleaner and safer than it was 20 years ago, the subway system is one of the world's largest and cheapest, with a flat fare of $2.25. Trains run around the clock. If you are travelling late at night, board the train from the designated off-peak waiting area, usually near the middle of the platform; this is more secure than the ends of the platform, which are often less populated in the wee hours.

Stations are most often named after the street on which they're located. Entrances are marked with a green and white globe (open 24 hours) or a red and white globe (limited hours). Many stations have separate entrances for the uptown and downtown platforms – look before you pay. Trains are identified by letters or numbers, colour-coded according to the line on which they run. Local trains stop at every station on the line; express trains stop at major stations only.

The most current subway map is reprinted at the back of this guide; you can also ask MTA workers in service booths for a free copy, or refer to enlarged subway maps displayed in each subway station.

City buses

White and blue MTA buses are usually the best way to travel crosstown and a pleasant way to travel up- or downtown, as long as you're not in a hurry. They have a digital destination sign on the front, along with a route number preceded by a letter (M for Manhattan, B for Brooklyn, Bx for the Bronx, Q for Queens and S for Staten Island). Maps are posted on most buses and at all subway stops; they're also available from the Official NYC Information Center (see p189). The Manhattan bus map is printed in the back of this guide. All local buses are equipped with wheelchair lifts. The fare is payable with a MetroCard (see left) or exact change ($2.25 in coins only; no pennies). MetroCards allow for an automatic transfer from bus to bus, and between bus and subway. If you pay cash, and you're travelling uptown or downtown and want to go crosstown (or vice versa), ask the driver for a transfer when you get on – you'll be given a ticket for use on the second leg of your journey, valid for two hours. MTA's express buses usually head to the outer boroughs for a $5.50 fare.

Rail services

The following commuter trains serve NY's hinterland.
Long Island Rail Road *1-718 217 5477 (or 511 within New York State), www.mta.info/lirr.* Rail services from Penn Station, Brooklyn and Queens to towns throughout Long Island.
Metro-North Railroad *1-212 532 4900 (or 511 within New York State), www.mta.info/mnr.* Commuter trains serve towns north of Manhattan and leave from Grand Central Terminal.
New Jersey Transit *1-973 275 5555, www.njtransit.com.* Services from Penn Station reach most of New Jersey, some points in NY State and Philadelphia.
PATH Trains *1-800 234 7284, www. panynj.gov/path.* PATH (Port Authority Trans-Hudson) trains run from six stations in Manhattan to various places across the Hudson in New Jersey, including Hoboken, Jersey City and Newark. The 24-hour service costs $2.

Taxis

Yellow cabs are rarely in short supply, except at rush hour and during unpleasant weather. If the centre light atop the taxi is lit, the cab is available and should stop if you flag it down. Get in and then tell the driver where you're going. (New Yorkers generally give cross-streets rather than street numbers.) By law, taxis cannot refuse to take you anywhere inside the five boroughs or to New York airports. Use only yellow medallion (licensed) cabs; avoid unregulated 'gypsy cabs'.

Taxis will carry up to four passengers for the same price: $2.50 plus 50¢ per fifth of a mile or per minute idling, with an extra 50¢ charge (a new state tax), another 50¢ from 8pm to 6am and a $1 surcharge during rush hour (4-8pm Mon-Fri). The average fare for a three-mile ride is $14, depending on the time and traffic. Cabbies rarely allow more than four passengers in a cab (it's illegal, unless the fifth person is a child under seven).

Not all drivers know their way around the city, so it helps if you know where you're going. If you have a problem, take down the medallion and driver's numbers, posted on the partition. Always ask for a receipt – there's a meter number on it. To complain or to trace lost property, call the **Taxi & Limousine Commission** (1-212 227 0700) or visit www.nyc.gov/taxi. Tip 15-20 per cent, as in a restaurant. All taxis now accept major credit cards.

Car services are regulated by the Taxi & Limousine Commission (see above). Unlike cabs, drivers can make only pre-arranged pickups. Don't try to hail one, and be wary of those that offer you a ride. The following companies will pick you up anywhere in the city, at any time, for a set fare.
Carmel *1-212 666 6666.*
Dial 7 *1-212 777 7777.*
GroundLink *1-877 227 7260.*

Driving

Car hire

You will need a credit card to rent a car, and you usually have to be at least 25 years old. All the companies listed below will add 19.875 per cent in taxes. Car hire is cheaper in the city's outskirts, and in New Jersey and Connecticut, than in Manhattan.
Aamcar *1-888 500 8480, 1-212 222 8500, www.aamcar.com;* **Alamo** *US: 1-877 222 9075, www.alamo.com. UK: 0871 384 1086, www.alamo.co.uk;* **Avis** *US: 1-800 230 4898, www. avis.com. UK: 0844 544 6666, www.avis.co.uk;* **Budget** *US: 1-800 527 0700, www.budget.com. UK: 0844 544 3470, www.budget.co.uk;* **Dollar** *US: 1-800 800 3665, www.dollar.com. UK: 020 3468 7685, www.dollar.co.uk;*

Enterprise *US: 1-800 261 7331, www.enterprise.com. UK: 0800 800 227, www.enterprise.co.uk;* **Hertz** *US: 1-800 654 3131, www.hertz.com. UK: 0870 844 8844, www.hertz.co.uk;* **National** *US: 1-877 222 9058, www.nationalcar.com. UK: 0845 120 2071, www.nationalcar.co.uk;* **Thrifty** *US: 1-800 847 4389, www.thrifty.com. UK: 01494 751500, www.thrifty.co.uk.*

Parking

Make sure you read parking signs and never park within 15 feet of a fire hydrant (to avoid a $115 ticket and/or having your car towed). Parking is off-limits on most streets for at least a few hours daily. The Department of Transportation provides information on daily changes to regulations (dial 311). If precautions fail, call 1-212 971 0771 for Manhattan towing and impound information; go to www.nyc.gov for phone numbers in other boroughs.

Cycling

The Manhattan Waterfront Greenway, a 32-mile route that circumnavigates the island of Manhattan, is a great asset: you can now ride, uninterrupted, along the Hudson River from Battery Park up to the George Washington Bridge, at 178th Street. Cycling maps and information are available from **Transportation Alternatives** (1-212 629 8080, www.transalt.org, closed Sat, Sun). **Bike & Roll** (1-212 260 0400, www.bikeand roll.com/newyork) is the city's biggest cycle-hire company, with nine outposts including Pier 84 (on the Hudson River at 43rd Street) and Central Park. Rates (incl helmet) start at $10 per hour, and you can rent at one branch and drop off at another for an extra $5.

Resources A-Z

Accident & emergency

In an emergency only, dial 911 for an ambulance, police or the fire department, or call the operator (dial 0). The following hospitals have emergency rooms:

Downtown Hospital *83 Gold Street, between Spruce & Beekman Streets, Financial District (1-212 312 5000). Subway 4, 5, 6 to Brooklyn Bridge-City Hall.*

Mount Sinai Hospital *Madison Avenue, at 100th Street, Upper East Side (1-212 241 6500). Subway 6 to 103rd Street.*

New York – Presbyterian Hospital/Weill Cornell Medical Center *525 E 68th Street, at York Avenue, Upper East Side (1-212 746 5454). Subway 6 to 68th Street-Hunter College.*

Roosevelt Hospital *1000 Tenth Avenue, at 59th Street, Upper West Side (1-212 523 4000). Subway A, B, C, D, 1 to 59th Street-Columbus Circle.*

Customs

US Customs allows foreigners to bring in $100 worth of gifts (the limit is $800 for returning Americans) without paying duty. One carton of 200 cigarettes (or 50 cigars) and one litre of liquor (spirits) are allowed. Plants, meat and fresh produce of any kind cannot be brought into the country. You will have to fill out a form if you carry more than $10,000 in currency. You will be handed a white form on your inbound flight to fill in, confirming that you haven't exceeded any of these allowances.

If you need to bring prescription drugs with you into the US, make sure the container is clearly marked, and bring your doctor's statement or a prescription. Marijuana, cocaine and most opiate derivatives, along with a number of other drugs and chemicals, are not permitted: the possession of them is punishable by a stiff fine and/or imprisonment. Check in with the US Customs Service (www.customs.gov) before you arrive if you're unsure.

HM Revenue & Customs allows returning visitors to bring £390 worth of 'gifts, souvenirs and other goods' into the UK duty-free, along with the usual duty-free goods.

Disabled

Under New York City law, facilities constructed after 1987 must provide complete access for the disabled – restrooms, entrances and exits included. In 1990, the Americans with Disabilities Act made the same requirement federal law. Many older buildings have added disabled-access features. There has been widespread compliance with the law, but call ahead to check facilities. **HAI** (1-212 575 7676, www.hospaud.org) has a database of NYC's cultural institutions on its website, which details accessibility and other features. All Broadway theatres are equipped with devices for the hearing-impaired, call **Sound Associates** (1-888 772 7686, www.soundassociates.com) for details.

Electricity

The US uses 110-120V, 60-cycle alternating current rather than the 220-240V, 50-cycle AC used in Europe. The transformers that

ESSENTIALS

power or recharge newer electronic devices such as laptops are designed to handle either current and may need nothing more than an adaptor for the wall outlet. Other appliances may also require a power converter. Adaptors and converters can be purchased at airport shops, pharmacies, department stores and at branches of electronics chain Radio Shack (www.radioshack.com).

Embassies & Consulates

Australia *1-212 351 6500.*
Canada *1-212 596 1628.*
Great Britain *1-212 745 0200.*
Ireland *1-212 319 2555.*
New Zealand *1-212 832 4038.*

Internet

Cyber Café *250 W 49th St, between Broadway & Eighth Avenue, Theater District (1-212 333 4109). Subway C, E, 1 to 50th Street; N, Q, R to 49th Street.* Open 8am-11pm daily.
NYCWireless *www.nycwireless.net.* This group has established dozens of hotspots in the city for free wireless access. (For example, most parks below 59th Street are covered.) Visit the website for information and a map.
New York Public Library *1-917 275 6975, www.nypl.org.*
Branches of the NYPL are great places to get online for free, offering both Wi-Fi and computers for public use. (Ask for an out-of-state card, for which you need proof of residence, or a guest pass.).
The **Science, Industry & Business Library** (188 Madison Avenue, at 34th Street, Midtown East), part of the Public Library system, has about 50 computers. All libraries have a computer limit of 45 minutes per day.
Starbucks *www.starbucks.com.* Many branches offer free Wi-Fi; there's a search facility on the website.

Opening hours

These are general guidelines.
Banks 9am-6pm Mon-Fri; generally also Sat mornings.
Businesses 9am or 10am to 5pm or 6pm Mon-Fri.
Pubs & bars 4pm-2am Mon-Thur, Sun; noon-4am Fri, Sat (but hours vary widely).
Shops 9am, 10am or 11am to 7pm or 8pm Mon-Sat (some open at noon and/or close at 9pm). Many are also open on Sun, usually 11am or noon to 6pm.

Police

The NYPD stations below are in central, tourist-heavy areas of Manhattan. To find the nearest police precinct or for information about police services, call 1-646 610 5000 or visit www.nyc.gov.
Sixth Precinct *233 West 10th Street, between Bleecker & Hudson Streets, West Village (1-212 741 4811).*
Seventh Precinct *19½ Pitt Street, at Broome Street, Lower East Side (1-212 477 7311).*
Midtown North Precinct *306 W 54th Street, between Eighth & Ninth Avenues, Hell's Kitchen (1-212 760 8300).*
17th Precinct *167 E 51st Street, between Third & Lexington Avenues, Midtown East (1-212 826 3211).*
Central Park Precinct *86th Street & Transverse Road, Central Park (1-212 570 4820).*

Post

Post offices are usually open 9am-5pm Mon-Fri (a few open as early as 7.30am and close as late as 8.30pm); some are open Sat until 3pm or 4pm. The **James A Farley Post Office** (421 Eighth Avenue, between 31st & 33rd Streets, Garment District, 1-800 275 8777 24hr information, www.usps.com) is open 24 hours daily for automated services.

Smoking

The 1995 NYC Smoke-Free Air Act makes it illegal to smoke in virtually all indoor public places. A law went into effect in 2011 that also bans smoking in public parks and pedestrian plazas and on beaches.

Telephones

As a rule, you must dial 1 + the area code before a number, even if the place you are calling is in the same area code. The area codes for Manhattan are 212 and 646; Brooklyn, Queens, Staten Island and the Bronx are 718 and 347; 917 is now mostly for mobile phones and pagers. Numbers preceded by 800, 877 and 888 are free of charge when dialled from within the US. To dial abroad, dial 011 followed by the country code, then the number. For the operator dial 0. Mobile phone users from other countries will need a tri-band handset. Public pay phones take coins and credit cards. The best way to make long-distance calls is with a phone card, available from the post office, chain stores such as Duane Reade and Rite Aid.

Time

New York is on Eastern Standard Time. This is five hours behind Greenwich Mean Time. Clocks are set forward one hour in early March for Daylight Saving Time (Eastern Daylight Time) and back one hour at the beginning of November. Going from east to west, Eastern Time is one hour ahead of Central Time, two hours ahead of Mountain Time and three hours ahead of Pacific Time.

Tipping

In restaurants, it's customary to tip at least 15 per cent, and a quick way to calculate the tip in NYC is to double the tax. For taxi tipping (*see p185*).

Tourist information

Official NYC Information Center
810 Seventh Avenue, between 52nd & 53rd Streets, Theater District (1-212 484 1222, www.nycgo.com). Subway B, D, E to Seventh Avenue. **Open** 8.30am-6pm Mon-Fri; 9am-5pm Sat, Sun.

What's On

The weekly *Time Out New York* magazine (www.timeoutnewyork.com), which hits newsstands on Wednesdays, is NYC's essential arts and entertainment guide. The best sources for all things gay is *Next* (www.nextmagazine.com); the monthly *Go!* (www.gomag.com) is geared towards girls.

Visas

Currently, 36 countries participate in the Visa Waiver Program (VWP; www.cbp.gov/esta) including Australia, Ireland, New Zealand, and the UK. Citizens of these countries do not need a visa for stays in the US shorter than 90 days (business or pleasure) as long as they have a machine-readable passport (e-passport) valid for the full 90-day period, a return ticket, and authorisation to travel through the ESTA (Electronic System for Travel Authorization) scheme. Visitors must fill in the ESTA form at least 24 hours before travelling (72 hours is recommended) and pay a $14 fee; the form can be found at www.cbp.gov/xp/cgov/travel/id_visa/esta/).

If you do not qualify for entry under the VWP, you will need a visa; leave plenty of time to check before travelling.

ESSENTIALS

Index

Sights & Areas

ESSENTIALS

ESSENTIALS

SEE OVER
101
SIGHTS!

CIRCLE·LINE SIGHTSEEING
at 42nd St.